# MAXIMUM MUSCLE BIBLE

F.Lepine Publishing


ISBN: 978-1-926659-32-9

www.MaximumMuscleBible.com

# TABLE OF CONTENT

# About

## ABOUT CHRISTIAN THIBAUDEAU

Coach Thib has worked with athletes from close to 30 different sports and is one of the only (if not the only) coach to have trained athletes that competed at the Crossfit Games, Olympic Games and the M. Olympia (not to mention several pro leagues). As such he is well versed not only on how to increase muscle mass and strength but also to do so in a way that will be transferable to athletic performance. He is a sought-after speaker, giving up to 20+ seminars in a year; he has written four books prior to this one as well as published two training DVDs covering various training methods. A passionate person about everything related to training, his own training combines bodybuilding, powerlifting, strongman and Olympic lifting to build a body that performs as well as it looks. Known as a great teacher and for making complex ideas easy to understand he participated with this book to help you learn methods that you can apply to your own training right now to spark new growth.

**www.ThibArmy.com**

## ABOUT PAUL CARTER

Coach Carter has spent almost 30 years of his life devoted to developing training and nutritional strategies that he has used to coach a myriad of athletes and help them find success. He has traveled across the world to speak and teach others how to use these methods in order to become stronger, bigger, and leaner. He has competed successfully in both powerlifting and bodybuilding, and has an athletic background in football, baseball, and martial arts. Coach Carter has written several books which have covered training for strength, mass, and even philosophical ideologies. Known as a "no BS" guy, Paul is sought after for his straight forward approach that combines real world results with scientific modalities.

**www.lift-run-bang.com**

# Preface

I am very excited to write this forward for Coach Thibs and Paul Carter. When it comes down to it, they embody everything I believe makes a great coach.

Let's talk CT. First of all, he lives in the trenches. He trains hard and smart, and has competed at a high level. Secondly, he is always trying to understand data and research to improve upon his methods, or to simply better understand the why of how things work. Lastly, he is not bound by this data and research. He is a creative thinker that does not sit and wait, rather he goes out and creates and evolves his ideas based on his deep desire to get better and better.

I would also like to speak about Paul Carter because I have traveled and presented with Paul internationally. Paul and Christian are very similar in many respects. In working with Paul, I have seen his desire to improve upon methods, not ignoring science, but not being handcuffed by it either, and being willing to experiment and always improve upon his methods. This to me is the mark of a true professional. It's never "well I figured everything out", it is a constant hunger to get better. Like with CT, I have the highest of regard for Paul and his intelligence, his witty humor, and the fact that he has successfully competed in multiple sports. He, along with CT, walks the walk.

I am sure you will learn a ton from Paul and Christian's work, and it will inspire you to also become a better coach, athlete, or simply a better you! I fully support these two and their efforts to give back to the community!

by John Meadows

# Introduction

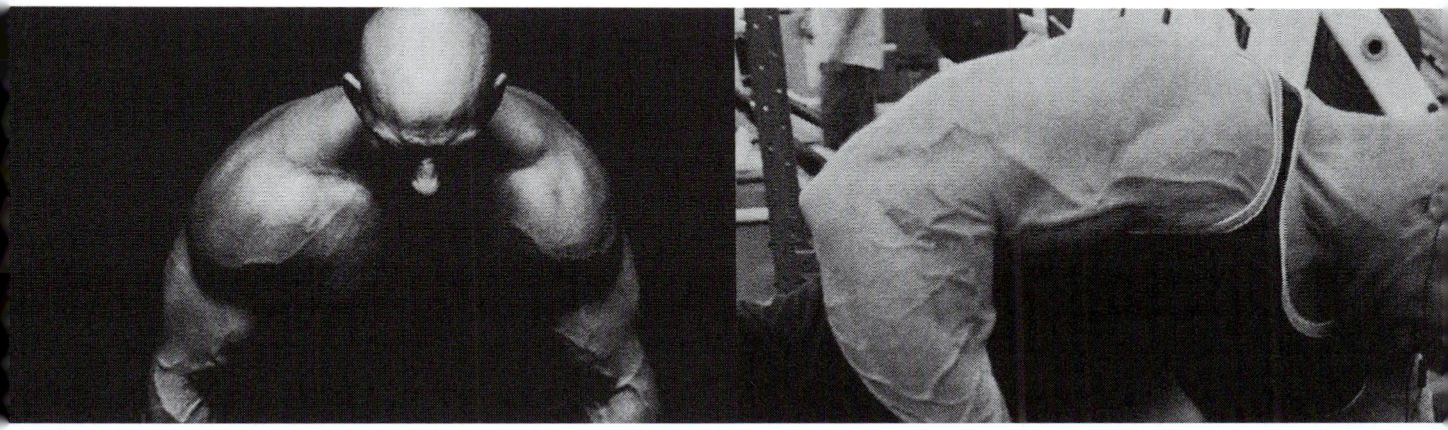

## The Process of Muscle Growth

Before one can make all the right choices in regards to training, diet, recovery and supplements, one must at least have a basic understanding of the process required to build new muscle mass, and how to create the most optimal and efficient environment to do so.

From a high-level overview standpoint, there are really only two factors:

1. Stimulus
2. Recovery from said stimulus.

The stimulus is obviously weight training. One must first train in a fashion that actually creates a stimulus for growth. The degree of this stimulus will vary depending on the qualification of the lifter.

A novice can do pretty much anything at first and see appreciable progress. This is because their body is in a maximal adaptation phase, and recovery is quick.

Once a trainee is past the initial stages of weight training—that is, the first 12 to 16 months—it will become exponentially harder to gain more muscle. When you are a novice, it doesn't take much stimulus to activate muscle growth and, because a novice is not very strong, the inroads on recovery are not very deep. Thus, as a beginner, you are in a very efficient stage to grow fast and recover easily.

As the body adapts to the repeated stimulus, it becomes more and more difficult to give the body a "reason to grow". The truth is that the body doesn't really want to carry an inordinate amount of muscle mass. Muscle mass requires a lot of calories to maintain, and that alone is terribly inefficient for survival. Therefore, there has to be a reason that it wants to grow more muscle mass, and that reason is training.

Understand that the process of muscle growth is essentially a type of survival mechanism. You ask the body to perform a certain type of physical work. To meet those imposed demands, it grows muscle tissue. This applies to virtually any physical aspect of life. People with physically demanding jobs often have a level of muscular development in accordance with what that job demands of them.

Your body doesn't know what a gym is. It just knows that it keeps being asked to perform repeated tasks that involve muscular exertion. To better equip itself to meet those demands, it adapts and grows.

Once these demands have been imposed enough times, and over a long enough period, growth becomes more difficult.

In order to further push the body past the limits it wants to stop at, we must ask it to do "more" in some fashion. We must also put it in the proper recovery environment so that it can grow. Without proper recovery, the growth process cannot take place. The recovery process is generally made up of proper rest and nutrition. Without recovery, the growth process is short-circuited and your time spent in the gym stimulating the growth process was for nothing.

The roadblocks to growth are comprised of not training properly and efficiently, and not supplying the optimum amount of rest and nutrition to meet the demands for that work.

The premise of this book is to help you get past these barriers, and take the guesswork out of understanding how to set up the most efficient training and nutritional modalities to grow.

# Chapter One: Nutrition

~ Paul Carter

## Real Protein Requirements

Over the years, there has been an enormous amount of debate with regards to the amount of protein needed to grow and recover from hard training. After all, amino acids—which are found in protein—are the building blocks of muscle. Without protein, it becomes damn near impossible to grow.

Because of the important role protein plays in muscle growth, people generally assume that more of it means more muscle growth. This is a common mentality throughout the lifting community:

*"If two sets work great, four sets will be even better."*

*"If 200 grams of protein a day makes me grow, then 400 grams a day will make me grow twice as fast."*

Unfortunately, it really doesn't work that way.

Muscle growth is a slow process. So long as you are training hard, and meeting your nutritional and recovery requirements, you will only grow as fast as your body will allow.

You cannot force-feed muscle growth. Once the stimulus for it has been put in place, it is then up to you to meet the demands for recovery. If those are met, you will grow. If they are not, you will not. It's that simple.

You will not grow faster by simply doing "more" of everything. There comes a point of diminishing returns. Not only that, but too much training can make it so that meeting the requirements of recovery are nearly impossible. At best, you will make zero progress. At the worst, overtraining syndrome (OTS) will set in (however, actually finding yourself in a state of overtraining is more difficult than you probably imagine).

No matter what someone tells you, it is vitally important to understand the balance with regards to stimulus versus recovery: you can't force muscle growth to occur at a faster rate by simply throwing more of everything at it.

More training
More food
More sleep
More supplements

It is important to find an equilibrium so that growth comes as fast as possible. Any more than that is not required. Think of it like filling up your car with gas. Once it's full, it's full. If you stand there pumping gas after the tank is full, what happens? The fuel spills out, and is wasted. You can't drive further because you pumped more gas.

That's what doing more than is required means, as well. It means wasted effort, wasted food and wasted time. This does not mean you don't have to train hard or eat enough; it means that understanding the appropriate balance of all these things will help you create the most ideal environment to grow in. And that is what you are after.

So how much protein does one need in order to meet the demands for recovery from proper training?

According to every piece of research we have seen on this, and through anecdotal evidence as well, it's about 1 gram of protein per pound of bodyweight (2.2 grams per kilo of bodyweight).

In fact, it's been shown that 0.8 grams per pound of bodyweight is actually enough. So, the truth is, you do not need to overload on protein in order to grow. As long as you're meeting the 1 gram per pound of bodyweight ratio, you will have your bases covered in regards to protein requirements.

The other question is: "Is this 1 gram per pound of lean body mass or total bodyweight?"

I would just go with total bodyweight to make it easier to calculate.

## Protein Sources

Now that we have established the amount of protein you need to create growth and recovery, let's look at where that protein should come from.

Lean cuts of red meat e.g. sirloin and flank
Chicken
Turkey
Tuna and other types of fish such as salmon, tilapia, trout, etc
Whole eggs and egg whites
Cottage cheese
Protein powder
This is by no means an exhaustive list of foods; however, it is a good starting point to build a solid diet from.

Since we have established that 1 gram per pound of bodyweight is the goal to hit on a daily basis for muscle growth, you now need to know how much protein is in these foods in order to accurately plan out an efficient diet.

4 ounces of chicken contains about 35 grams of protein
4 ounces of sirloin contains about 30 grams of protein
4 ounces of turkey contains about 19 grams of protein
4 ounces of tuna contains about 33 grams of protein
1 egg contains about 6 grams of protein
1 egg white contains about 3.5 grams of protein
1 cup of cottage cheese contains about 25 grams of protein
Depending on the protein powder, it's generally between 20 to 25 grams per scoop

With this information, it should not be difficult to plan out your meals/diet each day to make sure you meet your protein requirements.

Since I will advise you to split this out over five or six meals a day, simply divide that number by five or six to know how much you need to eat at each meal.

For example, if a 200 pound lifter needs 200 grams of protein per day, that's 200 divided by five. That means they need to eat 40 grams of protein per meal to hit 200 grams for the day.

Split out over five meals, using nothing more than the portions provided above, this is how that might look:

Breakfast: 3 whole eggs and 6 egg whites = 39 grams of protein
Snack: Protein shake with 2 scoops = 44 to 50 grams of protein
Lunch: 4 ounces of chicken breast = 35 grams of protein
Pre-training: Protein shake with 2 scoops = 44 to 50 grams of protein
Post-training meal: 4 ounces of sirloin = 30 grams of protein
Before bed: 1 cup of cottage cheese = 25 grams of protein

From the protein sources alone, this comes out to around 229 grams of protein per day. That is not including the protein that comes from other foods in those meals. So, as you can see, you don't have to gorge yourself in order to meet your protein requirements. These are not huge portions of food, and yet we exceeded the protein requirements for the day.

## Calories, Carbs and Fats

Believe it or not, counting calories is actually a fantastic and simple way to plan to lose fat or gain muscle. Understanding that all calories are not equal, however, is a very big part of efficient planning.

To elaborate, all foods have a thermogenic effect. This means that food itself requires energy to chew, swallow, and digest.

Protein takes the most energy to digest. Twenty to thirty percent of the calories from protein go towards digestion. With carbs, it's only about five to ten percent. With fat, it's around three percent max. Protein therefore has a higher thermogenic effect on your body than carbs or fats. It takes almost no calories to digest fats, and very little to digest carbs. This is a big reason why when we are dieting, we break the rule of 1 gram per pound of bodyweight for protein, and up it to 1.5 grams while reducing carbs.

Outside of the thermogenic effect of food, each nutrient has a different impact on hormonal response and even inflammation in the body. Eating 100 calories from gummy bears isn't the same as eating 100 calories from cream of wheat. Gummy bears will spike your insulin and provide no real nutritional value, while the cream of wheat will keep insulin low and is also packed with nutrients.

This is where the "if it fits your macros" crowd loses their argument when they say you can eat whatever you want, so long as it "fits your macros". 100 grams of carbs from candy or pop tarts doesn't have the same effect on the body as 100 grams of carbs from sweet potatoes or oatmeal—not when you start factoring in things such as the hormonal response and inflammatory response from food.

With that said, I still like to use total calories as the starting point for outlining a proper diet. From there, fill in your calorie needs with good, nutritious foods—not gummy bears, pop tarts, candy and ice cream.

## Guidelines

So, how do we do this?

Easy. We use your current bodyweight in pounds multiplied by a specific number to get your total calorie consumption starting point per day.

Before you can plan out these figures, you must first know what each macronutrient is worth from a calorie perspective.

1 gram of protein = 4 calories
1 gram of carbohydrate = 4 calories
1 gram of fat = 9 calories

We can now consider some basic guidelines for total calories per day to reach the goals of weight gain, maintenance or fat loss.

Muscle/weight gain = Bodyweight x 18-20
Maintenance = Bodyweight x 15
Fat loss = Bodyweight x 10-12

Remember, these are basic guidelines to give you a starting point. At bodyweight x 15, you may find that you gain weight or that you lose weight too fast (more than 1.5 to 2 pounds a week). But, this is a good place for most people to start.
Regardless of whether you need to lose body fat or gain mass, the one thing you must not do is go from one extreme of the calorie scale to the other. What I mean by that is that you don't want to suddenly reduce your intake from bodyweight x 25 to bodyweight x 10-12 overnight.

For fat loss, you will cycle your calories down each week until you get into the bodyweight x 10-12 range, and hold it there until the desired level of body fat is reached.

To gain mass, use this same procedure, but in reverse.

The reason you want to make changes slowly is so that the body can acclimate at a rate that doesn't throw it in to a state of shock. Adding too many calories too quickly will result in a quick net gain in fat. This is not what you are after. Conversely, a huge reduction in calories will cause your cortisol levels to rise, and your body will eat through fat and muscle, leaving you feeling weak, flat and fat at the same time.

None of these options are desirable.

## A Caveat to these Guidelines: Capping

As I noted earlier, there comes a point of diminishing returns on just "adding more". Therefore, we need to be cognizant of high points in regards to things like protein and total calories.

When you are dieting and reach bodyweight x 10-12, protein will be upped to 1.5 grams per pound of bodyweight, while reducing carbs to meet daily caloric goals. As noted, protein has a greater thermogenic effect than the other macros, so it's better to eat more protein while reducing carbs to shed body fat at a faster rate.

But there should be a cap on this. You don't need to shovel down 500 grams of protein a day in order to get lean. That would be very, very difficult to do and would make life pretty miserable for you and those that stay in proximity of you (protein farts, anyone?).

Therefore, the cap for protein is set at 300 grams per day, regardless of bodyweight.

Likewise, for gaining mass, there comes a point where it just isn't reasonable nor efficient to keep slamming down calories at a higher and higher rate. Dorian Yates—who was more than 300 lean pounds in the off-season in his bodybuilding prime—only consumed about 5,500 to 6000 calories a day. Since you are not Dorian Yates, the cap for total calories a day for gaining should be set at 5,000 (which is still generous).

Again, these are guidelines. If you know your body and know that you need more than 5,000 calories a day, eat more. However, for the majority of people, 5,000 calories of quality food and 300 grams of protein should be enough to create an anabolic environment for muscle growth.

Consider the following example of how to cycle into the proper ranges for muscle gain or fat loss.

Fat loss:

Week 1: BW x 15 (maintenance)
Week 2: BW x 14
Week 3: BW x 13
Week 4: BW x 12 (take protein to 1.5 grams per pound of BW, capping it at 300 grams per day)
Week 5: BW x 12
Week 6: BW x 11
Week 7: BW x 10 (stay here until desired level of body fat is reached)

Muscle gain:

Week 1: BW x 15 (maintenance)
Week 2: BW x 16
Week 3: BW x 16
Week 4: BW x 17
Week 5: BW x 18* (stay here until desired level of bodyweight is reached)

*If bodyweight x 18 = 5,000 calories a day, then cap it there. Otherwise, continue to bodyweight x 20.

## Deciding Whether to Get Lean or Gain Weight

Before you even start figuring out how many calories to eat per day, you must first ask yourself if you first need to gain weight or lose fat.

If you are above 15 percent body fat, you need to lose fat first. My recommendation is to get down to 9 to 10 percent and hold it there for a few weeks, before you increase calories to start gaining weight.

Once you get above 15 percent body fat, your body starts to accumulate fat at a much quicker rate. For the body to be primed to gain lean muscle mass, you need to be lean enough first. Being leaner means you are more insulin-sensitive, and your body will do a much better job of nutrient partitioning; that is, using the nutrients more efficiently to help promote growth.

Since I've already outlined the protein and calorie requirements, my guidelines for carbohydrates and fats are as follows.

## Fat Guidelines

20 percent of your calories should come from fats in the form of avocados, mixed nuts, olive oil, olives and peanut butter for monounsaturated fats; for omega-3 fatty acids fish like salmon and trout, flaxseed oil and walnuts.

## Carbohydrate Guidelines

Once you have your protein and fat requirements in place, simply fill in the rest of the calories with carbohydrate sources.

Carbohydrates should come from things such as oatmeal, sweet potatoes, whole wheat bread, brown rice and vegetables. Good options for post-workout (to be discussed in depth later) include cream of rice, jasmine rice and white potatoes.

This is not difficult.

Figure out your total caloric needs for the day.
1 gram of protein per pound of bodyweight until bodyweight x 12 in calories, when it becomes 1.5 grams per pound.
20 percent of calories from good fat sources.
Fill in the remaining calories from carbohydrates.

## Cheat Meals/Refeeds

Cheat meals have become a mainstay in dieting strategies. Every diet coach I know inserts them into their fat loss diets, and every person dieting talks about when and what their next cheat meal will be.

What is the purpose of the cheat meal, anyway?

Truthfully, it is to:

1. Provide a mental break from dieting; a reward system for being strict all week
2. Replenish glycogen stores
3. Increase leptin levels.

The first two are important with regards to wellbeing when dieting very hard. Having a "goal" at the end of the week to work towards helps a lot of people to stay focused on their eating during the week. It also serves the purpose of replenishing exhausted glycogen stores if one has been eating low-carb all week.

With that in mind, remember that you can "cheat" without actually eating junk food. Think of the word "cheat" as nothing more than a break from your limited macros for the day. So, you could sit down and pound down jasmine rice and potatoes for your cheat and do a great job of replenishing your glycogen stores, rather than eating pizza and burgers. Truthfully, this is a better option because of the third reason: leptin.

Leptin is the hormone in your body which controls satiety, or hunger. When leptin levels drop, it signals to your body that you need to eat more, and that's when cravings come on hard and fast. This happens to most people who diet hard for a long period of time.

When leptin levels are low for too long your metabolism will decrease, and getting rid of that last bit of fat becomes infinitely harder. A cheat or refeed will help to spike leptin levels and boost your metabolism again, shifting you back into a better state of fat burning.

To add, leptin is highly responsive to glucose metabolism. This means your body will do a better job of storing "clean" carbs as glycogen than processing meals which contain a mixture of fat, protein and carbs (what people have when they eat junk on refeeds).

A good baseline for a refeed or cheat meal is to take the protein back down to 1 gram per pound of bodyweight for the day, and then up the carbs to 150 percent of what you have been eating each day. Again, it's a better option to get these from clean sources rather than shoveling down junk food. You also won't feel as crappy afterwards, your muscles will feel fuller over the next few days, and your workouts will be awesome again.

Another factor to consider is how lean you are and how long you've been dieting. If you're really lean and have been dieting for several months, you may need a refeed or cheat more often, possibly twice a week. If you're not below 15 percent body fat yet, you probably don't need a cheat or refeed. Wait until you've actually earned one.

Use cheats or refeeds wisely, for their intended purpose. They are not a reason to blow up your diet. Also, remember that it's a cheat *meal* and not a cheat *day*.

## Breaking Down Meals for Easy Macros

Since your meals will be made up of protein, carbohydrates and fats, it's far easier to keep macros and calories on point if you limit the different kinds of food you eat to those sources.

Each meal should have one protein source, one carbohydrate source, and one fat source.

For example:

Breakfast:
Whole eggs and egg whites (protein and fats)
Oatmeal (carbohydrates)

Lunch:
Chicken breast cooked in olive oil (protein and fats)
Brown rice (carbohydrates)

If taste is an issue, add various spices to these meals to make them more entertaining. Eating plain anything will drive you insane after a while. Play with adding different spices and seasoning so that you don't throw yourself down a well lest you have to eat another plain chicken breast and cup of brown rice again.

Let me also add that you need to be aware of adding sauces. If you take a careful look on the label, most sauces contain pretty hefty amounts of sugars/carbs. So, if you are going to add them, make sure you add those calories and carbs to your daily macros and calories as well.

## Nutrient Timing

In order to understand the importance of nutrient timing, we must first understand who it really applies to.

Novice lifters, and even intermediate lifters, probably don't need to worry a great deal about nutrient timing in the way advanced lifters do. I would classify novice lifters as those in their first year of training, and intermediate lifters in their first three years of training.

From a muscular adaptation standpoint, if someone has been training very hard for three or more years, and has been very consistent with both training and diet, I would classify them as being in the more "advanced" stage.

The key word here is consistent. If you messed around off and on for three years, this does not apply. I am talking about those who have been at it hard and consistently on a daily and weekly basis for more than three years.

After three years of very hard and consistent training, the rate of muscular gain will have slowed significantly in comparison to the first couple of years. It is at this point, when an appreciable amount of muscle mass and strength has been obtained, that the lifter must pay more attention to detail in order to keep progressing at a consistent—albeit slower—rate.

## Beginner and Intermediate Nutrient Timing

For beginners and intermediates, it's simply enough to meet the demands for recovery. Eat a good meal one to two hours before training. This meal should be comprised of clean foods (I'm not going to debate what "clean" is) with a protein, fat and carb source. Something like two whole eggs with three egg whites and 30 grams of carbs from oatmeal or sweet potatoes will work well. Add in a fat source like a nut butter and this will help to slow down the digestion, so that the nutrient stream gets into the body at a slow but steady drip.

During training, I suggest using something like branch chain amino acids (BCAAs) or essential amino acids (EAAs).

After training have another quality meal within two hours.

For beginners and intermediates, this will suffice for recovery.

For advanced lifters, it's slightly different. It is critical for everyone who lifts to understand why these things are important, and how they make a difference.

## Advanced Nutrient Timing: Net Protein Balance
### (The Key to Optimal Growth)

As stated earlier, training is the stimulus for growth. It creates damage at a cellular level, and that damage has to be repaired.

The process for obtaining muscle growth cannot be completed unless muscle protein synthesis (MPS)—the process of removing or repairing damaged proteins and building new proteins that are replicas of the original—is greater than muscle protein breakdown (MPB).

Net protein balance is the weighing between MPS and MPB. If muscle protein synthesis is greater than muscle protein breakdown, net protein balance will be in a positive state. This means growth can and should occur.

If muscle protein synthesis is less than muscle protein breakdown you will lose muscle.

If muscle protein synthesis is the same as muscle protein breakdown, no progress/growth will occur at all.

MPS < MPB = Loss of muscle mass
MPS = MPB = No growth occurred, but no muscle mass was lost
MPS > MPB = Growth

The following needs to happen to make sure MPS is greater than MPB after training, so that net protein balance is in the positive.

**1. Eat a balanced meal before training**
It has been shown repeatedly that MPS is elevated when someone eats a meal with protein and carbs prior to training, compared to if they train fasted and ate afterwards. This is especially true if you supplement with leucine.

There's no reason to train fasted. I've read all the info on it and it's spotty at best in regards to benefits. The fact is that MPS spikes at a much higher rate post-workout if you have eaten *before* training, and when you combine the post-training meal. Anecdotally, I don't know a single huge guy that trains fasted. If he does, he's the exception—not the rule.

Yes, you can train fasted and still take advantage of increasing MPS by having a meal post-workout; however, you short-change the degree by not having a meal beforehand. The balance that is important here is that if MPS is not higher than muscle protein breakdown, or even if it's equal, your training session was literally a waste in regards to growing muscle. I will emphasize this many times so that you understand just how important this is.

**2. Supplement your training with BCAAs or EAAs and a simple carb source**
Highly Branched Cyclic Dextrin is my recommended carb source to use during training. How many carbs to consume during training will depend on the training session itself. For smaller workouts that are less intense 30 to 40 grams of carbs will work. For workouts such as legs, it will probably be closer to 80 to 100 grams. I recommend 5 to 10 grams of BCAAs or EAAs during training.

**3. Have a protein shake with a simple carb source after training**
You don't need to sprint to your car the second you finish your last set of the workout. MPS is indeed elevated for hours and hours after training (up to 48 hours in some cases). However, it has been shown that, for advanced trainees, getting a protein and carb source in very quickly after training promotes a higher degree of nitrogen retention than if they wait and eat a meal two hours later. For advanced lifters, this is a very important piece of the puzzle. Elevating MPS as much as possible post-workout means the chances for anabolism, or growth, will be much higher.

The reason for the carb source isn't to spike insulin. If you are having whey isolate post-workout (you should be) that alone will spike insulin. An insulin spike is needed post-workout as it reduces muscle protein breakdown. Remember, if MPS and MPB are equal, no growth will take place; it's not only about increasing MPS, but also decreasing MPB. Make sure you spike insulin post-workout by using something such as whey isolate.

To be even more exact, I recommend ingesting a protein shake that is half whey isolate, and half casein. Casein has been shown to do a better job of blunting MPB over an extended period because of its slow digestion rate. In my opinion, going with both whey isolate and casein is the most ideal option.

Carbs are still needed before and after training to keep cortisol low. When you are low on glycogen the body will release cortisol. Cortisol is another enemy of muscle growth because, while it does use free fatty acids for fuel, it also eats away at lean muscle tissue. So, it is very important to make sure to fuel up before and refuel after training with good carbohydrate sources. Post-workout, I recommend jasmine rice, white potatoes, and cream of rice with honey.

The ideal situation is to take in enough carbs so that you can train hard using *that* energy source, and then replenish them enough to fuel your next training session without taking in too many so that you get fatter. Cutting carbs is great for fat loss, but there is no benefit to going keto while trying to build muscle mass. No one goes keto and gets bigger. For guys who are dieting, I recommend planning the great majority of your carbs around the pre-, peri- and post-workout window. This is when your body will use them the most efficiently, with minimal risk of accumulating fat.

### *How much protein and how many carbs post-training?*

Generally speaking, your carbohydrate intake will depend on the severity of your training session - that is - your volume, intensity, how hard you trained, etc. For example, if you did an arm workout and are in a fat loss stage, you can probably keep carbs relatively low. If it's after a brutal leg training session, you will obviously want more carbs. For big workouts like legs and back, I recommend 0.8 grams of carbs per pound of bodyweight post-workout. For shorter or smaller training sessions cut that figure in half to 0.4.

From all the research we've seen, the requirement for maxing out MPS tends to be at an average of about 0.5 grams of protein per pound of bodyweight. So, if you're 200 pounds, that's 100 grams of protein coming in the post-workout window, and, depending on the type of training session, between 80 and 160 grams of carbs.

What I recommend is to take in half of those figures for the first meal post-training, and then the other half of them two hours later. In the example above, the first meal would contain 50 grams of protein and 40 to 80 grams of carbs. Two hours later, this would be repeated for the second meal. This should cover all your bases.

## Leucine

So as not to leave any stone unturned in regards to MPS, we must also cover the importance of leucine and its role in this process.

Leucine appears to be the key to making amino acids and branch chain amino acids work.

*A series of cellular studies has now clearly shown that leucine directly activates a critical compound in muscle called the mTOR (mammalian target of rapamycin). It turns out mTOR is like a molecular switch that turns on the machinery that manufactures muscle proteins and leucine is one of the major activators of mTOR. So leucine not only provides the building blocks for protein synthesis, it also plays a critical role in up-regulating the process. Even when an overabundance of amino acids are available to provide the building materials for new muscle, adding extra leucine augments protein synthesis rates further. The bottom line is that adding additional leucine to your diet is an effective strategy to maximize muscle anabolism after resistance exercise.*

*Source: http://www.nutritionexpress.com/article+index/protein/showarticle.aspx?id=807*

***How much leucine do you need?***

You should have 10 grams from the start of the pre-workout meal to the post-workout meal. A good recommendation is 2.5 grams before training, 2.5 grams during training and 5 grams after training.

## Conclusion

Nutrition is not as complicated as many people make it out to be. If you need to lose fat (those above 15 percent body fat) reduce calories and up your protein. If you need to gain mass, increase your calories over a number of weeks and hold it there until the desired bodyweight is reached (stop gaining when you reach 15 percent body fat).

Without proper nutrition, the recovery process from training cannot be completed. The fact is that without proper nutrition you *will not grow*. Period. Yet many consider nutrition to be the number two priority after training. If your nutrition isn't on point you will go almost nowhere. Nutrition determines both fat loss and the degree of muscle growth.

# Chapter Two: Stimulus Factors for Growth

~ Paul Carter

In the nutrition chapter, we talked about the two main factors in growing: the stimulus supplied for growth, and then meeting the demands for recovery through nutrition.

Now we're going to cover what a stimulus is, the different kinds of stimulus there are for growth, and how to implement those principles to take advantage of them.

## Progressive Overload

Progressive overload is the basic nuts and bolts of getting bigger, especially at the beginner to intermediate level. In essence, it simply means you must ask your body to lift heavier and heavier weights in order to grow.

Progressive overload is the basic foundation on which all mass-building comes from. After all, if you never lift more than you did on your very first day of training, your body would never change as there would be nothing for it to adapt to.

You can throw out every training principle there is; if you go from bench pressing 225 pounds for 10 reps maximally, to bench pressing 400 pounds for 10 reps maximally, you will have grown exponentially over the time it took to get there.

However, putting more weight on the bar isn't the only way to increase overload. Furthermore, as I will explain later, it may not even be the most optimal way to approach hypertrophy - depending on your qualifications as an athlete or lifter.

There are a myriad of ways to trigger progressive overload, as outlined below.

**Single Progression**
This means increasing a single factor in training. For example, instead of doing 225 x 8 reps, you shoot for 225 x 9 in the next workout. You could also add more weight the next week, such as 235, and then try to match the 8 reps you did at 225. Once the 235 x 8 is achieved, the lifter can then up the weight and work back to 8 reps, or work towards more reps at that weight. These are examples of single progression.

Single progression can also be applied to anything so long as it is only the addition of one factor.

For example:
Week 1: 225 x 8
Week 2: 225 x 2 sets of 8 (the addition of 1 set)
Week 3: 225 x 3 sets of 8

**Double Progression**
This involves increasing two factors in training, such as adding weight to the bar and increasing reps. So, instead of 225 x 8, you go to 235 x 10.

Just like single progression, double progression can be applied in other ways as well.

For example:
Week 1: 225 x 8
Week 2: 225 x 2 sets of 10 (the addition of more sets and reps)

**Triple Progression**
This involves increasing three factors in training. Here, you might add weight, reps and another set to training. In this example, instead of doing 225 x 8 reps, you might do 235 x 10 reps for 2 sets.

For example:
Week 1: 225 x 8
Week 2: 235 x 2 sets of 10 (weight was increased, a set was added, and more reps were done)

Single, double and triple progression are all examples of progressive overload, whereby you ask the body to do more work than it did during the previous workout.

You can also mix in each method of progression over the course of a training cycle, in order to take advantage of each type of overload.

For example:
Week 1: 225 x 8 (the starting point for progression)
Week 2": 225 x 10 (single progression—more reps)
Week 3: 225 x 12 (single progression—more reps)
Week 4: 235 x 2 x 10 (double progression—more weight and sets)

Week 5: 245 x 3 x 5 (double progression—more weight and sets)
Week 6: 245 x 4 x 6 (double progression—more sets and reps)
Week 7: 245 x 5 x 6 (single progression—more sets)
Week 8: 245 x 6 x 6 (single progression—more sets)
Week 9: 245 x 5 x 8 (single progression—more reps)
Week 10: 250 x 6 x 10 (triple progression—more weight, sets and reps)

Each one can be used at various times to create a new stimulus for the body to adapt to, to ensure that you are consistently giving it a reason to grow. However, with each one, there are benefits and drawbacks that must be understood in order to know when to apply them appropriately.

## Benefits and Drawbacks to Each Type of Progression

### Single Progression Benefits and Drawbacks

Benefits

- Easy to focus on a singular goal.
- Applies very well to lower volume training where the lifter is going near failure each week.
- Great for planning out longer training cycles, like strength peaking cycles.
- Makes tracking progress very easy.

Drawbacks

- Diminishing returns if one only chases rep PRs each week.
- Can get stuck for a long time hitting a certain rep total.
- Doesn't apply to volume training as well as the other approaches.

### Double Progression Benefits and Drawbacks

Benefits

- Allows for more variety in training.
- Applies very well to volume-style training.
- Provides more variables to judge training progress by.
- Works well with most volume and intensity training modalities.

Drawbacks

- Can cause plateaus quickly if one advances in both too fast.
- Not as applicable to training with higher intensities.

### Triple Progression Benefits and Drawbacks

Benefits

- Tremendous amount of stimulus for rapid growth.
- Great for beginners who tend to gain strength and size more rapidly.
- Provides a myriad of training variables to judge progress by.
- Works well with low intensity/high volume training modalities.

Drawbacks

- Very hard to factor in unless one plans very intelligently.
- Not as advanced lifter-friendly for longer cycles.
- Even more likely to bog the lifter down into a plateau if all are increased too quickly.

Of course, any of these points can be argued, and all of these approaches can be applied to almost any training program so long as they are used appropriately and intelligently. But, some apply better to certain training designs than others.

There are other forms of progressive overload or stimulus that should be mentioned here as well. For example, you can decrease time between sets to create more overload, or increase the frequency of training.

## Increasing Frequency and the Sliding Scale of F/V/I

Frequency is quite possibly the most important variable when it comes to growth. Frequency, volume and intensity are the cornerstones for creating an intelligent plan for hypertrophy. However, in my opinion, frequency probably has the greatest degree of potential for unlocking mass gains.

Of course, frequency, intensity and volume must all be managed in order to fit into the recovery model, lest one reach a state of overtraining or under-recovery.

I call this the sliding scale of frequency/volume/intensity (F/V/I) to meet the recovery variable.

**Frequency:** How often you train a lift or body part.
**Volume:** How much total work you do for a body part or movement in a training session.
**Intensity:** The percentage of one rep max you are using or RPE (rate of perceived exertion).

The single variable that cannot be violated when managing these three is, of course, recovery. If all three variables are too high, recovery will generally not be met. Two of the variables can be high, but the third variable needs to be lowered in relation to those two.

So, if you want to train many times a week, with a high intensity level, then you will need to lower the amount of volume you will be using in said programming. If you don't or can't train many times a week, then you can train heavier with more volume.

Depending on how you set up your training, you must remember to lower one of the three variables if the other two are high.

Frequency = High
Intensity = High
Volume = Low

Frequency = Low
Intensity = High
Volume = High

Frequency = High
Intensity = Low
Volume = High

There are other variations as well, but you get the general idea.

The reason frequency is possibly the most important factor with regards to hypertrophy training is because it gives you more chances to stimulate growth. So long as volume and intensity are dialed in to meet the standard of frequency you decide upon, and recovery is being met, then growth should come at a much faster rate.

This is why, generally speaking, bodybuilders are far more muscular than powerlifters, yet powerlifters are stronger. Bodybuilders usually train body parts multiple times a week, at multiple angles with high volumes, but they don't always go that heavy. Powerlifters tend to train each "movement" once a week on average (with bench sometimes being twice a week), and train with higher intensities (load on the bar) but with generally lower volumes (Sheiko aside).

From a muscle mass standpoint, it's probably more beneficial to train a body part more often with appropriate intensities, than to train it less often going balls out.

*However, you must also understand that by "training more often", it doesn't always mean you have to train more days per week.*

Depending on how you balance your split, you can train three or four days a week and actually hit body parts just as often as training six days a week (assuming body parts were hit twice a week during that time), but with more time for systematic recovery. That means, recovery of the body as a whole and not just localized muscle recovery.

Remember that every time you train very intensely, you deplete the body of fuels and reserves such as glycogen, BCAA, ATP, etc. Even if you are meeting all the requirements for nutrition and sleep, there is a finite amount of reserves for training that can be used. I will cover this more later.

For now, in this example, you can see that body parts can get hit twice a week while training only four times a week.

Day 1: Chest, Shoulders and Arms
Day 2: Legs and Back
Day 3: Off
Day 4: Chest, Shoulders and Arms
Day 5: Legs and Back
Day 6 and 7: Off

In the three times a week split below, you can hit body parts three times over a two-week period, rather than only twice if you were doing each body part once a week.

Week 1:
Day 1: Chest, Shoulders and Back
Day 2: Off
Day 3: Legs and Arms
Day 4: Off
Day 5: Chest, Shoulders and Back
Day 6 and 7: Off

Week 2:
Day 1: Legs and Arms
Day 2: Off
Day 3: Chest, Shoulders and Back
Day 4: Off
Day 5: Legs and Arms
Day 6 and 7: Off

There are benefits and drawbacks to both splits. With three days a week you have more time to recover based on your days off. However, because you need to cover more body parts per session training can get longer, and whatever is hit at the end of a training session can get less attention from an energy standpoint.

## Different Types of Tension and Stress

There are basically two things that happen when you lift weights in the gym: you take selfies in between sets, and hit on women that look good in yoga pants. Those are two things that should probably not be happening when you're in the gym to ride the gain train.

So, what two things are we now focusing on?

By lifting weights, you create both tension on the muscles and physiological stress in the body. Depending on the type of training you do, there are different types of tension and different kinds of stress.

**Concentric Contractions**
This is when the muscles shorten against resistance. It is also known as the "positive" portion of a rep, such as the raising of the weight on lateral raises.

**Eccentric Contractions**
This is when muscles lengthen against resistance. It is also known as the "negative" portion of the rep. Mind you, in this instance, the word "contraction" doesn't mean a shortening of muscle.

There are two interesting points about the eccentric portion of the rep:

1. It has greater potential for inducing growth than the positive portion of the rep.
2. You can lower a far greater percentage of weight than you can raise. This suggests that the body is resistant to lengthening muscles that are loaded.

We will take advantage of point number one during the programming and routine parts of this book. If you want to unlock every advantage with regards to growth, you can't leave a single stone unturned.

**Mechanical Tension**
This is a combination of both active tension, where the shortening of a muscle stops because tension is equal to the load, and passive tension, where the muscle is lengthened in an unloaded state, such as

a hurdler's stretch. With mechanical tension the muscles are activated while lengthening. This is using relatively heavy loads through a full range of motion in a movement as a means of stimulating growth.

**Metabolic Stress**
This is the build-up of acid in the muscles. It is the burning you will feel during high rep sets. The longer you rest between sets, the less metabolic stress you will place on the muscles during your training. This is why you should keep rest periods low for certain movements if you are trying to achieve greater metabolic stress. Very high repetition sets tend to create a lot of metabolic stress, and this is indeed a stimulus for muscle growth.

**Time Under Tension (TUT)**
This defines how long the muscles were under tension. If you do a set while lowering the weight in three seconds, not resting at the bottom, and then performing the positive portion of the rep in one second and not holding the contraction portion, then each rep had a TUT load of four seconds.

That looks like 3010 in regards to TUT per rep. This means three seconds for the eccentric, zero seconds for the bottom, one second for the eccentric, and zero seconds for the top/contracted position.

If you performed 10 reps using the above tempo, that means the set had a TUT load of 40 seconds.

TUT can play a major factor in unlocking more growth, if used correctly.

There are some caveats. If the lifter performs the negative portion of the rep under control—for example, lowering the weight in three seconds—then there is more tension created in the movement because momentum is reduced. This makes the muscles work harder.

The caveat here is that TUT still needs to adhere to the model of progressive overload. In other words, simply slowing down the degree of movement to achieve a specific TUT for a set isn't enough. The athlete still needs to strive to use intensities heavy enough to force adaptation. If you can curl 135 pounds with some degree of body English (cheating), but then decide to use a stricter form, paying attention to TUT, it won't do you any good if you reduce the resistance so much that the muscles aren't forced to adapt. For example, going from a semi-cheat curl with 135 for 10 reps to a strict curl using a 3010 tempo with 65 pounds for 10 reps probably isn't going to work. Weight on the bar is still important.

Like most things, the answer to using TUT lies somewhere in the middle. Using loads between 65 to 85 percent of your one rep max, depending on the movement, is ideal. Using a TUT of between 30 and 60 seconds using a 3010 tempo will be pretty efficient. That means you'll be shooting for sets of 8 to 15 reps using this tempo.

It must be noted that there's really not much of a benefit to using slower tempos on the concentric portion of the rep. The concentric portion doesn't hold a lot of potential for growth, and it will also significantly lower the degree of intensity that can be used on the set. As I noted previously, weight on the bar still matters. We can lower more weight than we can raise. When we use TUT for growth potential, we unlock more growth by placing emphasis on the negative and being explosive on the positive. This allows you to use the greatest amount of weight possible while also increasing tension to the greatest degree during the set.

The other factor is that TUT per entire session may play a significant role in muscle growth. That is, doing 10 sets of 8 reps with a 1010 tempo may not yield the same degree of hypertrophy as 10 sets of 8 with a 3010 tempo.

10 sets of 8 with a 1010 tempo @ 70% = 160 seconds of TUT
10 sets of 8 with a 3010 tempo @ 70% = 320 seconds of TUT

This is not something often considered when people factor in volume. Most people just look at volume in terms of sets and reps, and never think about the actual amount of time the muscles spend under tension in the training session. Once you factor that in, you can see that the "volume" of tension is vastly different.

In the example above, while the "volume" (total number of sets and reps) and the load are the same (70 percent) the amount of time the muscles spend under tension is twice as long in the 3010 scenario. Without a doubt, this means the muscles performed more work in the second scenario.

In this comparison, which one do you think created a higher degree of stress and stimulus for growth? It should be obvious.

## Forms of Progressive Overload vs. Forms of Tension

A well-rounded approach to building as much muscle mass as possible will take advantage of every principle that stimulates growth. However, the application or prioritizing those principles largely depends on the degree of development in the athlete and their level of experience.

For the lifter who has been training for, say, three years or less, different forms of progressive overload should make up the foundation of their training model, with less emphasis placed on other modalities. This is because there is still a lot to milk aside from just adding weight to the bar.

After a solid layer of muscle mass has been laid down and the athlete has been training consistently for more than five years, understanding how to apply as much tension—not only in a set but throughout whole training sessions—will pay much bigger dividends.

Think of it in the following terms. An advanced lifter who squats 605 may have to work very hard for the next few years to squat 635. If the lifter's focus is pure hypertrophy, adding 30 pounds to their squat might require an awful lot of work. However, in regards to leg growth, there may not be a huge difference. In other words, he would have done a lot of work for little in return concerning muscle mass.

This same lifter might instead focus on creating more tension in their movements over the same amount of time, and build significantly more muscle mass without adding much—if any—pounds to their squat. In fact, they may not squat at all during that time and still grow bigger wheels.

You have to ask yourself if your goal is to squat more or to have bigger legs? These things do not always go together, and you may have to get your head around this before you can maximize your training towards building muscle mass.

## Movement Initiation

One of the best ways you can determine if you are applying the greatest amount of tension on the muscle you want to work is by asking yourself this question: "Am I initiating the movement with the muscle I am trying to work?"

You may answer "yes" at first. But, if you are body aware, you may realize as you perform the movement that you are actually asking something else to fire before the muscle you are trying to isolate.

For example, I often see guys flex their traps before they do a barbell curl. This means the traps are taking some of the tension away from the biceps in order to start the movement. Consequently, the greatest degree of tension on the biceps is lost. If one was to lock down the scapula and elbows instead, and initiate the starting portion of the barbell curl with the actual biceps, tension in the biceps will be increased. That's what we want for every movement that is performed.

The reason a lot of people end up initiating a movement with a muscle that they aren't actually trying to work is because they choose a load that is too heavy. The thought is: "if I go heavy, I will grow." However, once you bring other muscle groups into play, and the execution of technique is no longer precise, tension will be shifted to other muscle groups and even to connective tissues and joints.

Show me a guy that does a lot of heavy, cheating reps and I will show you a guy that has joint issues. This isn't to say cheating is bad all the time. Once you hit a point of fatigue in a movement while using precise execution, it's okay to then use some controlled cheating to extend the set. However, you should get as close to muscular failure using perfect technique as possible before that happens.

Doing this will be a massive test of your ego. Remember, in the end, it's not weight on the bar that will ultimately determine growth. Weight on the bar is just a tool; it's what you do with that tool that is most important. To create as much tension as possible in a muscle group you need to perform the movement properly, with strict form and technique.

## Breakover Point

The breakover point is what I refer to as going from using a weight where you can apply the hardest contraction on to the selected muscle, to where you add weight and lose that feeling. It goes from being a movement where you are making the muscle work, to a movement where you are "moving weight through space".

Once again, if you are cognizant enough in your training and mind/body connection you will know when you have added too much weight and this happens.

The optimal weight is the heaviest that you can still apply the greatest amount of tension with. Light weights turn down the neural response in the body, and they cannot generate a high degree of tension. When weights are too heavy, it means tension is lost in the desired working muscle groups because other muscles are brought into play to assist in the movement.

Light and heavy are relative terms. What is heavy for one person, may be light for someone else; and what is light for one person, may be heavy for someone else.

You must find the weight that is heavy enough to generate the greatest amount of tension, with perfect execution, in the desired rep range for that movement. Once perfect execution has been exhausted because of fatigue, the lifter can then resort to not being as perfect in execution. But, if the lifter crosses the breakover point with the weight selected, then the muscle trying to be isolated will not receive the greatest amount of work in comparison to using less weight, with perfect form.

Be aware of what weights you select for your working sets. Getting greedy for more weight on the bar does not mean more muscle on your frame, and it often means that lagging body parts stay lagging, and joint pain can arise.

## Muscle Damage

Muscle damage is essentially microtears of the tissue which results in what everyone knows as delayed onset muscle soreness (DOMS). These microtears cause inflammation, which is the soreness we feel. When you think about why there is growth from this, it should make sense. Any time you have an injury, the body naturally responds to create inflammation in that injured area, to both protect it and initiate the healing process. In this case, that healing process means repairing the damaged muscle fibers and adapting to protect itself from future damage—which means the thickening and strengthening of those fibers over time.

This doesn't mean you should chase muscle soreness, as it's not indicative of growth. Lots of people adapt to a training protocol and still continue to grow, despite not always feeling sore.

Not only that, but there are drawbacks to getting too sore. If you're so sore that you cannot function properly, it probably means you've done more damage than can be repaired adequately.
This also means that the overall process of recovery will be so long that the muscle won't be able to be stimulated again in an efficient time period; thus, no growth will have occurred.

If you get so sore that you can't train that area again for a long time, you did too much and, by the time you get around to training it again, you've made no progress.

With all of that said, I do think a certain degree of muscle soreness is a positive sign that your body was forced to adapt to either a movement or degree of intensity. As long as your body is having to adapt to something that triggers muscle growth, progress should be forthcoming.

Also, remember that, over time, the body will become very good at adapting to high training intensities. This means you may not get sore, even if your training has been brutally hard. But is this a good thing?

## Adaptation and Fatigue Management

When the different stress factors of training are dialed in, and recovery is met, we grow. When the stress factors are too high, for too long, we overtrain.

The important part to remember is that stress is only good if the body is being forced to adapt to it. When we apply the same stress over and over again, without any change, the body will eventually fully adapt to that stress. At that point, you're simply training to incur more fatigue.

Think about that for a minute, and get really sad.

For those who tend to stay on the same routine for long periods at a time, and change nothing at all, you've been going to the gym to do nothing but make yourself tired. Once the body is fully adapted to a movement, load or stress, it has no reason to grow. It can already perform at the level you ask it to, and it can already perform the movement with great efficiency.

A visual example of this (from my article at Strength Sensei):

Week 1: Start a new routine, where you become sore from the change in movements and change in set and rep schemes.
Week 2: You perform better than in week 1, and soreness is still oncoming but not as bad as week 1.
Week 3: You perform much better than in week 2, and soreness is minimal.
Week 4: You perform much better than in week 3, and soreness is mostly non-existent.
Week 5: You perform slightly better than in week 4, with no soreness.
Week 6: You perform no better than in week 5, with no soreness.
Week 7: You perform no better than in week 6, or perhaps worse in some movements, with no soreness.

In this particular example you can see that the adaption curve peaks at about week 6. At this point, if the lifter changes nothing in their training, most of what occurs in each training session is the incurring of more fatigue debt.

The scenario above is pretty common. This is why I often do training in six week blocks and then decide if I need to take a few days off (deload), continue training as I have been (which means that, despite no soreness, I am still making progress), or change a few things around (which means progress has already slowed significantly or stalled).

This is one reason I am a big fan of having some base movements at the foundation of the program, but then rotate through different movements after that. In week one, I might bench press and then do incline dumbbell press afterwards, but, in week two, I might bench press and do dips afterwards. In week three, I would go back to doing incline dumbbell press and so on.

This is a good way to keep the body guessing and stop it from adapting to the same movements and loads too quickly. It also keeps the mind fresh so that you don't get bored of doing the same movements day in day out—one shouldn't underestimate the importance of staying excited about training.

In addition, remember that just because you reach a stage that looks like full adaptation, you don't need to overhaul everything. In fact, that's generally not a great idea. The best thing to do is start with simple changes to create the need for adaptation again, and go from there. Some ways to do this are:

1. **Change joint positions:** Move your feet or hands in or out. Bench with a closer or wider grip, squat with a closer or wider stance, change chin-up hand spacing, or change curl grips. Change the angle which certain joints move through space. It doesn't seem like much but, in a side lateral, if you concentrate on turning the elbows up, you will transfer a greater amount of stress on to the medial delts than if you have been allowing them to be more pointed towards the floor (try this out without weights and you will see). Change the military press you've been doing into a behind-the-neck press. You're still pressing overhead but the body must work much differently in each exercise.

2. **Change bar positions:** Going from high bar to low bar in the squat is still a squat, but it will bring certain muscle groups more into play while reducing others.

3. **Change tempo:** We covered this above. Something as simple as changing the tempo during a set his is enough to make the movement more difficult and, once again, it forces the body to adapt to a change. If you've been doing leg curls without paying attention to tempo, change to doing them with five second eccentrics and see if you don't wake up with sore hamstrings over the next few days. You didn't even have to change your routine: you just changed something in it that the body had to adapt to. This is how you keep the body guessing, and continually force it to adapt and grow.

## Time Between Sets

My opinion about time between sets is this: I rest long enough to recover between sets, and that depends on what movement I am doing and the protocol I am using. For example, if I am training for strength and using compensatory acceleration training where my focus is on being as explosive as possible with the weights, I will squat with a fairly light intensity (usually about 60 to 65 percent of my max), but I won't rest very long between sets—maybe only 60 seconds or so. If I am peaking for a strength competition, I will increase my intensity each week, and rest much longer between sets—possibly as long as five minutes.

If I am doing triceps pushdowns, I will move very fast between sets. This is not a very taxing movement, so there's no need to stand around for three to five minutes between sets.

## Conclusion

There is a myriad of ways to create stimulus for muscle growth. Your best bet is to understand the various ways you can use them together in a synergistic fashion, so that they work together to create growth in the fastest manner possible.

Some people say things like "you don't need to train heavy to get bigger" which is a poor, generalized statement. You will need to train heavier, over time, in order to grow. But there will come a point where adding more weight to the bar has a point of diminishing returns in regards to hypertrophy. This is where understanding the other factors that can incite growth come into play.

Some people will say, "you have to train heavy to get bigger. High reps don't build muscle." This is also not factually true, either, as we've seen both through studies and anecdotally that high reps with submaximal loads can—and do—build muscle mass.

A hypertrophy plan that uses each of these principles appropriately is most ideal and far more efficient. This way, you can keep yourself on the right path to growth, with the least amount of stagnation.

# Chapter Three: Simple and Effective Loading Schemes for Strength Development

~ Christian Thibaudeau

If your goal is to build bigger muscles, you have several different types of training at your disposal and I like to group them in two different categories. The first one is **muscle targeting** (more isolation or lighter work focused on squeezing a certain muscle), which will use more isolated or focused exercises, generally with a slower speed of movement to better be able to target the tension to the desired muscle. Training to failure or beyond (using rest/pause or drop sets for example) is normally desired to get the most out of muscle targeting training.

The second one is **heavy lifting/overload** in which you use bigger lifts in which you can move more weight. Here less importance is placed on lifting speed so that we can focus on pushing harder to be able to lift more weight.

Those who know how Paul and I work know full well that getting stronger is a very important part of building larger muscles.

The variable that has the greatest correlation with strength is the muscle's cross-section, or, in other words, its size. While this means that growing a muscle increases its strength potential, it also means that you will also build more muscle by getting stronger; especially if you do so using an intermediate rep range such as three to six reps per set (one to two reps have a much smaller effect on muscle mass, with adaptations to this range being mostly neural).

Furthermore, gaining strength or using strength-building methods affects how you build muscle in a number of ways.

1. **Training for strength increases neural efficiency**: The more force one must produce, the more fibers must be recruited. Lifting for strength obviously requires one to use heavier weights, which demands a greater force production. As such, when training for strength, you must recruit more muscle fibers and, interestingly, you must recruit more fast-twitch fibers earlier in your set. As such, those growth-prone fast-twitch fibers will get to perform more intense mechanical work, which will stimulate them to growth at a faster rate. But, even more interesting is the fact that you will become more efficient at recruiting fast-twitch fibers over time, and the intermediate and even slow-twitch fibers will take on fast-twitch properties (they won't become fast-twitch, but they will be more fast-twitch-like in the way they perform and respond to training). These two elements will make your muscles more responsive to other types of training. In other words, doing extensive strength work will make your body more responsive to hypertrophy training.

2. **Training for strength increases myogenic tone**: Hardcore lifters often make fun of what we call "being toned", which normally means having firm muscles. The average person often equates training to be toned with lifting light weights for sets of 15 to 20 reps, but it is in fact heavy lifting that gives you the greatest muscle tone. "Tonus", also called "myogenic tone", refers to a state of partial muscle activation, even at rest. It does not have anything to do with the muscle tissue being built differently. You can only make a muscle smaller or larger; you cannot build it out of soft or hard material. Muscle is muscle. What makes a muscle soft- or hard-looking is its state of activation. People with a highly efficient nervous system have harder looking muscles because they are kept partially activated by the nervous system. This is why people who are twitchy and overactive have greater muscle tone (we often refer to them as being "wiry"), while people who are relaxed, who never get stressed and who almost look lazy tend to have softer looking muscles. The most explosive athletes in sport also have the hardest looking muscles. By training for strength and power for a long enough time you will also develop that look. A lean powerlifter, sprinter or gymnast looks hard 24/7. Whereas a bodybuilder who only trains with pump techniques will double in volume during his workouts but quickly deflate afterwards.

3. **Training for strength increases "superficial hardness":** Another reason why training for strength and power gives you harder looking muscles is because this type of training specifically targets the fast-twitch fibers. These fibers are found in greater proportions closer to the skin (the superficial part of the muscle), as opposed to the deeper slow-twitch fibers. People who train for strength will thus develop more hardness through the specific development of the fibers closer to the surface of the muscles. That's also why bodybuilders who train mostly with lighter weights tend to build rounder muscles that don't look as hard and can look deflated when out of the gym.

4. **Training for strength stimulates the body's release of anabolic hormones:** While lighter work where the muscle is under tension for 40 to 70 seconds can lead to a high level of metabolites (lactate, hydrogen ions) and has been shown to increase the release of local growth factors (MGF, IGF-1, GH), heavy lifting leads to a greater level of free testosterone. While I'm not one to claim that transient

changes in hormones during training will make or break your training, they can certainly play a role in stimulating gains in the natural lifter.

5. **Training for strength "turns on" the nervous system for the rest of the session**: By lifting heavy early in the session, you turn on the nervous system. This is called "potentiation". Post-tetanic potentiation refers to a phenomenon whereby having the muscles produce a maximal effort consequently increases the capacity of the nervous system to recruit muscle fibers during subsequent efforts. In simple words, if you start a workout by lifting heavy, the hypertrophy work you do afterwards will be more effective because you will be able to recruit more muscle fibers. And the more muscle fibers you can recruit and fatigue, the more you will grow.

We can safely say that training for strength not only stimulates growth in itself but it will also make your body more responsive to your future training which will, in turn, increase your capacity to stimulate growth. I honestly believe that anyone interested in building a lot more muscle needs to train for strength in some regard, either by including specific strength phases during the year or including some strength work at the beginning of their hypertrophy workouts - preferably both. These approaches will not only build muscle in themselves, but they will also make your body more responsive to training in the future.

The basics of training for strength are fairly straight-forward: focus on lifting heavy weights during big movements and try to add weight to the bar over time. However, if the basics are simple, there are quite a few loading schemes and training methods that can deliver faster results when it comes to getting stronger. Furthermore, there is a difference between getting "1RM/competition stronger" and getting "stronger to build more muscle/look jacked". The former is all about improving your capacity to perform a maximal lift, while the latter is about making the muscles as strong as possible while adding size. It sounds similar, but it's not the same thing.

## 1RM Strength vs. Overall Muscle Strength

I could also call this "demonstrating strength vs. building strength". A competitive strength athlete involved in a 1RM sport (for example, a powerlifter or Olympic weightlifter) has the goal of being able to lift a maximal amount of weight on a few select movements (squat, bench and deadlift for the powerlifter, and snatch and clean and jerk for the weightlifter). While they need to build strength, it's only their foundation. In reality, maximizing efficiency in the competitive lifts as well as developing the capacity to turn everything on for one single effort are even more important than getting stronger overall. Look at elite weightlifters (especially those of the Bulgarian school of thought) who spend most of their time only doing snatches, clean and jerks, front squats and back squats. In powerlifting, while the Westside approach and the adaptations it spawned are still popular and they focus on building strength using a lot of assistance exercises, the most dominant lifters in the IPF (the less equipped, stricter federation)—the Russians, Ukrainians, Norwegians, etc—are now training very similarly to weightlifters by doing most of their volume on the competition lifts.

Coaching legend Ivan Abadjiev believed in extreme specificity of training. This means training as close as possible to your actual competitive event. In weightlifting, they compete in an all-out effort for one repetition in the snatch and clean and jerk. So, in training, they often do the snatch and clean and jerk very heavy for only one repetition. If you want to be good at displaying maximal results in one all-out effort, you must train in that manner. What I personally noticed is that strong non-competitive lifters tend to be stronger on their second or even third repetition in a heavy set. This is mostly a neural phenomenon: they have the muscle strength to move weight, but it takes a rep or two for their nervous system to be optimally turned on. Competitive lifters have to be good at doing maximum efforts, and that needs to be trained.

On the other hand, those who use strength training as a tool to build more muscle don't need to have the capacity to demonstrate strength in a one rep max effort. Training mostly with one rep sets will not build a lot of muscle; it will make you efficient at utilizing the muscle you already have.

**Note**: This is why Paul and I believe that competitive powerlifters need to allocate a good part of their training towards building more muscle. Muscle moves weight. There is only so much that you can accomplish through neural efficiency. While a powerlifter who already has plenty of muscle can afford to focus only on very low reps on the competition exercises, a powerlifter who still needs more muscle to perform optimally will need to include some form of hypertrophy work to reach peak performance. To some extent, the same holds true for weightlifters, but their requirement for overall size is lower since they don't require the same upper body strength, and their lifts are also more technique- and speed-based.

If your main goal is to build muscle, strength training should be seen as a tool to improve muscle density and size, and also increase neural efficiency to make subsequent training more effective. For those purposes, it is not necessary to perform sets of one or two reps or, more specifically, it's not necessary to *specialize* (do a lot of work) on those rep numbers.

## Basic Strength Training Parameters

Before getting into the more advanced material, it is important to know the basics: what type of reps, load and volume work is best to build strength. Then, once we understand what the proper "strength training zone" looks like, it will be easier to design and apply advanced loading schemes to accelerate results.

To me, there are two primary zones and one secondary zone when it comes to training for strength. They are:

1) Relative strength
2) Maximal strength
3) Functional hypertrophy.

### Relative Strength

This training zone focuses on improving your capacity to display strength in an all-out one repetition effort. We are talking mostly about one or two reps per set in training, although up to three reps per set can be used. This training zone works mostly via neural improvements and won't build a lot of muscle mass (which is why it's called "relative" strength, as it is about being strong relative to body weight by gaining a lot of strength without adding weight). Muscle could be built with this approach, but it would require a very high number of sets with near maximal weights which can't be sustained for long by most people.

**Maximal Strength**

This is a training zone where neural and muscular factors are both improved significantly. You can build muscle while training in this zone. You will also receive the neural benefits that heavy lifting can have on looks and size (looking harder, making subsequent training more effective, and waking up the nervous system for the rest of the session). I personally use the three to five rep range for this training zone, although four to six is used by some coaches. Personally, I feel as though there is a huge step between 5 and 6 reps—almost like six reps isn't real strength work. So I prefer to keep this zone to three to five reps per set. A bodybuilder who normally focuses on higher reps in training will likely be fine with four to six reps per set, however.

**Functional Hypertrophy**

This third zone is not a main strength zone since it's mostly aimed at building more muscle. However, it will still cause significant strength gains—albeit less than the two primary zones because of fewer neural improvements. This zone is best kept to isolation or to less demanding exercises when training for strength. The range for this zone is six to eight repetitions. It works well to help strength gains when using smaller movements (dumbbell triceps extension to improve the bench press, for example) because the range of motion (compared to the bench, for example) is shorter. Furthermore, the muscles are under tension for a shorter period of time during each rep: so you can afford to do more reps to get a good strength stimulation.

To recap:

**Relative Strength**

1 to 2 (or 3) reps per set
92 to 100% of maximum
Less than 9 seconds under load
5 to 8 sets per exercise (8 to 16 total reps)

**Maximal Strength**

3 to 5 reps per set
80 to 90% of maximum
10 to 20 seconds under load
4 to 6 sets per exercise (15 to 25 total reps)

**Functional Hypertrophy**

6 to 8 reps per set
70 to 80% of maximum
20 to 30 seconds under load
3 to 5 sets per exercise (20 to 35 total reps)

## Planning the Loading Schemes

Once we have defined the proper training zones, the next step to building a loading scheme is to decide how we will organize the workload. See, it's not only about doing work in the proper zone. How you organize your sets can affect both your strength and size gains.

There are six main ways to organize the sets in a strength session: straight sets, waves, contrasts, pyramids, ramps and plateaus. I will briefly present each type and then give you specific effective loading schemes for all types of loading.

**Straight Sets**
In this method, which is typical of Russian-influenced periodized strength programs, after warming-up, you perform all of your work sets with the same weight and do the same number of reps. For example, you do five sets of five reps with 80 percent of your maximum. With this approach, select a weight with which you can complete all your sets for the prescribed number of reps. It works mostly via the cumulative effect: the sets become more and more challenging as the muscle fibers fatigue. Fatiguing the fibers through heavy work is a strong stimulus. It is the easiest scheme to plan out.

**Waves**
Waves have always been a big part of my training repertoire. Basically, a wave is an ensemble of sets (normally three) that are progressively more challenging. Two or three such waves are done for an exercise during a session. Optimally, each subsequent wave is more challenging than the preceding one. For example, a 3-2-1 wave could look like this:

Set 1: 315lb. x 3
Set 2: 325lb. x 2
Set 3: 335lb. x 1
Set 4: 325lb. x 3
Set 5: 335lb. x 2
Set 6: 345lb. x 1

The wave works by increasing neural activation from set to set, and from wave to wave. It also plays on a psychological phenomenon where you will feel that each set becomes easier even though it gets harder. As you add weight, you reduce the reps; in your mind, it means less work, which puts you in a positive mindset and in fact makes the set easier! Then, when you start a new wave, you add reps but reduce the weight relative to your last set. When you unrack the bar, the contrast in weight makes it feel easier and increases your confidence to complete the set. The first set of the second wave is indeed heavier than the first set of the first wave, but all your brain thinks about is how it feels lighter than the set you just did.

In the world of strength, waves are very popular. For example, the best weightlifter in the world, Ilyia Illyin, as well as all the members of the Kazakhstan's national team use them extensively; however, instead of calling them "waves" they call them "attacks", which I've got to admit, sounds very cool!

**Contrasts**
Contrasts use two different types of loading done back-to-back. A series of pairs are performed in a workout. In that regard, contrasts are similar to waves but each series is composed of two sets instead of three.

One contrast series normally involves one set targeting maximal/relative strength development and one set either focusing on hypertrophy or power development.

For example:

Strength/Hypertrophy contrast
Set 1: 90% x 1
Set 2: 75% x 6
Set 3: 92.5% x 1
Set 4: 77.5% x 6
Set 5: 95% x 1
Set 6: 80% x 5 to 6

In this type of loading scheme, the strength sets serve a dual purpose: first, they develop strength and, second, they potentiate the nervous system, increasing muscle fiber recruitment for the hypertrophy sets and making them more effective for the purpose of stimulating growth.

Strength/Power contrast 1 (strength-speed emphasis)
Set 1: 90% x 1
Set 2: 50% x 3 (as explosive as possible)
Set 3: 92.5% x 1
Set 4: 55%% x 3 (as explosive as possible)
Set 5: 95% x 1
Set 6: 60% x 3 (as explosive as possible)

Strength/Power contrast 2 (speed-strength emphasis)
Set 1: Ballistic movement (jump squats, for example) 20 to 30% x 5
Set 2: 85% x 3
Set 3: Ballistic movement (jump squats, for example) 20 to 30% x 5
Set 4: 87.5% x 3
Set 5: Ballistic movement (jump squats, for example) 20 to 30% x 5
Set 6: 90% x 2 to 3

These illustrate two possible ways to pair up strength/power exercises. There is a brief rest between the two sets of a pair (for example, 60 seconds between Set 1 and Set 2) and a longer rest between the end of a pair and the beginning of a new one (for example, three minutes between set 2 and Set 3).

**Pyramids**
A pyramid can either be ascending (increasing the weight while decreasing the reps on each set) or descending (increasing the reps but decreasing the weight on each set). Within those schemes, we can also have a broad or narrow pyramid. When it comes to strength development, it's best to use a narrow pyramid, while a broad one can be better for hypertrophy.

Broad means that the difference in weight (and reps) is large between the heaviest and lightest sets of the pyramid; narrow means the opposite (there is a small difference between the two extremes).

Here are examples of each type of pyramid:

Broad ascending pyramid
Set 1: 12 reps @ 60%
Set 2: 10 reps @ 65%
Set 3: 8 reps @ 70%
Set 4: 6 reps @ 75%
Set 5: 4 reps @ 80%
Set 6: 2 reps @ 85%

Narrow ascending pyramid
Set 1: 6 reps @ 65%
Set 2: 5 reps @ 70%
Set 3: 4 reps @ 75%
Set 4: 3 reps @ 80%
Set 5: 2 reps @ 85%
Set 6: 1 rep @ 90%

Broad descending pyramid
Set 1: 2 reps @ 90%
Set 2: 4 reps @ 85%
Set 3: 6 reps @ 80%
Set 4: 8 reps @ 75%
Set 5: 10 reps @ 70%
Set 6: 12 reps @ 65%

Narrow descending pyramid
Set 1: 1 rep @ 95%
Set 2: 2 reps @ 90%
Set 3: 3 reps @ 85%
Set 4: 4 reps @ 80%
Set 5: 5 reps @ 75%
Set 6: 6 reps @ 70%

You will notice that in the descending pyramids you can typically use more weight than on an ascending one. The reason is that, with the ascending scheme, you build up fatigue while you are working toward the heavier sets. In the descending pyramid, you do the heavier sets in a fresher state and you also potentiate the nervous system for the higher rep sets, making them more effective.

From a physiological and neural standpoint, the descending pyramid pattern makes more sense. However, the value of ascending pyramids should not be discounted. For example, the 5/4/3/2/1 ascending pyramid is a favorite of Paul's and mine.

I personally find the benefit of the 5/4/3/2/1 scheme for strength is that, even though the weight gets heavier with each set, in your mind it actually gets easier because you have to do less reps. So, right off the bat you have a better mindset with each set. Thus, even though you have more fatigue in theory, the better mindset leads to a better performance.

While a broad ascending pyramid will cause a lot of fatigue that will hurt performance in the later sets, a narrow ascending one will not have the same problem. Gradually increasing the weight also prepares you psychologically for the heavier sets.

The broad descending pyramid can also be used by those wanting to build strength and size: the heavier sets potentiate the lighter ones, giving better results. But when it comes to building strength, I would stay away from broad ascending pyramids (ironically, it seems to be the most popular one in the average gym pop).

**Ramps**

This method is similar to an ascending pyramid in that the load is increased every set. The main difference is that you use the same number of repetition per set throughout the exercise. Practically speaking, you start at 60 to 70 percent of your maximum and then gradually work up until you hit the maximum weight you can lift in good form for the prescribed number of reps. Ideally, I like to have about six to eight sets in a ramp. Sometimes, if it's a very good day, you might be able to get nine or ten because you are able to work up higher than expected, but six to eight is a good range to shoot for. Sure, it looks like a lot, but in reality only about four or five of those sets will actually feel like work sets with maybe two feeling like a challenge. Why do the other sets then? To properly prepare for the heavier sets, get in the groove and wake up the nervous system. You do this without creating too much fatigue because the early sets are low volume and submaximal efforts.

For example, let's say that we do a ramp to a 3RM and your max is around 350 pounds. It's safe to assume that your 3RM should fall between 315 and 330 pounds, and that your starting weight should be between 210 and 245 pounds, likely 225 (you should do one or two warm-up sets prior to that, of course). Let's say that you plan on going from 225 to 325 pounds in six to eight sets. The theoretical ramp might look like this:

Set 1: 225 x 3<br>
Set 2: 240 x 3<br>
Set 3: 255 x 3<br>
Set 4: 270 x 3<br>
Set 5: 285 x 3<br>
**Set 6: 305 x 3**<br>
**Set 7: 320 x 3**<br>
**Set 8: 325 to 330 x 3, depending on feel**

The sets in bold are those that will be a good challenge/work set. In those sets, your focus should be pushing as hard as possible. In the previous sets, the goal is to fine-tune technique and get in the groove. The worst mistake you can make is to do those first four to five sets half-assed. See these as practice sets; make them feel and look like a maximal effort. If you use loose form on these early sets, you won't turn in an optimal performance in the true work sets.

**Plateau**

This method combines elements of the pyramid and straight set approach. You use two or three different loading zones (reps and weight) and do two or three sets with each weight/zone.

For example:

Triple plateau of two sets; ascending
Set 1: 5 reps @ 75%
Set 2: 5 reps @ 75%
Set 3: 3 reps @ 87.5%
Set 4: 3 reps @ 87.5%
Set 5: 1 rep @ 92.5%
Set 6: 1 rep @ 92.5%

Triple plateau of two sets; descending
Set 1: 2 reps @ 90%
Set 2: 2 reps @ 90%
Set 3: 4 reps @ 82.5%
Set 4: 4 reps @ 82.5%
Set 5: 6 reps @ 77.5%
Set 6: 6 reps @ 77.5%

Double plateau of three sets; ascending
Set 1: 6 reps @ 75%
Set 2: 6 reps @ 75%
Set 3: 6 reps @ 75%
Set 4: 3 reps @ 87.5%
Set 5: 3 reps @ 87.5%
Set 6: 3 reps @ 87.5%

Double plateau of three sets; descending
Set 1: 2 reps @ 90%
Set 2: 2 reps @ 90%
Set 3: 2 reps @ 90%
Set 4: 5 reps @ 80%
Set 5: 5 reps @ 80%
Set 6: 5 reps @ 80%

Triple plateau low-high-low
Set 1: 5 reps @ 80%
Set 2: 5 reps @ 80%
Set 3: 1 rep @ 92.5%
Set 4: 1 rep @ 92.5%
Set 5: 3 reps @ 87.5%
Set 6: 3 reps @ 87.5%

Triple plateau, high-low-high
Set 1: 1 rep @ 95%
Set 2: 1 rep @ 95%
Set 3: 5 reps @ 82.5%
Set 4: 5 reps @ 82.5%
Set 5: 3 reps @ 87.5%
Set 6: 3 reps @ 87.5%

Note that I only give examples using strength parameters since this is the subject of this chapter, but the same principle can be applied with different rep ranges.

## Effective Loading Schemes for Strength

The following are some foolproof schemes for building strength. Note that you can also use advanced methods like clusters, extended sets, paused reps and the like to build strength. These will be covered in the next chapter about advanced methods of strength development.

## Straight Sets Schemes

Straight sets are often overlooked when it comes to planning training programs. Why? Because they aren't "sexy". People love to use more complex patterns, feeling that it's more advanced. Truth be told, if you feel that something is more cutting-edge, it might actually give you better results simply because you are more motivated to do it.

Honestly, the key to gaining strength is doing hard work with the proper intensity. In that regard, straight sets are just as effective, and easier to plan, than more complex patterns. At a certain point, you just have to "do work".

Here are some good loading schemes to use if you are training to build strength.

| STRAIGHT SETS LOADING SCHEMES | |
|---|---|
| **Scheme** | **Description/Notes** |
| 6 x 1 @ 90% | This is a "quick gain" plan if you desire to peak the strength you already have. It will work for two to three weeks, but beyond that you will begin to spin your wheels and risk an injury. |
| 5 x 2 @ 87.5% | Personally, I see "2s" as the equivalent of "1s" for those who don't compete in strength sports. I would much rather have a non-competitor train toward establishing a 2RM than a 1RM. When it comes to stimulation the "2s" aren't that different to "1s", but they are a lot less neurologically demanding. |
| 6 x 3 @ 85% | To build strength, this is one of the most effective straight set approaches you can use. It has just the right amount of overall mechanical work to stimulate long-lasting strength gains (due to both neural and muscular adaptations). However, the number of reps per set is low enough relative to the intensity to allow you to dominate each rep, while reinforcing proper lifting technique and avoiding burning out the nervous system. |

| | |
|---|---|
| 5 x 4 @ 82.5% | Similar to the preceding scheme. In reality, 6 x 3 will not have a significant difference in results to 5 x 4. The latter is a quicker way of getting your volume done. I personally notice a huge mental difference between doing 3 and 4 reps. For me, 3 is more effective because 4 starts to feel like a lot of work. When training for strength, 3s give me the best results. But bodybuilders used to doing sets of 8+ reps will not have that barrier. |
| 5* x 5 @ 80% | 5* sets of 5 with 80% is an extreme scheme as it falls slightly outside of the optimal number of reps for that intensity level. Most people should shoot for 3 or 4 actual work sets with 80% and do 1 or 2 sets at a more conservative poundage like 70 to 72.5%. |
| 4 x 6 @ 77.5% | This is a good "middle of the road" scheme that allows you to get stronger while building muscle. It's equally effective for both. Bodybuilders who are used to higher reps will get plenty strong with sets of 6, but strength athletes used to doing heavier might not find that this is a strong enough stimulus to lead to maximal strength gains. |

**Note**: The percentages are a good starting point. You have some leeway depending on how you are feeling that day. When training for strength (not testing for strength), you should not allow reps where form breaks down.

## Waves Schemes

Waves are one of the most effective ways to quickly stimulate strength gains. They only work well with low and moderate reps. Why? Because the goal is to use the heavy set(s) of a wave to potentiate yourself for the high(er) reps set of the next wave. If you create too much fatigue, you will lose that effect.

### The Potentiation/Fatigue Relationship

Every time you perform a set—heck, every time you perform a repetition—two major things happen. One increases your capacity to perform (potentiation) and another decreases it (fatigue).

Potentiation is what is called a "muscle contraction aftereffect". When a muscle contracts hard, the nervous system and muscle becomes "turned on" and, for a certain period of time, their capacity to produce force is increased: either due to a stronger neural drive or more sensitive neuromuscular junction. This phenomenon is called "potentiation". The more force one has to produce, the greater the effect on potentiation. Two types of muscle contractions work well for this: heavy lifting and explosive work. The lower weight/higher rep sets do not require the same level of force production and, as such, do not lead to the same amount of potentiation.

We have all noticed that when doing a set of deadlift, military press, bench or squat with a heavy but not maximal weight (85 to 90 percent, for example), the second rep almost always feels easier than the first one. We've also done protocols that called for, for example, several sets of two to three reps with the same weight, and noticed that the second and even the third set felt easier than the first one. These are two prime examples of potentiation.

Note that potentiation for a heavy effort lasts for up to four to five minutes, but peaks at around two minutes after a set and is kept very high for up to the three minute mark. This is why rest intervals should be three minutes or less when training for strength (if you want to take advantage of the potentiation effect). We've all taken five to six minutes or more between sets only to find that we've "gone cold" and our performance suffered; this is mostly due to the loss of potentiation, not cooling off (that won't happen in such a short period of time).

Fatigue is a side effect of muscle action: you deplete energy stores, increase waste product in the muscles that make it harder for them to contract hard, deplete neurotransmitters, etc. The more fatigue you accumulate, the greater the impact on your capacity to perform. As such, the more reps you perform in a set, the more fatigue you create. For many goals (hypertrophy, fat loss and resistance, for example), this is something we look for. But, for strength gains, it can hurt our capacity to do heavy work and thus makes it harder to get a maximum stimulus.

Waves using higher reps (10/8/6, for example) will thus create more fatigue while leading to less potentiation, in effect, missing the boat on what waves are designed for.

Here are good wave loading schemes to use for strength development.

| WAVE LOADING SCHEMES | |
|---|---|
| **Scheme** | **Description/Notes** |
| 2/1/1 wave | I like to call this the "PR wave". It's the scheme I like to use during a session where the goal is first to get a lot of strength work done and, second, ideally end in a PR. It's similar to the 3/2/1 wave but it builds less fatigue from set to set. The advantage is that you will reach a stronger lift at the end, but the downside is that you get a little less stimulation. That is why I like to use it when the goal is to get the highest number possible. The first wave starts at about 87.5% x 2/90% x 1/92.5% x 1. You add weight on each wave (normally the second set of the first wave becomes the first set of the second wave, etc.), and you continue doing waves until you miss a rep. Ideally, you shoot for three waves. If you complete four, the starting weight was too conservative, so adjust it next time. |
| 3/2/1 wave | This is similar to the 2/1/1 wave, but the goal isn't so much to reach a high number as to create a larger training effect. In that regard, the sets of 3 are your key sets and the sets of 2 and 1 are there mostly to potentiate the "3s". Use the same starting percentages as the 2/1/1 wave. Ideally, shoot for three waves. If you complete four, the starting weight was too conservative, so adjust it next time. |

| | |
|---|---|
| 5/3/1 wave | For the next three schemes, you only perform two waves due to the high volume on each wave. The first wave should be conservative: use weights that you know you'll be able to lift solidly for all the reps. On the second wave, use weights that you know will challenge you and will make it hard to complete all the reps. |
| 6/4/2 wave | The 5/3/1 wave is more of a pure strength wave. It will build tons of strength since it addresses both the neural and muscular components optimally. The 6/4/2 wave is similar but will have a slightly greater impact on muscle mass and slightly less on strength. I could refer the 6/4/2 wave as the "5/3/1 wave for bodybuilders"; it will work best for those used to doing higher reps, while the 5/3/1 will work best for those used to lower reps. It's a mental thing. Here, you also only perform two waves. |
| 7/5/3 wave | I was hesitant to include the 7/5/3 wave scheme since I see it more as a hypertrophy wave than a strength one. It will build strength, don't get me wrong, but it will have a greater impact on size than strength. With that in mind, I suggest going harder on the first wave and decreasing the weight slightly on the second wave as the cumulated fatigue will be greater than the potentiation effect. After the first wave, even if you went easy, your performance will suffer. |

## Contrast Loading Schemes

Contrasts are one of my favorite ways to train. You can create two distinct training stimuli (strength and hypertrophy, for example) while focusing on one at a time, getting more out of each set. You can also use the aftereffect of a set to make the next one more effective.

The "original" contrast set approach was developed by the former Romanian (and later USA) National weightlifting coach, Dragomir Cioroslan, who called it the "mixed neural drive/hypertrophy program". I learned it from Charles Poliquin, who simply called it the 1-6 principle.

This method is the perfect example of a contrast. I will use it as an example to show you what we look for when designing a proper contrast loading scheme.

To simply explain what constitutes a properly planned contrast scheme, I'll go over it point by point.

1. A contrast loading scheme doesn't work in terms of "sets"; it works in terms of a unit of two sets called a "series". Each of the two sets in a series work together and are independent from the other series in the scheme. For example, in a 1-6 contrast, each series is made up of one set of one heavy repetition and one set of six repetitions with a lighter weight.

2. In a series, the first set is used to make the second set more effective—not just to get a training effect by itself. Specifically, we are looking for a potentiation effect from that first set. As we saw earlier, this means that the first set in a series must either be heavy (90 percent or more) or explosive

and cause little muscular/metabolic fatigue. The second set in a series is where you work for the quality you are looking to improve the most. For example, the 1-6 approach is aimed mostly at building muscle with the set of six being the most important part of the contrast, and the set of one being the tool to make the second set better.

3. Potentiation peeks at around two minutes after the conclusion of a set. The ideal rest period between the first and second set of a series is, therefore, two minutes.

4. The second set in a series causes more metabolic fatigue (especially if it's done to stimulate hypertrophy). We don't want fatigue to interfere with the next series. So, the rest period between series (after the conclusion of our set of six reps in the 1-6 example) should be about three minutes to allow for a fuller recovery. We don't want to take more than that since, after five minutes, the potentiation effect is rendered insignificant.

A contrast loading template would appear as follows.

<u>Series 1</u>
**Set 1**: Used to potentiate the nervous system; either near-maximal/maximal effort or explosive work; low reps to avoid fatigue.
*2 minutes of rest.*
**Set 2**: Used to stimulate the adaptations we are looking for. These are the sets which create the greatest training effect.
*3 minutes of rest.*

<u>Series 2</u>
**Set 1**: Normally, we can go slightly heavier than the first set of the first series.
*2 minutes of rest.*
**Set 2**: Again, we should be able to go a bit heavier than the preceding series, because the nervous system is more turned on.
*3 minutes of rest.*

<u>Series 3</u>
**Set 1**: Depending on the scheme you used, you might be able to go even heavier than the second series, but you might also stick with the same weight or even decrease it. The goal is not to hit a max; we only need to lift something heavy (at or above 90 percent) to potentiate the nervous system.
*2 minutes of rest.*
**Set 2**: Same as above. Normally, I like to go a bit heavier on that last set and work to failure, even if we are not able to get all the planned reps in.
*End of scheme.*

**Note:** The higher the reps, the less the performance depends on the nervous system activation level. For example, sets of six reps primarily target hypertrophy but are still heavily reliant on the nervous system, whereas a set of 12 or 15 reps is more limited by metabolic and fatigue factors than neural ones. As such, when using a contrast approach, I believe using higher reps for the second set of your series isn't maximally effective. After all, the whole purpose of the contrast is to potentiate the nervous system with the first set of a series to improve the result of the second set in a series. If we are using a rep number that is less dependent on the nervous system, potentiating it won't make the contrast maximally effective.

| CONTRAST LOADING SCHEMES | |
|---|---|
| **Scheme** | **Description/Notes** |
| 1-3 contrast | This is a pure strength contrast. I believe that sets of 3 reps are optimal to build strength, and sets of 3 with a heavy weight (85 to 90%) are highly affected by neurological potentiation. So, this makes this scheme one of the best ways to build strength. The sets of 1 teach you to demonstrate strength. You have the two elements of "being strong on a lift" present: building strength and being able to demonstrate it in one maximal effort. For the sets of 1, use 92% to 97% (up to 100% on a good day, but that's not the goal), and for the sets of 3, use 85% to 90%. |
| 1-6 contrast (or 1-5) | Of course, I could have included 1-3, 1-4 and 1-5. In reality, 1-4 isn't really that different from 1-3. You can do 1-4 instead of 1-3 if you want, but it is not different enough in training effect to justify making it a separate scheme. 1-6 (or 1-5) is a contrast where hypertrophy and strength are equally developed. As such, it is the best contrast scheme to use for most of us: bodybuilders wanting to get stronger while working on adding mass, and powerlifters looking to gain muscle without neglecting their strength. For the sets of 1, again use 92% to 97%, and for the sets of 6 (or 5), use between 77% and 85%. |
| 1-8 contrast | 8 reps are the highest I'd consider going for the second set of a series—more than that and it's kind of pointless—because the potentiation created by the set of 1 won't have much of an effect on the performance of the higher reps set. 1-8 will build a bit more muscle than 1-6, but a little less strength. Yes, the sets of 1 allow you to stimulate strength, but you don't have enough mechanical work at a higher percentage of your 1RM to be optimal for strength development. However, it will still lead to some strength gains while you are working mostly on adding some more mass. The sets of 8 reps will be done with a weight between 70 and 80%. |

**Note**: I often get asked "*can I do two reps instead of one for the first set of each series?*" Well, you can do anything you'd like, but I wouldn't recommend sets of two instead of one for the "primer". Firstly, the neural activation will not be higher with two reps versus one, since activating depends on the force produced and not the amount of work done. Secondly, sets of two reps will cause a bit more fatigue than sets of one. So, the net gain in performance for the next set (which is the result of the potentiation and fatigue factors) might be less than with sets of one. As far as stimulation goes, you won't get much more out of 2s than singles. Finally, the purpose of the first set in a series is to prime the nervous system for the second set, not to stimulate a lot of gains in itself.

## Pyramid Loading Schemes

As I mentioned earlier, when training for strength, the pyramid types that are effective are the narrow and broad descending pyramids as well as the narrow ascending one. The broad ascending one isn't really effective for building strength, as too much fatigue accumulates before you reach your heavy sets.

| PYRAMID LOADING SCHEMES | |
|---|---|
| **Scheme** | **Description/Notes** |
| Narrow descending | This can be 1-2-3-4-5, or 2-3-4-5-6, or 3-4-5-6-7, or 4-5-6-7-8. I'm not going to bore you with individual descriptions of these four schemes as they are fairly similar in that they all develop strength and size. The first two are a bit more slanted toward strength, and the last two toward hypertrophy. Which one you prefer to use doesn't really matter, as your results will be pretty similar from one to the other. |
| Broad descending | This can be 1-3-5-7-9, or 2-4-6-8-10, or 3-5-7-9-11, or 4-6-8-10-12. Again, there is not much of a difference. Relative to the narrow descending pyramids, the broad ones tend to favor size gains more than strength gains. In this case, the first 2 sets in the pyramid are mostly activation/potentiation tools to make the last 3 sets more effective. |
| Narrow ascending | This can be 6-5-4-3-2, or 5-4-3-2-1. I wouldn't use other schemes because using higher reps for the first set might lead to too much accumulated fatigue, which will hurt performance in the heavier sets. |

***Why always five sets?***
When training for strength, I find that a minimum of four work sets are necessary to get optimal results from an exercise. I find that everything turns on a notch on the third set. From there, I like to have at least two other work sets. Because the volume in a pyramid is fairly high (for strength work), due to the higher rep sets, I would not extend the pyramid to six sets. Four would work, and can be used if you are tired on that day. But, if you are feeling good, five sets are better than four.

## Ramp Loading Schemes

I already explained pretty much everything about ramps. Honestly, it's fairly simple: you pick a rep number, and gradually work up towards the maximum amount of weight you can handle for that specific number of reps. You do that by only doing the number of reps selected, even in the earlier/lighter sets. That way, you gradually amp up your nervous system and get your body prepared to handle bigger weights without causing too much fatigue.

Because we want to avoid building up fatigue, I feel that ramping is best kept for sets of one, two or three reps. Those with great work capacity can go up to four and five, but most people should stick to one to three reps for a ramp. Higher reps cause too much fatigue and too little activation to be effective as a ramp.

## Conclusion

Training for strength is very important, even if you are primarily interested in building more muscle. Strength training will:

1. Allow you to use more weight when doing bodybuilding work in the future, making these sessions more effective at stimulating growth.

2. If you do strength and hypertrophy work in the same session, doing the strength work first will make the following hypertrophy work more effective by turning on the nervous system; thereby leading to greater muscle fiber recruitment (and stimulation).

3. Doing a period of focused strength work in your year of training will improve your neural efficiency. You will improve your capacity to recruit fast-twitch fibers. And the fast-twitch fibers are a lot more prone to growth than the slow and intermediate fibers; the better you are at recruiting and fatiguing them, the more muscle mass you will stimulate.

4. Heavy strength work can increase muscle hardness both by increasing myogenic tone and stimulating the development of the fast-twitch muscle fibers that tend to be more superficial, while the slower fibers are deeper.

# Chapter Four: Special Training Methods for Strength and Size

~ Christian Thibaudeau

While utilizing effective loading schemes is enough to give you optimal results for a *looooooong* time, utilizing special methods to build either strength or size can help get you out of a plateau, fix a specific weakness, or accelerate your gains.

I'm always hesitant to write about special methods of training because people tend to abuse them. It's human nature to want to take the fastest road to our destination… and with changing our body being very emotional, it's even more likely that you will look for every shortcut possible to get there. We see special training methods as being more effective and superior to regular training and, as such, we easily fall victim of using too many of them for too long, too often!

Understand one thing: yes, special strength training methods can be more effective than regular training if you understand how they work and how to use them. But anything that provides the opportunity for a stronger training effect also carries a downside; it can make you stagnate faster if not used correctly. Providing a stronger stimulus can lead to faster adaptations, but it can also drain your capacity to recover and it can desensitize you to regular training. When you become desensitized to training (that is, when your body is used to receiving a very strong training stimulus and doesn't respond to more normal ones), you constantly must push the envelope when it comes to the amount and intensity of the training stress to continue progressing. You might have to go so hard at every session to stimulate gains that you risk overtraining, just to do enough to progress. It's a catch-22 situation: it's hard to train at a high enough level to stimulate gains, but if you train too hard your body will have a hard time recovering, which will itself diminish your gains.

So, while special strength training methods are "cooler" and indeed more effective if used correctly, they can also hurt your long-term progress if abused. It is therefore important to understand how they work and what they do, so that you can pick the right one for your needs and use them at the right frequency and dose.

*What is a special strength training method?*
A special strength training method refers to modifying either the way the structure of a set is done (for example, doing reps to failure, resting 15 seconds and doing a few more reps with the same weight) or how the individual repetitions are performed (for example, lowering the bar extremely slowly).

This allows us to:

1. Perform more work at a given intensity level, or continue to do work once you reach a level of fatigue that would normally prevent you from doing more reps. Some examples are cluster variations, rest-pause sets, drop sets, mechanical drop sets and growth factor sets.

2. Put a stronger than usual stimulus on a certain part of the range of motion. Some examples are partial reps, double contractions, accommodating resistance, functional isometrics, and taking pauses during the reps at key points in the range of motion.

3. Put more emphasis on a certain type of muscle action than when doing regular reps. Some examples are lowering the weight very slowly, adding resistance during the eccentric portion of a lift or taking pauses during the reps.

4. Put more emphasis on one muscle involved in a multi-joint movement. This mostly refers to pre-fatigue supersets, post-fatigue supersets or pre/post-fatigue supersets.

5. Increase training density to stimulate the release of more anabolic hormones and get a greater metabolic increase from training. Antagonist supersets, complexes and EMOMs are good examples.

In this chapter, I will present my favorite special strength training methods for strength and size, and explain what they do and how demanding they are on the body (less demanding methods can be used more often).

## Category One: Extending Sets

In this category will be all the methods where you do more work than you should normally be able to. This is done by taking short rest periods between reps or a group of reps; by taking a medium pause at the end of the set and then doing more reps with the same weight; by reducing the weight at the end of the set to be able to continue doing reps; or by decreasing the range of motion at the end of the set.

1.1 Using Intra-Set Pauses

This is referred to as "clusters". Basically, each set is a series of mini-sets ranging from one to five reps (normally one to three) and we use 7 to 15 seconds of rest between these mini-sets. The goal is to either get two to three more reps than you should be able to do with a given weight, or to use three to five percent more than you could normally for a given repetition number.

Why are clusters so effective? The simple explanation is that clusters allow you to perform more work than you would normally be capable of at a given weight, and the very brief rest between reps is not enough to lose the "set effect" (or repeated bout effect). The short rest period allows you just enough time to replenish some ATP in the muscles to continue performing at a high intensity, but it's not enough time to lose the benefit of doing sets of multiple repetitions—which is to fatigue the muscle fibers more because they have to perform more than one bout of effort.

I've always believed that the key to making muscle grow optimally and getting as strong as possible is to do the most to recruit the high threshold motor units—more commonly known as the fast-twitch fibers. These fibers not only have a faster, stronger contraction, but they also have a more important growth potential. If you want to grow optimally and get beastly strong, you need to target those fibers.

The high threshold motor units are named as such because they are only recruited when a very intense muscular effort is needed. It takes a lot to activate them. The number factor involved in recruiting them is the intensity of the load relative to your maximum. In other words, the closer a weight is to your maximum in a movement, the more the high threshold motor units will come into play.

A counter argument is that you can also recruit the fast-twitch fibers by using lighter weights but going to failure. The explanation is that, as you perform reps with a light weight, you create fatigue which makes the movement more difficult and therefore means the last few reps are actually of maximal effort and require the participation of the high threshold motor units.

That is true. And I do believe that when training with isolation work, working to muscle failure is the way to go. However, the value of heavy lifting is that you not only recruit the fast-twitch fibers sooner in the set, you also improve their capacity to "twitch" rapidly. Each "twitch" produces force so the higher the "twitch frequency" the more force a fiber can produce. And heavy lifting is the best way to work on that element (rate coding). By improving motor unit recruitment and rate coding you increase muscle strength, which will also help you gain more muscle size in the future.

One thing I'd like to add is that it's not enough to just recruit a muscle fiber to stimulate it to grow and get stronger. To quote Zatsiorsky: "A muscle fiber that is recruited, but not fatigued, is not trained." (Zatsiorsky V. Science and Practice of Strength Training. Human Kinetics. 1995.)

It's not enough to just recruit more fibers; you must fatigue them. It thus requires the repeated bout method. That is why doing heavy sets of one or two reps won't work well to make you bigger; you recruit a lot of fibers, but you don't fatigue them. Even if you do several sets of one or two reps, you still recover between sets, which means that it requires a lot of sets to grow.

Clusters take care of that problem. You have the heavy loads (90 to 100 percent) that help you recruit a maximum amount of muscle fibers, and you still have the repeated bout effect by doing reps to failure in your set. The fact that you have short rest intervals is enough to allow you to do more total reps by replenishing some ATP, but not enough to allow the fibers to recover. They get more and more fatigued so, when you reach the end of the set, you have not only recruited them but also fatigued them. This means maximal growth.

Below are some effective cluster strategies.

**Classic Cluster (5 x 1, with 10 seconds of rest)**: In the classic cluster, your goal is to perform five repetitions with a weight you would normally use to do three reps with. You do so by taking 10 seconds of rest between each repetition. Be sure to re-rack the weight after each rep. Start counting the rest when the body is unloaded of the weight (when it's back on the rack). This is one of the most effective methods to gain strength and it also has a decent effect on muscle mass. Note that we cannot put a ceiling on the number of mini-sets per set. For example, we could simply say you should use a weight you could do three reps with and do as many mini-sets of one rep (with 10 seconds of rest) as possible. But, most of the time, it will fall between four and six reps.

**Double Cluster (5 x 2, with 12 seconds of rest):** This is the same approach as the classic cluster, but with more volume. The goal is to perform 10 repetitions in total, grouped into mini-sets of two repetitions, with a weight you would normally use to do six or seven reps. Again, you re-rack the bar after each mini-set. You can also shoot to do as many mini-sets as possible with a 6-7RM load but, again, it will almost always fall between four and six mini-sets. This is a type of cluster that will greatly affect muscle mass as well as strength, especially in those who are used to traditional bodybuilding-type training, as opposed to powerlifting training.

**Triple Cluster (5 x 3, with 12 seconds of rest):** This is more of a pure hypertrophy cluster. The goal is to perform a total of 15 repetitions with a weight you would normally use for a 10 to 12 rep set. This is done via mini-sets of three repetitions. You can actually use less rest than 12 seconds at the beginning of the set and increase the duration as you progress through the cluster. The first three mini-sets tend to feel very easy, so taking shorter rest periods will make the method more effective.

Note that once you understand the principle behind clusters, you can make up your own versions. For example, you can combine a double and classic cluster by doing something like 2-2-2-1-1. That is, eight total reps with a weight you would use for five to six reps.

### 1.2 Rest-Pause Extended Sets

Once again, the goal with rest/pause sets is to do more reps than you normally could with a given weight. This time, we don't take pauses inside the bulk of the set; rather, we go to failure or close to it in one set. When you reach the point of failure, or close to it, you rest for a short period of time, and then attempt to get a few more reps with the same weight. The process can be done once, twice or even three times in a set.

**Single Rest-Pause Set:** This if your basic rest-pause set where you work up to failure or technical failure with a given weight, then rest 10 to 15 seconds and try to get a few more repetitions, again working to failure or close to it. This can be used for strength by using a weight you can get three to five reps with in the initial portion of the set, or for developing size by using a weight you can get six to ten reps with in the initial portion of the set.

**Double Rest-Pause Set**: Similar to the single rest-pause approach, in this method you simply add a second rest-pause at the end of the second portion of the set. You can take up to 20 seconds of rest between the second and third part of the set. A set might look like this: 7 reps/rest 15 secs/4 reps/rest 20 secs/3 reps. This can be done for strength or size using the same parameters as above.

**Triple Rest-Pause Set:** You will be surprised to learn that this is, once again, just like the previous two; you simply add a third rest-pause, making the set an ensemble of four mini-sets. A set might now look like this: 7 reps/rest 15 secs/4 reps/rest 20 secs/3 reps/rest 20 secs/2 reps. You may notice this doesn't look too different from the 5-4-3-2-1 approach we discussed earlier. The difference is, in the rest-pause approach, you go to failure or close to it on every mini-set and, as such, you can't predict the number of reps you will get. In the 5-4-3-2-1 method, the goal is not to reach failure but rather to get all the prescribed reps done; if you go to failure on any of the mini-sets, you likely won't get there.

Of course, the double and triple rest-pause methods produce a greater stimulus within your muscles, so many people will be tempted to primarily rely on these. Keep in mind, though, that these methods are more stressful on the body and will affect the performance of the subsequent sets more than a single rest-pause set. As such, it is smart to cycle the use of single, double and triple rest-pause sets.

### 1.3 Drop Sets

Drop sets are well-known to most lifting enthusiasts since they—along with supersets—are one of the first intensity methods that we learn when we begin to lift for size. The principle is simple: you work up to or close to failure with a certain weight, and then drop the weight in order to continue on with the set. The goal is, again, to allow the target muscle to continue working once it's too fatigued to do more with the original weight.

I will not give you all the options possible with drop sets. There are essentially three factors you can play with to create your own versions:

**Customizable Option One – The Starting Point:** Here I'm talking about the load and number of reps you start your set with. With drop sets, I don't lie to start with more than eight or maybe ten reps, because the average weight of the set will be too light to provide maximal results. Drop sets should also only be used to increase muscle mass; they are not adequate/optimal to build maximal strength. As such, the three possible starting points are 1) a load you can get four to six reps with 2) a load you can get six to eight reps with and 3) a load you can get eight to ten reps with. If you plan on doing multiple drops in a set, or doing a large drop, I suggest starting with four to six reps. If you are only doing one drop, or a smaller drop, the other two zones will work well, too.

**Customizable Option Two – The Number of Drops:** You can do as many drops as you want, provided that you are still lifting some weight by the last one! For example, if you start doing dumbbell lateral raises with 20 pounds and want to do five drops, it's pretty much useless since you'll have to use 2.5 pounds at the end—which won't do much except burn energy. As a rule of thumb, I personally don't drop any lower than 50 percent of the original weight. For example, if I'm doing curls with 80 pounds I won't finish with less than 40 pounds. This is not an obligation, but I find going any lower than 50 percent to be counterproductive; if you want to do more work, it's better to do one more set than drop below 50 percent, if you ask me. Still, you can decide to do one, two or three drops, depending on how good you feel that day.

**Customizable Option Three – The Size of the Drops:** This is heavily influenced by how many drops you do (if you do five drops, it will be hard to make them big), but not entirely. You can do one drop and make it a small one—something like eight reps with 100 pounds + two reps with 90 pounds. The advantage of smaller drops is that you keep the average weight high; this will take advantage of the muscle damage way of stimulating growth. If you make larger drops, you will be able to do more total repetitions but the average weight will be lower and, as such, you will rely more on the growth factor accumulation and mTOR activation rather than muscle damage to stimulate growth. Just because doing more total reps is more painful (more lactate accumulation due to burning more glycogen), it doesn't always make it more effective. Both work via different pathways and both can be used.

I'll be honest with you: drop sets are not among my own favorite techniques, but I do use them from time to time, mostly on isolation exercises.

## 1.4 Variable Range of Motion Sets

The basic principle of this training method is simple: you perform regular reps to a point close to failure. When you reach that point, you shorten the range of motion to 1/2 or 1/3 reps in order to continue with your set. This is one of my favorite intensity methods. I find it very effective because you keep a high level of tension on the muscles (as you keep the same weight during the whole set), which will increase the production of growth factors. It allows you to combine a fairly heavy load with a longer time under tension, thereby stimulating growth via two different pathways at once.

Note that you can do either "half" of the range of motion for your partials. For example, when you do a bench press, you could follow your full reps with bottom-half reps (from chest to elbows at 90 degrees) or with top-half reps (from above elbows at 90 degrees to lockout), depending on which muscles you want to target. Of course, in some movements it will only be possible to do reps in one half of the movement (for example, doing bottom-half squats when you reach a point close to failure on full squats doesn't work), in which case the partials are done in the stronger portion of the movement.

The number of partial reps performed is not important. What is important is how you perform your partials. Partials reps should be done slower than full reps as such that a half-rep takes you almost as much time to complete as a full rep. That is key: go slower and don't use momentum to do your partial reps.

This method works equally well with isolation exercises and compound movements. It can be quite effective to build strength and size simultaneously. To focus more on strength, do three to five full reps and then partial reps to failure on a big compound movement. For size, I like to start with six to eight full reps for compound movements and eight to ten full reps for isolation exercises.

## Category Two: Overloading a Certain Point in the Range of Motion

This category includes methods for both strength and size development. What we want to do is place a larger than usual stress on a specific point or portion of the range of motion; to increase the work performed and strengthen that specific point in the range of motion (to correct a sticking point, for example), or to have a certain muscle perform more work than the other muscles involved in the exercise (to grow a lagging body part, for example).

### 2.1 Partial Reps

This option is mostly to build strength. It consists of performing only a specific portion of an exercise's range of motion. It can be used for two main purposes:

To get your nervous system and Golgi tendon organs (GTOs) used to handling supramaximal loads, and to become more comfortable handling heavier weights.
To strengthen a specific angle in the range of motion, thereby correcting the sticking point of the exercise.

In the first option, you only perform the strongest portion in the range of motion. The actual distance the bar travels should be at least one-third of the range of motion. The goal is to use a weight that is significantly heavier than the one you can use over the full range of motion. One of the benefits of this technique is to become psychologically used to handling very heavy weights. A lot of the time, a big lift such as a squat or bench is failed before it even starts, when you unrack the weight and it feels heavy and psychs you out. Getting used to handling heavier than normal weights, even if they are for partial repetitions, will accustom you to the feeling of maximal weight and you won't feel intimidated when you unrack your regular heavy sets.

The other benefit is physiological: your muscles have protective mechanisms to reduce risks during the course of physical work. One of these mechanisms are the GTOs, which are basically force gauges at both ends of the muscle (where the tendons begin). Their role is to inhibit further force production if they sense that the muscle is already producing too much of it and, in turn, risking tearing itself if more force is produced. The bad thing is that the GTOs are overprotective in average people. Non-trained individuals can only produce about 30 percent of their force potential due to an overly conservative protective mechanism. The more experience with heavy lifting you have, the less conservative the GTOs become. Lifting supramaximal weights over partial ranges of motion is a good way to desensitize the GTOs; it's a way to tell them that "hey, I used 50 pounds more than you think I can lift and I didn't tear anything". Over time, this approach will desensitize the GTOs, thereby allowing you to use a greater portion of your force potential.

In the second option, you start the concentric part of the movement just above your sticking point. Why just above and not *at* the sticking point? Because, by nature, the sticking point is a weaker part in the range of motion, so starting the movement there will greatly reduce the amount of weight you can use. By starting just above it, you will be able to use more weight and that will lead to greater strength gains. And don't worry—there is carryover of the strength gains for 10 to 15 degrees. For example, if you initiate your movement at a knee angle of 100 degrees, the strength gains will carry over to an 85 degree knee angle. By starting *just* above the weak point (one to two inches above), you will thus have the greatest gains possible at that sticking point.

For partial reps, there are three main set-up options. Although similar, they have some important differences in training effect. These options are to start the lifts from pins in the power rack (or putting the bar on blocks for the deadlift), using boards (on your chest for the bench press) or a box (to sit on during the squat), or to do the rep normally but with a shorter range of motion (for example, setting up like a regular bench but only going down halfway).

**Partial Lifts from Pins:** From experience, this is the option that allows you to lift the most weight for a given position. Firstly, because the bar is supported without you being involved, you can set up perfectly on every repetition. You also waste less energy because there isn't really an eccentric phase. Another characteristic—which can be a pro or con depending on how you look at it—is that, with lifts from pins you go from zero force production (because your muscles aren't supporting the load at the beginning) to maximum force to fight the inertia. As such, you can increase the rate of force development and starting strength, not just strength. The downside is that you will never have a similar situation in the regular full range lift; thus, the strength gain will not always be 100% transferable. Another drawback of lifts from pins is that you don't really work on the precision of the eccentric phase. Most people simply bring the bar back on the pins after each rep, not focusing on using a proper bar path or controlling the load. As such, this can be hard to transfer to a movement where transitioning from the eccentric to the concentric *is* important. In conclusion, it is probably the best method to increase concentric strength in a muscle or group of muscles, but those strength gains can take a while to transfer over to the full movement.

**Partial Lifts from Boards or a Box**: These are a staple of many powerlifters' training. Bench press with a stack of boards on your chest, lowering the bar to the boards and acting as if the boards *are* your chest (in other words, keep the same bench press mechanics as during your full range bench press). Or, squat down to a box. Relative to the pins, this option is more transferable to the full range lift since the dynamics of the movement are kept. For example, in the board press, even when the bar is on the board, you are still supporting it and your body is still under load. Resting the bar on the boards is the same as resting it on your chest, because the board is in contact with the chest and the resistance is therefore transferred to the chest/body through the board. You also must execute the eccentric phase properly, and switch from lowering to lifting. Therefore, it's important to execute these lifts in exactly the same way as you would a regular strength lift. See the board as your chest, not a board you need to rest the bar on. Imagine that the boards are not there, and your chest just got a whole lot bigger! The downside with lifts from blocks is that you can't use as much weight as with lifts from pins. In fact, some lifters aren't much stronger from boards. You won't have as much GTO desensitization as with lifts from pins, but the strength gains you make will be immediately transferable to the full range lift.

**Partial Lifts Without Support**: This last option consists of doing a regular repetition but with a shorter range of motion. For example, you squat halfway down and then stand up. This also has a great transfer to the full range movement and, if done properly, can be really effective in strengthening a sticking point. Why? Because not only do you have to lift from just above the sticking point, you also have to break the downward movement of the bar when you arrive at the weak area, and that requires even more force. It's also easier to maintain a lift when it is similar to the full range movement. The biggest drawback is that it's hard to be consistent with the range of motion used. With boards, a box, or pins it's easy because you have a "target" telling you exactly where to lower the bar to. In the case of free partials, you have to use your judgement and few people can hit the proper depth over and over. So, while it is a method that has potential, its application isn't optimal. I personally like to use it for the military press, as it's easier to judge depth since I can give myself targets such as "lower to forehead", "lower to nose", "lower to eyes", and so on. It can also be used on machine exercises fairly easily. But, for squat and bench, it's harder to do properly.

**Note**: Partials tend to be used more often to develop strength, but they can also be used as a hypertrophy tool. For example, doing top-half close-grip bench from pins or five board presses for fairly high reps will really hit the triceps hard with a heavy load. When using partials for hypertrophy, I like to increase the reps over what I normally would do. For example, where I would use six to eight reps for a full range movement, I'd use 10 to 12 partials.

## 2.2 Variable Resistance

This refers to using training tools that allow you to change the amount of resistance to overcome various parts of the lift. Specifically, the use of resistance bands or chains added to the barbell.

Both chains and bands increase the amount of resistance as the bar progresses through the range of motion. In other words, the closer you are to completing the lift, the higher the resistance will be. The bands do this by being stretched more, which makes them pull the bar down harder, and the chains do this by being heavier off the floor (the chains are on the floor at the beginning of the lifting phase and are lifted as you lift the barbell). There is also the reverse band set-up in which you hang the bar from the top of the power rack using bands. As you add weight, the bar will go down. The band is more stretched at the bottom, which lightens the load. As you lift the barbell up, the bands are stretched less which reduces the "help" given and thus increases the load.

While all three change the force curve in a similar way they each have different effects. Chains only add weight, while the bands actually try to pull you down. The latter is more stressful and the increase in resistance is more exponential, while the chains provide a more linear increase.

For that reason, chains can be used quite often whereas bands are best used for two to four week cycles. Note that the reverse band set-up is the less stressful of all variable resistance methods, and it can be used with a much higher volume of work than the two others.

Traditionally, variable resistance work has been used to train for strength. It was popularized by the Westside Barbell crew who used all three methods for both explosive lifting (to force you to accelerate from the start to "beat" the bands/chains) and for maximal lifting (to increase resistance where the powerlifting gear helps less).

However, they also have their place in training for increased muscle mass. What these tools do is make the whole range of motion more challenging. Normally, in a big lift, the first half of the range of motion is hard but it gets easier as the barbell goes up. This is true for two reasons:
Mechanical advantage in the second half of the movement.
In the latter part of the lift the barbell is already moving, and it's easier to overcome a barbell moving in the direction you want it to go, than a static one.

For that reason, half of the lift is actually sub-optimal in terms of muscle tension, which means less muscle fiber fatigue and less stimulation. With chains or bands, you can make the whole range of motion maximally effective. It also helps you maintain constant tension more easily during a set, as the increase in resistance forces the muscles to contract hard.

There is no doubt that doing more typical bodybuilding work, and focusing on constant muscle tension will work well with variable resistance methods. You should shoot for 6 to 12 reps per set. As long as you reach a point close to failure within that zone when using variable resistance, it will work. There is no need to be too prissy about details in that specific case.

## Category Three: Emphasizing the Eccentric or Isometric Components of a Lift

Both eccentric and isometric actions play a big part in muscle growth. Traditionally, the eccentric phase of a lift has been associated with stimulating more growth. The fact that emphasizing it also tends to cause more muscle soreness has led people to believe that accentuating the eccentric works mostly by increasing muscle damage. While this can be part of the equation in some cases, I believe that the bigger reason why accentuating the eccentric leads to more growth is because emphasizing the eccentric leads to a greater mTOR activation, and that is the most powerful training-controlled factor to increase protein synthesis/muscle growth.

As far as isometric actions go, it can play three roles. Firstly, it has been shown that you can recruit 10 percent more muscle fibers during an isometric action, and turning on more muscle fibers will mean more growth. Secondly, it increases time under tension. By adding isometric pauses/holds during a set you place the muscles under tension for longer which, as we have seen earlier, will lead to more growth stimulation, provided that the load is kept high enough. Lastly, pausing during a set increases the accumulation of metabolites in the muscle as well as helps to create a hypoxic state (lack of oxygen). This occurs because when a muscle is kept contracting hard, blood cannot enter in the muscle, which prevents the metabolites from being taken out and oxygen from being transported in. Both of these will increase the release of local anabolic growth factors.

So, you can turn regular repetitions into intensity methods simply by emphasizing the eccentric phase of the lift or by adding pauses in your lift.

The first one is straight-forward: you simply make the eccentric portion of the repetition harder by lowering the weight slowly while tensing the muscles hard. Another option is to have a partner apply pressure on the barbell during the eccentric phase of the lift, making that phase harder. A third option works well with machine exercises; it's called the 2/1 technique whereby you lift the weight with two limbs (for example, leg extensions with two legs) and lower it down slowly with one limb.

As for the pauses, you can use them for several purposes:

1. **To take the stretch reflex out of the movement**: When a muscle is stretched under load, the stretch reflex is activated to help you lift the weight (like stretching a rubber band and releasing it). This is good for performance, but not so much for muscle work as the stretch reflex takes over the role of active muscle contracting during the first part of the lift. Taking a two second pause before lifting the barbell greatly deactivate the stretch reflex and, as a result, the muscles must do more of the work.

2. **To increase time under tension**: While a pause to increase time under tension can be done at any point in the range of motion, I find that the t
wo best positions to do the hold is at the mid-point of the range of motion and at the peak contraction position (on exercises offering the possibility to hold a peak contraction). I find this method especially

useful for movements with a very short range of motion like shrugs and calf raises. In these movements, the range of motion is so short that it is hard to place the muscle under load for long enough to stimulate maximal growth without resorting to ultra high reps. The work at the peak contraction helps solve that issue.

3. **To create an occlusion effect**: As we mention a few times in this book, preventing blood from entering the muscle because of a sustained, intense contraction increases the release of local growth factors. A method I really like is doing a static hold (either at mid-point or peak contraction) for 30 seconds, and then doing your six to ten repetitions. I find this to be very effective to stimulate growth and to increase mind-muscle connection. A variant that is also very effective is to do your 6 to 12 reps and then hold for as long as you can.

## Category Four: Pre- and Post-Fatigue Supersets

Supersetting is quite possibly the oldest form of intensity method. It consists of coupling two exercises together, taking minimal rest between the two (note that giant sets, which are supersets of more than two exercises, are similar). While there are several types of supersets, the two main ones consist of (1) coupling exercises for the same muscle group and (2) coupling exercises for opposing muscle groups.

In this method, we will focus on the first category: same muscle supersets. The goal of these supersets go well beyond simply creating a mega pump. While the mere act of using two exercises for one muscle group back-to-back will work, by extending the time under tension the target muscle is under and increasing lactic acid accumulation—which, in turn, increases the release of growth factors while also causing more fatigue on the muscle fibers (both of which can lead to growth)—you can get more out of your supersets if you plan properly.

To me, one of the biggest benefits of same-muscle supersets is to improve the recruitment of a lagging muscle group within a big compound movement, thereby making this exercise more effective in the future.

Take the bench press, for example. If someone is really strong in the delts and weak in the pectorals, the chances are that the delts will do more work than the pectorals when bench pressing. Even though that person would do the bench press to build their chest, they will get more front deltoid growth and only accentuate the imbalance between the delts and pectorals. We can use supersets to teach your body to use the pecs better in the bench press. In time, you will become better at making the pectorals the prime movers in the bench press.

To do this, we rely on a phenomenon called "enhanced feedback" and we do a method called pre-fatigue supersets to do that. The working mechanism is to do an isolation exercise for the lagging muscle group (pectorals, in our example) prior to doing the big lift. For example, supersetting a set of pec deck machine flys and bench press.

This creates a pump in the pectorals before doing the bench press. The result is, that when you bench press you will feel your pectorals much more, as you will have improved mind-muscle connection to your pectorals during the bench press. Over time, you will become better at feeling and flexing your pecs while bench pressing; which is the first step in making that muscle the prime mover in the exercise.

**Note**: The counter-argument is that by pre-fatiguing the pectorals before bench pressing, you will make them even weaker, which will force your body to rely even more on the delts and triceps. The other argument is that you will be forced to use less weight on the bench press, which might make it less effective at stimulating growth. Both comments are true and valid. However, you must understand what the purpose of pre-fatigue supersets is. Yes, they will stimulate growth, but that's not the main reason why you should do them. The main reason is to learn to use a muscle in a big lift. It's an investment for future gains. Let's say that your chest is weak, and you have been bench pressing for 10 years without feeling it in your chest. Is it not worth it to bench press a little less weight for four weeks so that, for the rest of your life, the bench press will become an effective tool to build your pecs?

Furthermore, while pre-fatiguing the pectorals might make them weaker, it also turns them "on" for the bench press. So, while the logical thing to assume is that they would be less involved when pre-fatigued, in reality, they might very well be involved *more*, especially at the beginning of the set. They will tire out more quickly, but this way at the end of the set the pectorals are fried, contrary to when you do heavy bench pressing by itself.

So once again, pre-fatigue supersets (isolation + compound) are tools to improve your capacity to use a lagging muscle group in a compound movement. They work with any big lift (all bench press variations, overhead presses, squats, deadlifts, rows, pull-ups, etc). It's simply a matter of identifying the muscle that is not involved properly in the big lift, and selecting an isolation movement for it.

The second option is to do the opposite: start with the big lift and then do an isolation exercise for the target muscle group. This is called post-fatigue and is primarily a hypertrophy tool, not a motor learning tool (learning to integrate a lagging muscle group in a big lift). The working principle is really simple. In a big lift, several muscles share the load. At the end of the set, it is the ensemble of muscles that is not able to produce enough force as a group, but chances are that the individual muscles still have some power and have not been fully stimulated. By adding an isolation exercise for your target muscle, you can fully fatigue that muscle and thus increase growth stimulation.

This method should be used with ample rest periods between sets (but no rest between exercises), to allow you to use more weight on the big lift.

Note that a variant exists where you do the compound lift and then two or three isolation exercises—one for each of the muscles involved in the big lift. For example, a giant set of bench press + pec deck flyes + dumbbell triceps extensions + dumbbell front raises.

Post-fatigue is a better method versus pre-fatigue for immediate/direct hypertrophy. But pre-fatigue is a good investment for future gains if you have problems getting a muscle to grow from a big compound lift.

To quickly recap:

**Pre-Fatigue** (isolation + compound): Primarily a tool to improve your capacity to integrate a muscle in a big lift. But, like every superset method, it has a good impact on hypertrophy via an increase in time under tension and an increased production of lactic acid.

**Post-Fatigue** (compound + isolation): A pure hypertrophy tool that allows you to stimulate maximum growth to one muscle using a mix of a heavy compound lift and a fully fatiguing isolation movement.

## Category Five: Density Methods

Training density refers to the amount of work done per unit of time. Increasing density basically means fitting more work in a set period of time or doing the same work in less total time.

There are several benefits to having a higher training density:

1. **It keeps you better focused:** When you take shorter rest periods and keep moving, you always keep your mind on training and you don't let your mind wander. This better training focus is often what separates those who get okay and those who get great results.

2. **It leads to a better hormonal milieu**: Higher density of training is normally associated with a greater release of growth hormone, local growth factors, and a higher free testosterone level. A higher density also leads to less cortisol output for a given training volume. In other words, the anabolic hormones are higher and the catabolic one is lower.

3. **It increases caloric expenditure**: Although we aren't lifting to lose fat, it's always nice to jack up energy expenditure if that helps us get leaner while adding muscle mass. A higher density of work increases caloric expenditure during training as well as in the period post-training.

4. **It provides health benefits, specifically for the cardiovascular system:** The higher density of work keeps your heart rate elevated for longer, which will improve cardiac efficiency and help keep the vascular system in top shape.

Personally, I've always liked to train fast, and Paul is the same way. Taking too long between sets gets me out of the zone and cools me off, not to mention that data on post-tetanic potentiation (the increase in neural efficiency following an intense effort) shows that the boost in performance you get from a set peaks after about two minutes. While some of it is sustained for as long as five minutes, the sweet spot as far as potentiation goes seems to be two minutes—long enough to recover but short enough to get the neural potentiation benefit.

Of course, performance remains my main goal. If cutting rest intervals too much leads to a drop in lifting capacity, then it's not a good trade-off.

Besides simply reducing rest intervals, there are other methods that allow you to increase training density. Below are some of them.

**Antagonist Supersets**: This method consists of pairing two exercises for opposing muscle groups or movement patterns in a superset. There is no, or little, rest between both exercises and a moderate rest period after a set of both has been done.

For example:
A1. EZ bar preacher curl x 8 to 10 reps
15 seconds of rest
A2. Decline dumbbell triceps extension x 8 to 10 reps
75 seconds of rest
If you do four sets like that, it will take you about 10 minutes. If you were to do both exercises by themselves for four sets each, it would take you approximately 14 minutes (given 75 seconds of rest

between sets). This provides almost a 30 percent increase in training density without changing any other parameter and performance would not suffer either—in fact, it might be better.

Logical pairings are as follows.

**Muscle Group Pairings**
Biceps/Triceps
Pectorals/Upper back
Quads/Hamstrings
Anterior and lateral delts/Rear delts and rhomboids
Abs/Lower back
Calves/Tibialis

**Movement Pattern Pairings**
Upper body vertical pushing/Upper body vertical pulling
Upper body horizontal pushing/Upper body horizontal pulling
Arm flexion/Arm extension (not really different to biceps/triceps)
Scapular elevation (shrug)/Scapular depression (pec minor dip, for example)
**I wouldn't train the lower body with antagonist movement patterns because there is too much cross-fatigue. With the lower body, I prefer to use one big movement and an isolation movement for the antagonist exercise. For example, back squats + lying leg curls OR Romanian deadlifts + leg extensions. Something like front squats + Romanian deadlifts would fatigue the lower back too much and you wouldn't perform well on either of the exercises.*

**Mechanical Drop Sets**: This is one of my favorite training methods. It consists of pairing three similar movements. They should work the same basic pattern (for example, upper body pressing) but include some slight variations that make some of the movements "stronger" than others. For example, standing dumbbell press, incline dumbbell press and flat dumbbell press should be done back-to-back with the *same weight*. This is like a drop set but, instead of dropping the weight, you change the exercise to a stronger one that allows you to continue getting reps.

For example:
A1. Overhead dumbbell press x 8 reps (close to failure)
10 seconds of rest, then move on to:
A2. Incline dumbbell press x maximum reps (close to failure)
10 seconds of rest, then move on to:
A3. Flat dumbbell press x maximum reps (to failure)
Rest 2 to 3 minutes.

This can be done for low (two to five) or moderate (six to eight) reps for the initial movement. The number of reps for the other two exercises will depend on your tolerance for work.

**Good Pairings:**
Overhead press + Incline press + Flat press (dumbbell or barbell)
Close-grip bench + Wide-grip bench + Normal bench*
Dumbbell flyes + Dumbbell power flyes (greater bend in the elbows) + Dumbbell press (incline, decline or flat)
Behind-the-neck pulldowns + Pronated pulldown in front + Supinated pulldown in front
Seated row, torso leaning forward + Seated row, at 90 degrees + Seated row, leaning back

Bent-over row with torso parallel to the floor + Bent-over row at 60 degrees + Bent-over row with low back swing
Dumbbell lateral raise + Dumbbell front raise + Dumbbell front raise one arm at a time (alternating)
Narrow-grip barbell front raise + Mid grip barbell front raise + Wide-grip barbell front raise
Front squat + Back squat narrow stance + Back squat wide stance (good luck!)
Romanian deadlift + Snatch deadlift + Sumo deadlift* (good luck!)
Leg extension, with feet turned in + Leg extension, with feet neutral + Leg extension, with feet turned out*
Leg curl, with feet turned in + Leg curl, with feet neutral + Leg curl, with feet turned out*
Reverse preacher curl + Preacher curl + Standing curl
Reverse dumbbell curl + Dumbbell curl + Dumbbell hammer curl
Rope triceps extension, while opening hands + Rope triceps extension, with hands together + Rope triceps extension, while leaning forward

*Put the movements in order from the weakest to the strongest so that you can continue to do reps. Some people might be stronger than others in some movements. For example, someone can be weaker in the Romanian deadlift compared with the snatch deadlift, while others will be the opposite. Go with the order that represents your own strengths and weaknesses.

**Barbell/Dumbbell Complexes:** These were made popular by Istvan Javorek (Javorek complexes) and John Davies (Bear complex). They consist of doing several (three to six) barbell or dumbbell movements with the same object, ideally without dropping it and without stopping. This is quite common among Olympic lifters.

For example, a Bear complex works as follows:
Power clean + Front squat + Overhead press (bring the bar behind your neck) + Back squat + Behind-the-neck overhead press (bring the bar back in front). This is *one* repetition. Typically, you would do three to six repetitions (cycles) without rest.

A variation would be to do all the reps for each movement before moving on to the next. In which case, I would change the order to something like:

5 Power cleans + 5 Overhead presses (bring the bar behind the neck) + 5 Behind-the-neck presses + 5 Back squats (bring the bar in front) + 5 front squats

This is very demanding work. While it can be used to build muscle and strength, it is primarily a conditioning tool. However, other simpler complexes can be used to build muscle mass.

For example:
5 Upright rows + 5 Bent-over rows (torso parallel to the floor) + 5 Shrugs. Also note that the reps per exercise can change; you could do 5 upright rows, 8 bent-over rows and 12 shrugs if there is a large strength difference between movements.

Another example:
3 Upright rows + 5 Hang power cleans + 5 Overhead presses + 10 Shrugs

You can play with the reps to get the training effect you want.

**EMOMs**: This is a concept that is very popular among CrossFit athletes. It consists of starting a new set with each new minute. For example, you start a set at 0:00, the next set starts when the clock hits 1:00, and then the third set starts when the clock hits 2:00, and so on. This approach works best for low rep sets using moderately heavy weights (70 to 80 percent). Up to three to five reps per set can be used, but I personally prefer three reps per set. Typically, I perform EMOMs for 8 to 12 minutes. Why not just give 8 x3 @ 80 percent? Because having to beat the clock keeps you in the zone. It's weird but it puts you in a different mindset. I've had many CrossFit athletes get personal best lifts during EMOMs, even with the fatigue accumulation, where I told them to increase the weight on every set. It keeps their mind focused on ***doing*** instead of overthinking (worrying about the weight, their technique, etc.).

For bodybuilding or strength purposes, I like two to three reps per set for 8 to 12 minutes (after warm-up) using 70 to 80 percent of your maximum.

## Conclusion

Listen, I'll be honest. The real key to getting bigger and stronger is simply to work hard—harder than you even think you need to. When you work this hard, any program will get you results. Using "cutting-edge" training methods will not do anything for you if you don't give it all you've got when you are in the gym. You cannot compensate a lack of effort with an overscientification (yes, I made that up) of your training. *But,* if you are already training as hard as you can, using some of these methods will certainly put your gains into overdrive!

# Chapter Five: Isolation Work

~ Christian Thibaudeau

## Why, When and How

The value of the big lifts to accumulate size and strength is well understood and accepted by the vast majority of serious iron addicts. Nobody can dispute that progressively getting stronger on lifts such as the bench press, overhead press, squat, deadlift, front squat, row, pull-ups and dips will lead to a significant increase in overall size and muscularity.

Anybody who has built an impressive amount of muscle mass, especially if they did it naturally, included a hefty dose of big compound movements in their training. The relative proportion of these lifts versus isolation work will vary depending on who you talk to, but it is very rare to find someone with significantly above average muscle mass who didn't gain a lot of strength on the big basic lifts throughout their lifting career.

Still, I see a pretty common trend in the various gyms I visit: those who are doing "body building" rely more and more on isolation exercises and less and less on the big compound movements. Keep in mind that I'm using "body building" (two words) and not "bodybuilding". The latter refers to those who compete in bodybuilding, while the former refers to those who hit the gym only to build muscle and look better without any competitive plans.

As a result, the average "natural" gym patron doing "body building" actually has less muscle than the average powerlifter and even the average CrossFitter. Don't laugh—it's true. I work with all three types of athletes and see tons of them every day!

I recently saw three women preparing for a figure competition. They pumped away on dozens of isolation moves and when they finally did the big lifts, it was with baby weights "to avoid making the waist too big". Well, these three women, who were training and eating specifically to get muscular and lean, carried a lot less muscle mass than all the CrossFit women I'm training. Most of the latter were leaner and more aesthetic, too. They all deadlifted, squatted and pressed heavy, and did pull-ups, dips, and the Olympic lifts, with barely any isolation exercises.

Yes, the top bodybuilders have more muscle than the top CrossFitters and powerlifters. But when you take average the participants of all three activities, the body builders training specifically to build muscle often have the less impressive physique of the bunch.

Yet still we see more and more isolation work and less big lifts.

***Why?***

**They Only Look at the Current Picture**

We are all the same. We want to know how the top guys train, and train like them. The average gym rat doesn't lack desire and training intensity but, instead, they lack confidence in doing the right thing to get results. He is insecure about his training, and fears wasting his time. That is why you see so many articles on training "like the pros". Doing the program that a pro bodybuilder is doing puts your mind at rest, as "if he's doing it, it must work". Here are the problems with that idea:

1. You shouldn't do what he is doing now, but what he did when he was at your level of development. A lot of bodybuilders built most of their size on the big basics. However, when they reach a certain level it becomes more and more grueling to keep pushing those big lifts up, and it also becomes more dangerous. Even if your muscle strength increases, tendon strength is much slower to follow. When a top pro can rep out 405 pounds for 12 on the incline bench press, continuing to push that lift higher and higher might not be worth it from a risk/reward standpoint. By the same token, that pro bodybuilder who can do high reps with 405 pounds on the bench will likely be able to do very strict lateral raises with 40 to 50 pounds or more, getting a good muscle squeeze on them. You might need to use 15 to 20 pounds to get the same quality squeeze. Sure, you can use the 40s, but you will be swinging away and not getting much out of the exercise. Now, here's the deal. You can't get the same stimulus from 15 to 20 pound dumbbells as you can from 40 to 50 pound ones. Sure, relatively speaking, the load might be the same compared to your limit strength but, in reality, the load imposed on the body is much lower and won't be as effective. When you have the strength to do strict, squeezed and controlled isolation work with fairly heavy weight, it will build more muscle than doing the same with lighter weights. As such, someone who built a strong foundation with the big lifts will benefit more from isolation work than someone who is weaker and doesn't have that base.

2. Here's a shocker—pro bodybuilders (and most competitive guys, even those who claim to be "natural") are using drugs to promote growth. What works great for them might not work as well for a natural trainee. I'm not just talking about growth drugs making everything you do more effective, but about drugs changing the way your body reacts to training—it completely changes your physiology. A lot of people think "okay, he's using drugs so I won't get as many gains but what he does will work the same with me at a slower rate". It doesn't work like that. See, training creates a physiological signal that tells the body to build muscle. There are many ways to do that and several different physiological signals exist (I'll talk about them later). When someone uses drugs, he is artificially creating one of these signals, and actually keeping it elevated 24/7. So, the need to create the signal isn't as important. You have much less need to create a strong growth-promoting signal to get results. A drug-using lifter can easily use less big lifts and more isolation exercises and grow optimally, because the anabolic trigger has already been stimulated. He only needs to tell his body which muscle to hypertrophy. In that sense,

he can simply let the drugs initiate the anabolic process and use the training to target that hypertrophy. A natural trainee needs to use training to both create a strong anabolic response and target growth. That is why the "average pro bodybuilder training" isn't likely to work well on you. That said, more and more pro bodybuilders are training the smart way. It used to be that competitive bodybuilders hired "prep gurus" who were really nutritionists/drug experts and didn't provide much training advice. Now, more and more top bodybuilders are turning to training experts for actual programming. The result is that they use less and less drugs while getting better results.

## The Feel Factor

We tend to believe that the more we can feel a muscle working and the better pump we can create, the more we can make that muscle grow. Since it's much easier to feel the target muscle during an isolation exercise than during a big lift, we instinctively assume that the isolation work is more effective.

There is *some* truth in that reasoning. I believe that if you don't feel a muscle working during a set, or feel that it worked after a set (if it is tired, pumped or tensed/toned), then you aren't stimulating it optimally. It is also a fact that beginners have—for the most part— a bad mind-muscle connection, and they have a hard time feeling their muscles doing the work during big compound lifts. However, they easily feel the muscle doing the job when doing isolation work.

Doing an exercise and not "feeling" it anywhere is not actually rewarding. Add to that the instinct of gravitating towards the exercises that give the best pump, and you have the perfect excuse for beginners to stick to isolation work. The problem is that they stick to that habit. I believe that a lifter wanting to build a lot of muscle should learn to feel the target muscles working during the big lifts, rather than avoiding them and going for the easy option.

So, yes, feeling the muscle working is important, but learning to feel it during the big money lifts is even more important. It's a skill that will do more for you as a lifter than any magical program, training tip or secret exercise ever will.

## Big Lifts are Hard Work

As much as I'd like to believe that everybody who wants to build a lot of muscle is willing to put in the work, the truth is that most aren't. Let's face it: squats, deadlifts, rows, pull-ups and so on are more demanding than curls, rope triceps extensions and lateral raises. Honestly, if you are someone looking for the easy way out, I'm not really interested in working with you! So, I won't expand much more on this topic. Simply understand that a lot of people will try to convince you that the big lifts are bad and less effective for X, Y and Z reasons. Most of the time, the person is simply looking to justify their lack of heart and recruit you to their bandwagon to feel better about being a pussy.

I think it's fair to say that, by now, you understand how important it is to push your big lifts up and how important it is to learn to feel the target muscles doing the work during the big lifts.

*"But isn't this the chapter on the value of isolation work?"*

Yes, it is!

*"Then why all the hate on isolation exercises?"*

I'm not hating on them. I'm only putting things in perspective so that you understand when, why, and how to use isolation exercises.

## The Main Problem with the Big Lifts

The big compound lifts are those that will allow you to use the most weight. They create the greatest overall stimulation in your body and have the strongest impact on the nervous and hormonal systems. For those reasons, they should be the cornerstone of any good mass-building program.

However, they have one major drawback: they hit your strongest muscles more than your weakest ones.

You might be using the bench press to build up your chest. But, if your deltoids are overpowering your chest they will take most of the load. As a result, the deltoids will receive more stimulation and thus will progress faster. This will make the deltoids even more dominant relative to your pectorals, which will make recruiting (and stimulating) the pecs even more difficult.

So, unless you have perfect muscle balance (which is very rare) and levers, you cannot build a balanced and complete physique with only the big basic lifts. There will always be some muscles that will be less stimulated than others and, the more you progress, the greater the gap between your strong and weak links will become.

This causes three problems:

1. It increases the risk of injuries
2. It decreases your performance potential
3. It will make it impossible to build a fully developed physique.

As you can see, while the big lifts should be your main focus, isolation work is also necessary to ensure maximum performance, a complete physique, and a reduced risk of injuries. But it needs to be used properly.

Understand that the body has a limited capacity to recover from training. You can't just throw in garbage volume to get a pump. Every exercise you use in a program should have a precise and well-defined goal, and it needs to be the best solution to accomplish that goal. Sometimes, the best tool to get the job done is an isolation exercise.

## The Purposes of Isolation Work

There are three main purposes of isolation work, as follows.

**1. Learning to feel a muscle:** I believe that if you do not feel a muscle working during a set or that it worked after it (muscle pump or increased tension post-set), then you aren't properly stimulating that muscle.

Stimulation starts with recruitment, and the first sign of recruiting a muscle optimally (that is, recruiting a lot of muscle fibers during the execution of the exercise) is feeling that a muscle is under tension and doing work while performing an exercise.

As we mentioned earlier, it is harder to feel a muscle working during a big compound lift than during an isolation one. The big lift involves many muscle groups, so someone who isn't used to exercising might have problems focusing on one main muscle group to stimulate. The training stress might also be distributed among the participating muscles in such a way that it's hard to feel it anywhere specific.

During an isolation exercise, you can put your mind on one muscle. Instead of focusing on trying to involve the target muscle, you can think about not only contracting it, but tensing it as hard as you can during the exercise. This will teach you to get the most out of a muscle. In that regard, isolation work can be used to develop not only your capacity to use and feel a muscle working, but also to utilize it to the maximum extent by producing an intense contraction.

**2. Learning to integrate a muscle in a complex movement**: Exercise theorist Paul Chek used to say "*isolate then integrate*". What he meant by that is that you start by learning to use a specific muscle. When you can do that properly, you learn to keep feeling that muscle working optimally when doing a more complex lift.

When someone is at a certain level of development and has lagging muscle groups, they will most certainly tend to rely on their strengths during big compound lifts. This is, in large part, is because his mind-muscle connection with the "weaker/lagging" muscle group is not good. To correct the situation, one can use isolation exercises combined with compound ones to improve mind-muscle connection via what I call "enhanced feedback".

Enhanced feedback refers to doing an isolation exercise for your target muscle prior to doing your big lift. This can be done as a superset, in which case we call it "pre-fatigue superset". As explained in chapter four this is when you do the isolation exercise then, without any significant rest, you move on to the main lift. Alternatively, it can be done in straight sets fashion, by doing three to four sets of the isolation exercise prior to doing your sets of the main movement.

In both cases, the goal is to increase the feeling of the target muscle by creating a pump via an isolation exercise.

The "pump" from the isolation exercise increases intramuscular tension/pressure and, as a result, you feel the muscle much more. When you switch to the compound movement, you still have an augmented feeling in the target muscle and that will help you learn to integrate it in the main movement.

Opponents of this method will be quick to point out that you will not be able to use as much weight on the big lift and, as a result, you will stimulate less overall growth. I can't argue with that—it's true.

However, you have to keep in mind why you are using this method and why it works.

Pre-fatigue should be used first and foremost as a tool to learn to integrate a lagging muscle group in a compound movement. See it not specifically as a hypertrophy tool, but as an investment in your future gains. Once you are able to program your body to better recruit the lagging muscle group while doing a big compound lift, your future gains will be all the more impressive. The big lifts allow you to place the greatest stress on the muscles, but not being able to place the stress on the muscles you want to build will make the process sub-optimal.

That said, you will build muscle with pre-fatigue methods. The fact that you are pre-fatiguing the lagging muscle group will allow you to fully fatigue it when doing the compound lift, whereas if you did the compound lift only, the lagging muscle (which you aren't yet effective at recruiting during a compound lift) would be left relatively unfatigued and thus under-stimulated.

Yes, the pre-fatigue method isn't optimal to build strength, and it might lead to less growth in the other muscle groups involved in the main lift. However, keep your mind on the prize: correcting a muscle imbalance.

**3. Correcting a muscle imbalance that is holding you back**: Learning to integrate a lagging muscle group into a big compound lift is a good investment for the future. But we can also use isolation exercises to speed up the catching-up process.

While gaining strength on the big money lifts is a solid way to build muscle, it's also possible to stimulate growth via lighter isolation work if used properly. That's because there are three main ways to stimulate the muscle-building process.

## Sidebar: The Three Roads to Hypertrophy

**Road One: Heavy Mechanical Loading:** Here, we are mostly talking about using a fairly heavy load which places mechanical stress on the muscle fibers. If the volume of intense mechanical loading is high enough, it will force the body to strengthen the muscle fibers by increasing their thickness and strength. Note that volume is also of importance here; a very low volume of work, even if it is very intense, is unlikely to lead to structural changes in the muscle fibers as the adaptations will be mostly neural. Take note that I believe that very low volume/very heavy loads can lead to injuries, because the neural improvements exceed the strengthening of the muscle fibers' structure. As a result, you can produce more force than your structures are able to handle safely.

**Road Two: mTOR Activation:** mTOR, or mechanistic/mammalian target of rapamycin, is a cell signaling pathway that plays a huge role in cell growth. For us iron addicts, it's interesting to note that it is the main regulator in stimulating hypertrophy—via an increase in cell proliferation and protein synthesis. In other words, if you activate the mTOR pathway, you will initiate the muscle-building process. Lifting weights/resistance training has the greatest impact on mTOR activation (a large caloric consumption also has an effect) and, among "lifting activities" the eccentric portion of the lift has the greatest impact. We used to believe that eccentric actions had the greatest impact on muscle growth (which is true), because it led to more muscle damage. We now know that it's because of its great impact on mTOR activation. Studies have shown that slow eccentric actions where the muscle is producing maximum tension (tensing the muscle hard) are optimal for mTOR activation, even with a light weight. So, you can stimulate growth with fairly light weight if you do the eccentric portion very slowly while keeping the target muscle as tensed as possible (and tensing a specific muscle is more easily done with isolation exercises).

**Road Three: Growth Factor Release**: Research on occlusion training (performing an exercise with restricted blood flow to the target muscle) has shown that it is possible to stimulate as much growth with very light loads (as low as 30 percent of 1RM) as with heavy weight when reducing oxygen/blood entry into the muscle. What happens is that the hypoxic state (lack of oxygen) inside the muscle, as well as the accumulation of waste products (specifically lactate), increases the release of local growth factors. These growth factors then stimulate protein synthesis and thus muscle growth. I'm not a huge fan of occlusion training, but you can get a similar effect by performing an isolation exercise using a constant tension technique. That is, move the weight slowly up and down while flexing the muscle as hard as possible at all times—never relaxing it. As long as the muscle is kept contracted, blood cannot get inside the muscle and you create an occlusion, with its growth factor-boosting effect.

**(END OF SIDEBAR)**

Don't be scared to use isolation exercises. If you build up a decent physique that has "holes" (lagging muscle groups on an otherwise well-developed body), chances are that you won't fix them with big compound movements. You need to use the proper isolation exercises to cure the problem.

*"But I am using isolation exercises and my lagging muscles aren't growing."* Then, it's likely that you aren't doing them properly.

As I explained, it is perfectly possible to stimulate growth via isolation exercises, but you have to do them right. To reap the maximum out of isolation exercises, you need to employ a repetition style that promotes the use of roads two or three. Road one will always work best with heavy compound lifts.

## How to Perform Isolation Exercises

When doing isolation work, do not think about lifting weights; think about flexing a muscle against resistance. People tend to lump together any exercise that involves "lifting". The truth is that compound movements and isolation exercises are two different tools. They are used for different purposes and work for different reasons. Is it so hard to understand that they should thus be done differently?

While it is generally advised to shoot for gradually using more weight (while maintaining proper form) with the big lifts, it's not really of prime importance when using isolation exercises.

You stimulate growth with isolation exercises mostly by activating mTOR and stimulating the release of local growth factors— not by placing a big mechanical stress on the muscles. As such, progressive overload isn't nearly as important as doing the reps the right way to stimulate the growth factors.

When doing isolation work, there is a perfect weight. This is a weight that is light enough to allow you to squeeze the muscle hard on every inch of every repetition, never losing the feeling for the muscle during the set, but heavy enough to lead to muscle fatigue/failure (or close to it) in 50 to 60 seconds or less of work. If after being under load for over 60 seconds you still haven't reached failure, the load is too light.

It is my opinion that isolation exercises should be done with the constant tension repetition style. This means that the muscle must be kept tensed/contracted as much as possible during the whole set.

To do that, both the lifting/concentric and lowering/eccentric portions should be done under control. It doesn't necessarily have to be super slow, but there should be no momentum created. Something like a three to four second eccentric and two second concentric works well.

It's not enough to use the proper rep speed/rhythm; you must also voluntarily squeeze/tense/contract the muscle as hard as you can during both phases of the lift. Imagine that you are flexing your target muscle while lifting the weight. I often tell my clients to imagine that they are doing a photoshoot and the photographer might be snapping a picture of your muscle at any time, so make sure that your muscle looks flexed and hard!

The other element is the transitions, between the lifting and subsequent lowering as well as the transition between reps. To get the most out of isolation exercises, you want to avoid pausing during the transitions. Keep moving smoothly while keeping the muscle contracted.

This repetition style will maximize the release of growth factors.

With isolation exercises, I don't really focus on the number of reps but, rather, on the duration of the set. An optimal isolation set would last about 45 to 50 seconds, keeping the tension constant. This is what will lead to the greatest accumulation of lactate, which will also increase the release of growth factors.

## When to Use Isolation Exercises

Isolation work can definitely be effective to build muscle mass. But it can also be easily overdone. Big compound lifts are somewhat self-regulatory; after doing five sets of squats all-out, chances are that you won't feel like doing five sets of front squats, then five sets of deadlifts and then five sets of lunges. Contrary to big lifts, isolation exercises do not cause much systemic fatigue. And feeling a muscle pumped is pretty cool. So, it's much easier to overdo isolation work than compound movements. I've seen plenty of people doing six or more exercises for biceps for a total of 25 to 35 sets in a workout. But I'm yet to see someone do 25 to 35 sets of squats or deadlifts!

Yes, the compound lifts take more out of you, so you can indeed tolerate more sets of isolation exercises. But, when you fatigue a muscle and its muscle fibers it doesn't care what type of exercise caused the fatigue. While doing 30 sets of biceps might not have a huge systemic impact, it can sure fatigue the biceps excessively.

Add to that the fact that big compound lifts themselves work the muscles that you are targeting with your isolation exercises, and you will see that you might be doing too much isolation work for your own good, and may be slowing down your progress because of it.

First and foremost, isolation exercises should be used to fix a weak point. They are supplemental work for muscles that aren't growing at an optimal rate compared to your other muscles, or for muscles that are holding your performance back in the big lifts.

If a muscle is growing rapidly from the big lifts you are doing, so much so that it's overpowering your other muscle groups, there is no need to do a lot of isolation work for that muscle. Remember that you have a limited capacity to adapt to physical load. You only have a certain amount of "training money" to invest on exercises. So, make sure to invest wisely by allocating isolation work only where it's needed. Remember, isolation work is there mostly to correct a weakness (aesthetic- or performance-related). There is no obligation to do a ton of isolation work for every single muscle equally.

## Basic Training Parameters for Isolation Work

We will cover more advanced training methods in future chapters. But, if you decide to use regular sets of isolation exercises, you should follow these training parameters.

**Sets**: 3 to 5 per exercise
**Rhythm/Style:** Constant tension with a fairly slow, momentum-free movement speed
**Duration/Reps per set**: 40 to 60 seconds/set or 8 to 15 reps per set
**Rest between sets**: Incomplete rest (45 to 75 seconds)
**Exercises per body part:** 1 to 4, depending on the severity of the weak point.

## Conclusion:

When it comes to building muscle, isolation work can indeed contribute either as a direct mean of stimulating growth in a specific muscle, or indirectly by improving your capacity to recruit a muscle and then integrate it more easily in the big strength lifts—making that muscle more responsive to these big money movements. However, chose your isolation exercises wisely because you have a limited capacity to tolerate training stress. Isolation work must be selected for a specific purpose: to correct a weak link that is not growing enough from the big basics. You don't have to use isolation for all your muscles. If a muscle is growing fine from the big basics alone there is no need to "waste" training money on doing isolation work for that muscle. Every exercise can be a tool that will help you reach your goal, it's only a matter of using these tools optimally.

# Chapter Six: Extended Methods for Growth

~ Christian Thibaudeau

As much as it pains me to admit it, the muscle must be under load for a significant period of time to stimulate maximum growth. In other words, the muscles must spend enough time performing actual mechanical work for them to grow at the fastest rate possible.

How long does it have to be under load? When talking strictly about stimulating as much growth as possible without regard to maximal strength gains, the target time under load is 40 to 70 seconds for a set. If you use a fairly controlled movement rhythm then we are talking about 8 to 12 reps per set, and if using slightly faster movements, it can go as high as 20 reps per set.

Personally, I prefer to reach that time under load via a combination of several variations of an exercise in one set, rather than doing all the reps with one movement. Firstly, because it allows me to use more weight, secondly because it's mentally easier to do five to six reps of three variants than 15 to 20 reps of the same movement. Using slight variations of an exercise will also allow you to hit more muscle fibers with each set.

Remember that it's not the number of reps that is important, but simply how long a muscle is placed under load.

When talking about mechanical loading to stimulate growth, the formula for success could be simplified as:

"Growth stimulated = Load x Time under load".

In other word, a strategy that allows us to place the muscles under the greatest load for long enough will cause the most growth.

If the set is very long (more than 70 seconds) but the load used is very light, we won't place maximum mechanical stimulation on the muscles.

If the load is very heavy but the set doesn't place the muscles under load for long enough (less than 30 to 40 seconds), the mechanical stimulation will not be optimal either.

That doesn't mean that you can't stimulate growth with heavier/shorter or lighter/longer sets, but it's simply not optimal for mechanical stimulation.

To get the best of both worlds— a heavy enough load and a long enough time under load—I use four main methods that use variations of the same exercise in one set. Briefly, these methods are:

1. **Mechanical drop sets:** This method uses three technique variations of the same exercise, done in succession (with 5 to 10 seconds of rest between exercises) going from the weakest to the strongest to allow you to use the same weight for all three exercises.

2. **Multi-contraction sets:** This method uses only one exercise but utilizes three types of contraction/repetition styles during the set, with a very brief rest period between repetition styles (5 to 10 seconds), going from the hardest repetition style to the easiest one. The same load is used for all types of contractions.

3. **Growth factor sets:** This method is used mostly with isolation exercises and it uses different exercises targeting one muscle group, without necessarily being variations of the same movement. Once again, the same weight is used for all exercises and no rest intervals are used between exercises. The goal here isn't so much about completing X amount of reps with a certain weight but, rather, keeping the muscle loaded for 60 to 70 seconds.

4. **Variable range of motion sets:** This method uses only one exercise, but the range of motion is reduced as fatigue sets in. You start with the full range of motion, which is harder, and gradually reduce it to be able to keep the muscles under load for as long as possible with a heavy load. The goal is not to complete a certain number of full and partial reps, it's just to keep the muscles loaded.

## Mechanical Drop Sets

Mechanical drop sets have been one of the main hypertrophy tools I have been using for about 10 years. I even recorded a DVD on this method about eight years ago. But it still works! I especially like to use this approach with athletes and people who are focused on strength and performance as much as muscle mass. As I'm writing this (June 2015), I'm using it extensively with two CrossFit athletes preparing to compete at the CrossFit Games.

Mechanical drop sets use three variations of one movement pattern. They are done in succession with a brief rest (5 to 10 seconds—just enough to reset and clear a bit of lactic acid). The three exercises are arranged in order of weakest to strongest. This will allow you to go close to failure on the first one, and still be able to do reps on the second one, and then again on the third one.

A classic example would be to start with a dumbbell high incline press, then move on to a dumbbell low incline press, and finish with a flat dumbbell press.

The benefits of this approach are that:

1. Like a regular drop set, you can continue to have the target muscles do mechanical work, even when you reach the point of failure (or close to it—I advise stopping one rep short). But, contrary to the traditional drop set, you do not lower the load to increase the time under load.

2. You can hit more fibers by using slightly different angles.

3. You can do more work per unit of time therefore increasing density, which leads to many positive hormonal responses and more hypertrophy.

4. It's mentally easier because, even though you are doing a lot of work, it doesn't feel like it because you are changing movements during the set.

### *How many reps?*

Out of the three variations that compose a mechanical drop set, only the target reps for the first exercise are planned, because you never know how much fatigue you will build up from exercise to exercise and how much stronger you will be in the latter variations. For example, someone who isn't much stronger on the flat dumbbell press than the incline dumbbell press will not be able to do a ton of reps on the flat press, whereas someone who is significantly stronger on the flat press might get six to eight reps on the last leg of a set.

Use a weight you can get five to seven reps with on the first movement of a mechanical drop set, and then do as many as possible on the other two. You want to be able to perform at least three reps of the last two movements, but ideally five. If you can't get to three, it's okay to take a little bit more rest between the exercises. Ideally, you will stick to 5 to 10 seconds but, if you absolutely have to, you can go up to 15. Hopefully, that won't be necessary. In an ideal world you would perform 15 to 20 total reps in a mechanical drop set, but anything between 12 and 20 is acceptable.

### *What exercise combinations should be used?*

Once you understand the basic concept (three similar exercises, going from the weakest to the strongest) it's pretty easy to come up with many effective combinations as shown below. Keep in mind that not everybody has the same strength balance, so you might need to change the order of some supersets. For example, some people are stronger sumo pullers than conventional. So, if I prescribe a mechanical drop set of 1) Romanian deadlift 2) Sumo deadlift 3) Conventional deadlift, you might need to switch up the order of the sumo and conventional.

**Chest**

**A.** High incline dumbbell press (60 degrees) + Incline dumbbell press (30 degrees) + Flat dumbbell press
**B.** Reverse-grip bench press from pins + Wide-grip bench from pins + Bench from pins
**C.** Close-grip bench press + Wide-grip bench press + Bench press
**D.** High incline reverse-grip dumbbell press + Incline reverse-grip dumbbell press + Flat reverse-grip dumbbell press
**E.** Reverse-grip dumbbell press + Neutral-grip dumbbell press + dumbbell press

**F.** Reverse-grip dumbbell incline press + Neutral-grip dumbbell incline press + dumbbell incline press
**G.** Pec deck machine flye, supinated + Pec deck flye, hands low + Pec deck flye, hands in line with shoulders

**Back**
**A.** Lat pulldown behind neck + Lat pulldown in front, with pronation + Lat pulldown in front, with supination
**B.** Pull-ups, pronated + Pull-ups, supinated + Pull-ups, neutral-grip
**C.** Seated row, leaning forward as much as possible + Seated row, with torso 45 degrees + Seated row, with torso 90 degrees
**D.** Rope straight-arm pulldown + Kneeling rope row, with torso forward + Kneeling rope row, with torso backward
**E.** Bent-over row, with torso parallel to floor + Bent-over row, with torso 45 degrees + Bent-over row, with momentum
**F.** Bent-over dumbbell row, pronated + Bent-over dumbbell row, supinated + Bent-over dumbbell row, neutral
**G.** Machine reverse flye, with hands high (head level) + Reverse flye, with hands shoulder height + Reverse flye, with palms down
**H.** (In front) Lat pulldown, wide pronated + Lat pulldown, close pronated + Lat pulldown, supinated

**Deltoids**
**A.** Dumbbell Arnold press + Dumbbell shoulder press + Dumbbell push press
**B.** Behind-the-neck press + Front press + Push press
**C.** Standing dumbbell press + High incline dumbbell press (60 degrees) + Incline dumbbell press (45 degrees)
**D.** Dumbbell lateral raise on 30 degree bench + Dumbbell lateral, seated straight + Standing dumbbell lateral, slightly cheated
**E.** Dumbbell front raise, seated straight + Dumbbell front raise on 30 degree bench + Standing dumbbell front raise, alternating
**F.** Barbell front raise, narrow-grip (8 inches) + Barbell front raise, shoulder-width + Barbell front raise, wide-grip
**G.** (Smith machine) Behind-the-neck press + Front press + Reverse-grip front press

**Quads**
**A.** Front squat + Narrow stance back squat + Regular/wider stance back squat
**B.** Split squat, with back foot elevated + Split squat, with both feet on floor + Split squat, with front foot elevated
**C.** Leg press narrow, with feet low + Leg press hip-width, with feet in the middle of the surface + Leg press wide, with feet high
**D.** Leg extension, with feet turned in + Leg extension, with feet neutral + Leg extension, with feet turned out
**E.** Walking lunges, with very short steps + Walking lunges, with medium steps + Walking lunges, with long steps
**F.** Back squat, with heels elevated (1.5 to 2 inches) and narrow stance + Back squat, shoulder-width + Back squat, wide

**<u>Hamstrings/Posterior chain</u>**

**A.** Romanian deadlift + Sumo deadlift + Conventional deadlift
**B.** Romanian deadlift, with toes elevated (1 to 1.5 inches) + Romanian deadlift + Sumo deadlift
**C.** Arched back good morning, with toes elevated + Arched back good morning + Wide squat
**D.** (Lying) Leg curl, with feet turned in + Leg curl, with feet turned out + Leg curl, with feet neutral
**E.** (Lying) Leg curl, dorsiflexed + Leg curl, with feet neutral + Leg curl, plantarflexed
**F.** Romanian deadlift, with feet turned in + Romanian deadlift, with feet turned out + RDL, with feet neutral
**G.** (Seated) Leg curl, with feet turned in + Leg curl, with feet turned out + Leg curl, with feet neutral
**H.** (Seated) Leg curl, dorsiflexed + Leg curl, with feet neutral + Leg curl, plantarflexed

**<u>Biceps</u>**

**A.** (Preacher bench) Dumbbell reverse-grip curl + Dumbbell curl + Dumbbell hammer curl
**B.** (Standing) Dumbbell reverse-grip curl + Dumbbell curl + Dumbbell hammer curl
**C.** (Preacher bench) Reverse EZ bar curl + Wide EZ bar curl + Narrow EZ bar curl
**D.** Steep angle preacher curl + 45 degree preacher curl + Standing curl
**E.** 45 degree seated dumbbell curl + Standing dumbbell curl + Standing alternating dumbbell curl
**F.** Steep angle reverse preacher curl + 45 degree reverse preacher curl + Standing reverse curl
**G.** Extra-wide barbell curl + Wide barbell curl + Narrow barbell curl

**<u>Triceps</u>**

**A.** (Lying) EZ bar triceps extension to forehead + EZ bar triceps extension to nose + EZ bar triceps extension to neck
**B.** (Lying) Dumbbell triceps extension, supinated + Dumbbell triceps extension, pronated + Dumbbell triceps extension, neutral
**C.** (Lying) Dumbbell triceps extension, pronated + Dumbbell triceps extension, neutral + Tate press
**D.** (Incline) Dumbbell triceps extension, supinated + Dumbbell triceps extension, pronated + Dumbbell triceps, neutral
**E.** (Incline) Dumbbell triceps extension, pronated + Dumbbell triceps extension, neutral + Tate press
**F.** (Decline) Dumbbell triceps extension, supinated + Dumbbell triceps extension, pronated + Dumbbell triceps extension, neutral
**G.** (Decline) Dumbbell triceps extension, pronated + Dumbbell triceps extension, neutral + Tate press
**H.** (Cable, EZ bar) Triceps extension, supinated + Triceps extension, pronated and wide + Triceps extension, pronated and narrow
**I.** (Cable, rope) Triceps extension, opening the rope at the bottom + Triceps extension, keeping hands together + Triceps extension, with a slight cheat.

### *Can this method be used for strength?*

Although this is primarily a hypertrophy method, it can also be used to build strength by recruiting more muscle fibers when training a movement.

When training for strength, I recommend six to nine total repetition, which means two to three reps per exercise. Challenge yourself, but avoid failure and breaking form when training for performance.

***How many sets?***

With this method, you build up a lot of muscle fatigue quickly. So, there is no need to perform a high number of sets. Three is about right for most people, while some can handle four. I prefer that you go harder on fewer sets than to keep more in the tank to be able to complete more sets.

If you are using this method to build strength (so using less reps), you can perform four or five sets.

***How many complexes per muscle group?***

When using this method, I normally only use one combination per muscle per workout. This is obviously not all that is done during the workout. I personally count three sets of mechanical drop work as equivalent to six regular sets. So, if you tend to respond well to 12 to 15 sets per muscle group, and you use a mechanical drop set combo for three sets (equivalent to six regular sets), it means that you can perform six to nine other work sets.

It is possible to perform two different complexes but, in that case, you should drastically reduce the amount of work spent on other exercises during your workout.

## Multi--Contraction Sets

In case you didn't know, there are three main types of contractions a muscle can do:

1. **Eccentric**: This is where a muscle produces force while it is being lengthened. In most exercises, this is the "lowering or returning" part.

2. **Concentric**: This is where a muscle produces force while it is being shortened. In most exercises, this is the actual "lifting" part.

3. **Isometric**: This is where a muscle produces force without changing length (so no movement). This is often called "holding".

When you do an actual repetition, all three contractions are normally present to some extent, especially the concentric and eccentric phases.

You can perform these phases in different ways. The concentric and eccentric phases can be done very fast, under control (roughly two seconds), slowly (three to four seconds) or super slowly (more than five seconds). The isometric can be avoided, can be done briefly (one to two seconds), for a moderate time (three to nine seconds) or for a long time (more than 10 seconds).

When doing a rep you can "construct" your repetition style by mixing different elements, and you can vary the type of contraction during a set to be able to produce more work at a given load. This will also help to recruit different fibers, because different types of muscle actions have different recruitment patterns. For example, during an eccentric emphasis you recruit less total fibers but more fast-twitch fibers, and during an isometric action you recruit more total fibers, and so on.

This method, like the mechanical drop set, will use three different contraction types. The same weight is used for the whole set, and 5 to 10 seconds can be taken between each contraction type. Start with the most demanding rep style and finish with the easiest one.

The "weakest" contraction type is the concentric, with the isometric being second, and the eccentric being the strongest. But you can change the order by changing the conditions (doing the phase more slowly, for example). Note that the same rep rule applies as for the mechanical drop set: start by doing four to six reps for the first part, and then shoot for three to five for the other two.

Here are some good examples:

1) Three pauses (two seconds) during the concentric phase of each rep + Three pauses during the eccentric phase of each rep + Normal reps.

2) Slow eccentric/Slow concentric + Slow eccentric/Fast concentric + Isometric hold at mid-point for max time.

3) Three pauses (two seconds) during the eccentric and concentric + Three pauses during eccentric/normal concentric + Isometric hold at mid-point for max time.

4) Slow eccentric/Long pause in bottom/Fast concentric + Slow eccentric/Fast concentric + Normal reps.

5) Slow eccentric/Pause (two seconds) during concentric at mid-point + Slow eccentric/Normal concentric + Isometric hold at mid-point.

6) Normal reps + Isometric hold at mid-point for max time + Eccentric-only (partner to help during concentric).

### *Can this method be used for strength?*

This method can be used to build strength, too. Anything that increases muscle fiber recruitment will have a positive effect on strength—not to mention that "muscle lifts weight" while the nervous system plays a key role in maximum force production. All things being equal, a bigger muscle will be a stronger muscle. Methods that are effective at building muscle while increasing motor unit recruitment will have a significant impact on maximum strength.

Just like with mechanical drop sets, to build strength with this method I suggest shooting for six to nine total reps, or two to three per contraction type.

### *How many sets?*

This method seems to be a little less demanding than the mechanical drop sets, so I normally like to use four sets. In my experience, four sets of this type of work is equal to about six regular sets. If you are using this method to build strength (with lower reps) do five to six work sets.

***How many complexes per muscle group?***

Again, it depends on the amount of volume you like to perform per muscle group. It would be possible to perform four sets of this approach and three sets of a mechanical drop set. This would be equivalent to 12 work sets, which is well-tolerated by most. You can also do four sets of this method and six to eight sets of other work for your target muscle.

## Growth Factor Sets

Contrary to the mechanical drop set where you stick to very similar movements, growth factor sets use different movement patterns. The goal is to create the largest, most uncomfortable pump in a muscle group. This method is often referred to as "giant sets". While it is possible to use compound exercises, isolation moves are the key elements in this method. We do not shoot for big weights, but instead focus on keeping a constant tension on the muscles. The objective is to keep a muscle group under load for 60 to 70 seconds, with most of that time spent with the muscle under tension (if you lift with acceleration, you partly deload the muscle during part of the range of motion). Do not think about lifting weights; think about flexing a muscle against resistance.

Try to avoid taking rest between exercises in this method.

Here are some of my favorite combinations for each muscle group.

**Chest**
**A.** Dumbbell squeeze press + Dumbbell flye + Dumbbell press
**B.** Dumbbell flye + Dumbbell power flye (more bend in the elbows) + Dumbbell press
**C.** Incline dumbbell flye + Incline power flye + Incline dumbbell press
**D.** (Pulley shoulder level) Cable cross-over, close to body + Cross-over, in front + Cable press
**E.** Chest dips (torso leaning forward) + Dumbbell flye + Dumbbell press (same weight as flye)
**F.** Dumbbell flye + Dumbbell press + Push-ups
**G.** Incline dumbbell flye + Incline dumbbell press + Push-ups, with feet elevated

**Back**
**A.** Straight-arm pulldown + Lat pulldown, pronated + Lat pulldown, supinated
**B.** Bent-over rear delt raise + Seated row, pronated + Seated row, supinated
**C.** Shoulder height pulley face pull + Low pulley rope row + Shoulder height pulley row to chest
**D.** Straight-arm rope pulldown + Low pulley rope row + Seated row with low pulley rope
**E.** Straight-arm pulldown + Lat pulldown, supinated + Dumbbell pullover
**F.** Pull-ups, supinated + Straight-arm pulldown + Dumbbell pullover

**Deltoids**
**A.** Dumbbell lateral raise + Dumbbell front raise + Dumbbell Arnold press
**B.** Dumbbell lateral raise + Dumbbell front raise + Dumbbell Cuban press
**C.** Barbell Cuban press + Barbell front raise + Barbell upright row (shoulder-width, 6 inches from body)
**D.** Dumbbell lateral raise + Dumbbell Arnold press + Dumbbell press
**E.** Dumbbell lateral raise + Dumbbell front raise, all the way above your head + Dumbbell front raise

**F.** Front raise, with chest supported on 45 degree bench + Seated Dumbbell lateral raise + Dumbbell front raise

**Quads**

**A.** Leg extension + Walking lunges, with short steps + Dumbbell squat
**B.** Leg extension + Hack squat machine + Bodyweight squats
**C.** Leg extension + Leg press + Chair hold on wall (max time)
**D.** Leg extension + Front squat + Back squat
**E.** Leg extension + Front (or back) squat + Leg extension (half the weight, shooting for 20 to 30 reps)
**F.** Leg extension + Front (or back) squat + Leg extension isometric hold at peak for max time
**G.** Walking lunges + Dumbbell squat + Chair hold on wall (max time)
**H.** Chair hold on wall (max time) + Hack squat machine + Bodyweight squats
**I.** Chair hold on wall (max time) + Leg press + Bodyweight squats
**J.** Chair hold on wall (max time) + Front (or back) squat + Bodyweight squats
**K.** Chair hold on wall (max time) + Hack squat machine + Leg extension
**L.** Chair hold on wall (max time) + Leg press + Leg extension
**M.** Chair hold on wall (max time) + Front (or back) squat + Leg extension

**Hamstrings/Posterior chain**

**A.** Leg curl + Dumbbell Romanian deadlift + Dumbbell walking lunges, with long steps
**B.** Leg curl + Romanian deadlift + Back extension
**C.** Dumbbell dead walk + Dumbbell walking lunges, with long steps + Dumbbell Romanian deadlift
**D.** Glute-ham raise + Back extension + Dumbbell Romanian deadlift
**E.** Glute-ham raise + Back extension + Leg curl
**F.** Glute-ham raise + Dumbbell Romanian deadlift + Leg curl
**G.** Dumbbell dead walk + Dumbbell Romanian deadlift + Dumbbell sumo squat
**H.** Leg curl + Dumbbell Romanian deadlift + Dumbbell sumo squat

**Biceps**

**A.** Reverse-grip cable curl + Cable curl + Dumbbell hammer curl
**B.** Reverse-grip EZ bar curl + Pull-ups (supinated, close-grip) + EZ bar curl
**C.** Reverse-grip cable curl + Pull-ups (supinated, close-grip) + Cable curl
**D.** Pull-ups (supinated, close-grip) + Wide-grip EZ bar curl + Narrow-grip EZ bar curl
**E.** Reverse-grip preacher curl + Reverse curl + Dumbbell hammer curl

**Triceps**

**A.** JM press + Lying dumbbell triceps extension (neutral) + Diamond push-ups
**B.** JM press + Lying dumbbell triceps extension (neutral) + Rope triceps extension
**C.** JM press + Close-grip bench + Diamond push-ups
**D.** JM press + Close-grip bench + Dumbbell triceps extension (neutral)
**E.** Close-grip bench + Lying dumbbell triceps extension (neutral) + Diamond push-ups
**F.** Close-grip bench + Lying dumbbell triceps extension (neutral) + Rope triceps extension
**G.** Dumbbell triceps extension + Triceps dips (elbow tight, torso upright) + Diamond push-ups
**H.** Dumbbell triceps extension + Triceps dips (elbow tight, torso upright) + Rope triceps extension

***Can I use this method for strength?***

Growth factor training focuses on flexing the muscles against a resistance, trying to make a light weight feel hard by tensing the muscles as hard as possible during every inch of every rep. Because of that, it is not effective to build strength in itself. When used in conjunction with heavier training, however, it can help by pulling more nutrients into the muscles that were worked with heavy weights beforehand.

Anything that builds muscle can help with strength. So, the muscle you will build with this approach will be functional, but the actual gains in strength on the big lifts from this method will be small if it is not used in conjunction with heavier lifting.

***How many sets?***

With the growth factor method, perform three work sets per complex. More than that will not give you anything more. After three good sets, you will have achieved a maximum pump and released a lot of growth factors. Doing more work on the same complex will not give you anything more; you might even lose some pump.

***How many complexes per muscle group?***

I do not count growth factor sets as more than one regular set, even if you are performing three exercises. This is because the mechanical loading is actually fairly low and you aren't causing any muscle damage (only the release of growth factor). Three sets of a complex are therefore equal to three regular sets.

If you only perform growth factor complexes in one workout, you can do up to four different ones (for a total of 12 sets). You can also add one or two complexes at the end of a workout where other methods were used.

## Variable Range of Motion Sets

You are stronger in partial movements than in full movements—I hope nobody is left flabbergasted by this one! For example, on the big compound lifts (bench press, squat, deadlifts, military press, dips) you are stronger if you only have to perform the last half or last quarter of the concentric phase. If you go down into a half squat, you'll be stronger than if you go down into a full squat. And, if you only go one quarter of the way down, you will be even stronger. Again, I hope this isn't a shock for anybody.

Another way of extending a set is to continue performing reps when you near failure, but reduce the range of motion.

For example, you might start by doing front squats. When you feel that you won't be able to complete another solid full repetition, you switch to only going down halfway. When you feel that you won't be able to complete more reps, you then switch to doing only quarter-reps.

This is fairly simple. There are only two things I want you to pay particular attention to:

1. On your partial reps, use the exact same technique as you would on the full lifts. In other words, the half-squat position of your partial reps should be a carbon copy of what you look like when you hit the mid-point of a full squat.

2. Stay in full control of the weight during the partials and do not do short, choppy reps. The goal is not to move weight, but to load the muscles.

This method works best with big, compound lifts, especially the squat, front squat, bench press, military press and pull-ups (for the pull-ups, the partial reps would be from the low position to lifting yourself halfway or one-quarter of the way up). It can also work with many isolation exercises (for example, leg curl, leg extension, preacher curl, lateral raise, front raise, etc.).

Why does it work? Aren't we usually saying "partial reps for partial results" and making fun of those half-reppers?

While it's true that *only* doing partial reps isn't very effective, doing those half-reps still places a mechanical load on the muscles and tendons. The muscles are still fully tensed when under load during a partial lift. If the partials are done after you already did the full movement close to failure, the partials then become effective by maintaining the target muscle under tension; therefore, creating more stimulation than if you would have stopped. Furthermore, in the squat, partial reps target mostly the quads and especially the vastus medialis. Doing the partial reps at the end of a set will amplify the development of that part. The same could be said about the triceps and the partial bench press, and the biceps and partial pull-ups.

Another benefit is that it will strengthen the muscles responsible for holding a solid lifting posture since these are solicited as much on half-reps as on full reps.

### *How many reps do I do?*

With this method, just like the mechanical drop sets and multi-contraction method, you plan the number of reps only for the first part of the exercise: the full reps.

When using this method to build size, pick a weight you can get six to eight reps with if using a compound movement, or eight to ten if doing an isolation exercise.

The number of half- and quarter-reps isn't prescribed. You should aim for as many half-reps as possible and then as many quarter-reps as possible while maintaining perfect form and control over the weight at all times.

### *Can this method be used for strength?*

YES! It is actually a very effective method to build strength. Obviously, start with lower reps in the full movement—three to five or even one to three depending on your goal and the training phase you are in. The same rules apply for the half- and quarter-reps: do as many as you can while respecting the exact positions you would in the full lifts, and control the weight at all times.

### *How many sets?*

When using this method to build size, I recommend doing four sets. If you are using it for strength (with less reps), I suggest five or even six work sets.

### *How many complexes do I do?*

If you are using a big lift with this method only do one per muscle group. You can add other stuff in your session, but not another variable range of motion complex for that muscle group.

If you are using only isolation exercises with this method, you can use two different ones. And you will be able to perform four to six sets of another type of lifting method for that muscle group.

## Conclusion

When it comes to mechanical loading, these four methods are my favorite ones. The mechanical drop sets, multi-contraction method and variable range of motion technique are especially effective because they combine both a long time under load and a high average load. This will result in maximal hypertrophy stimulation and rapid gains in both strength and size.

# Chapter Seven: Mass for Powerlifting

~ Paul Carter

The title for this chapter is "Mass For Powerlifting" and not "Powerlifting For Mass".

I have to point that out because, after more than a decade of doing powerlifting-specific training, I can tell you for certain that powerlifting-style training is a very inferior method for building mass compared to bodybuilding or very specific hypertrophic-style training.

This will rub some people the wrong way, but there's no denying that bodybuilders are far more muscular than powerlifters. After all, bodybuilders train specifically for mass, while powerlifters train for moving maximal weight.

This doesn't mean there are no muscularly developed powerlifters. Indeed, there definitely are. However, if a powerlifter's focus was to solely get bigger— especially to increase his lean muscle mass to raise his strength ceiling—he would need to do things aside from just training for the competition lifts.

In fact, a lot of powerlifters lack development muscularly because they can often become "minimalists" with regards to movement selection.

While the squat, deadlift and bench press will create a solid foundation of mass they will also leave one incomplete from a muscle mass perspective, if they make up the bulk of one's training program.

It takes more than the big three to maximize muscle mass and overall development.

## Targeting Appropriate Muscle Groups for Powerlifting

A powerlifter would want to approach mass training a little bit differently to a bodybuilder. Obviously, each is trying to gain mass for entirely different reasons.

The bodybuilder is trying to gain mass to create the most complete, balanced and symmetrical physique he or she can to present to a panel of judges.

The powerlifter is trying to gain mass so that the new muscle translates to bigger lifts on the platform. After all, as noted, more muscle means a higher strength ceiling. You can talk about central nervous system this and that all day but at the end of the day, muscle is what moves weight and more muscle means the potential to move more weight.

That is why it's important to understand that, as a powerlifter, how you set up training for mass will probably look far different from how a bodybuilder sets up training for mass.

## Primary and Secondary Movers, and Weak Points

Despite the fact that everyone has their own unique leverages, everyone—for the most part—uses the same primary, secondary and tertiary movers in the squat, bench and deadlift.

The bench is mostly pecs, triceps, and deltoids; with the lats and upper back playing a support role.

The squat is quadriceps and glutes; with the hamstrings, erectors and upper back all playing a role as well.

The deadlift is quite a mixed bag, depending on how you perform it. But, assuming you are a conventional puller and your technique is dialed in, your legs will perform the push off the floor, and then the back and glutes perform the "pull" from over the knees (the glutes perform hip extension to assist with lockout). We will just say the posterior chain (the glutes, hamstrings, lats, traps and rhomboids) are all vitally important in developing mass for a stronger pull.

The degree to which they are used can vary depending on the technique employed by the lifter.

For example, a very wide squatter will bring more hips into play, whereas a close stance squatter will activate more of the quadriceps. A close-grip bencher will need more triceps strength, whereas a very wide-grip bencher will ask the pecs to do more work.

This doesn't negate the fact that you still need to make your strong points stronger, and your weak points stronger as well. Basically, you need to get bigger and stronger all over.

One principle lost on a lot of powerlifters is, because of your leverages and individual make-up, your sticking point will always be at the same place unless you change your technique. And, when you do, you will have a sticking point there as well.

Your "weak point" is generally going to be the transition point where the distribution of the weight is lessened across the larger muscle groups involved, and the smaller ones must complete the lift.

An example is the area where the pecs become close to maximally shortened in the bench press, where the triceps then have to take over to complete the lift.

The train of thought about this has been that if you fix your weak points, the lift will go up. And it will; until you reach a weight that exceeds your ability to press, squat or deadlift it. Then the same sticking point will resurface. This is because the shorter the range of motion is, the less musculature is involved in lifting the weight.

The part that is also missed in that is that you can miss a lift not just because of a weak point, but because the primary mover isn't strong enough to get you through the transition point to finish the lift. If the primary mover can't generate enough momentum to get through the transition point so the secondary mover can finish, you will fail to complete the lift.

That is why, when we talk about training for mass for powerlifting, we need to change the train of thought from training the movements to making the primary and secondary muscles grow—all while still training the lifts themselves but with less of an emphasis.

## Inclusion of the Big Three

Despite the fact that we are talking about gaining muscle mass, the actual lifts involved in competing still need to be trained to keep the motor cortex primed in regards to movement patterns.

What this means is that you still need to practice the lifts so that you maintain your "groove" with them, and still have to practice to perfect your technique. This way, when you transition either into a block of volumizing the competition lifts or into a peaking cycle, you're not spending as much of that time trying to perfect form.

However, because this is about gaining mass that is applicable to the big lifts, you will place less of an emphasis on actually doing the big three, and more of an emphasis on building the body parts involved in them.

For quite some time, "movement kings" have frowned on such ideologies: *"You don't train body parts; you train movements."*

No, you do both. You understand the difference in moving weight through space (training movements), and making the muscle work against resistance (making the muscle work).

The difference in the two is that when you train to move weight through space, you're not trying to emphasize one particular muscle group over another. So, while it's virtually impossible to actually isolate off a muscle group, you can indeed become body aware enough to ask certain muscles to do the majority of the work with particular movements.

Some movements lend themselves to this function more efficiently than others. Flyes tend to exclude the triceps from doing very much work, while they ask the pectorals to do the great majority of it. Conversely, in the standard barbell bench press, you aren't trying to isolate anything off. You're actually trying to bring the maximum amount of muscle groups into play, in order to move as much weight as possible. Although you can perform a bench press in the realm of "making the muscles work", it's more efficient to use it as a "moving weight through space" exercise because of the degree of weight that can be moved with it.

With that said, let's talk about how we will keep the big three in the program.

## Rate of Perceived Exertion (RPE)

RPE is nothing more than a way to apply a degree of effort to a set. That is, rather than program by intensity (degree of one rep max), you go by "feel" that day, and work up to a certain RPE programmed for a particular rep range.

This is what the RPE scale looks like:

*RPE 10: Maximal effort. No more reps could be done.*
*RPE 9: Near maximal effort. One more rep could have been done.*
*RPE 8: Very hard. Reps don't move fast but two to three more reps could have been done.*
*RPE 7: Somewhat difficult. Bar speed is fast when maximal effort is applied.*
*RPE 6: Top end of warm-ups. Bar moves fast with moderate force applied.*
*RPE 5 and below: Essentially falls into warm-up sets.*

Remember that the RPE scale can be applied to any rep range, and not just one rep maxes.

For example, if the lifter goes into the gym to squat, and works up to 315 pounds for an all-out set, where a sixth rep could not have been done it would appear as follows.

Squats: 315 x 5 @ RPE 10

The RPE scale can therefore be applied to virtually any set to give an idea of the difficulty of it.

Since we've already established that we want to simply keep the motor patterns fresh in regards to the big lifts, and apply our energy towards bringing the muscle groups involved in the big three up, we are going to keep RPE relatively low. The volume dedicated to the big three will also be low.

For the big three that means, after warm-ups, working in nothing higher than a RPE of 7.

Below are the guidelines.

Bench Press: Warm-ups, then 2 sets of 8 @ RPE 7.
Squats: Warm-ups, then 2 sets of 5 @ RPE 7.
Deadlifts: Warm-ups, then 3 sets of 3 @ RPE 7.

Remember that RPE is based on how the movement and weights feel on that day, so the numbers you will use each week may vary.

On a day that you are bench pressing and feeling awesome, you might do 315 x 2 sets of 8 @ RPE 7. The next week, however, you may feel under the weather, and end up settling on 275 x 2 sets of 8 @ RPE 7.

It's important to be honest with yourself during these times, and stick to the program. On the days where you feel awesome, you may be tempted to add more sets or extra weight that will bring the RPE into the 9 or even 10 range.

DO NOT DO THIS.

If you are having an off day, don't fret the fact that you are using less weight on the competition lift than last week. So long as you stick to the RPE scale, you're still asking the body to work at the same degree of effort.

Save your energy for the movements that follow, and are designed to bring up your muscle mass through volume and lagging muscle groups. Remember, this is not the phase to bring up the competition lifts. This phase is designed to *build* on that phase when you decide to implement it (which is beyond the scope of this book).

## Movement Selection

Just because we aren't going to apply a lot of effort into building the lifts for this phase, doesn't mean we aren't going to train using a similar movement pattern for them. In fact, we want that to be a big part of this program.

We want to be able to build mass in the muscle groups that are primarily responsible for maximizing the lifts but, in order to do that, we must be intelligent about movement selection outside of the big three. We will call these "primary support movements".

We still want to press, squat, and pick things up off the floor, however, we want to use movements that are similar to the competition lifts to ensure there is as much transfer to them as possible.

For bench pressing, this means exercises such as incline pressing and dumbbell bench pressing.

For squats, it means exercises such as front squats or hack squats.

For deadlifts, it means stiff-legged deadlifts and bent-over barbell rows.

We also want to pick movements based on building mass and strength in various transitions of the three lifts.

For example, if your technique is dialed in on the deadlift but you are slow off the floor, it means your legs need to be stronger. This means more quad and hamstring strength and mass is required.

If you are a wide-grip bench presser, then you need more pec mass to get off the bottom and more triceps to finish at lockout. If you are a close-grip bench presser, then the triceps play a somewhat bigger role, since they will kick in earlier in the movement and have a longer "stroke" to complete the lift.

Putting this all together, we need to take the following into account:

1. Pick similar movements to the competition lifts to get maximal carryover
2. Develop the primary working groups maximally for the competition lifts
3. Pick movements that address each phase of the lift, i.e. bottom of the squat, start and finish of the bench press, and deadlift.

With that defined, let's create a list that fits the criteria of primary support movements that are similar to the competition lifts. These movements are also defined as "moving weight through space".

## Primary Support Movements

<u>Primary Support Movements for the Bench Press</u>
Dumbbell bench pressing
Incline pressing (barbell and dumbbell variations)
Decline pressing (barbell and dumbbell variations)
Close-grip bench
Wide-grip bench
Overhead pressing (any kind—yes—I know this doesn't qualify as a similar movement pattern, however, we're making an exception because you still need strong shoulders)

<u>Primary Support Movements for the Squat</u>
Front squat
Hack squat
Safety bar squats

<u>Primary Support Movements for the Deadlift</u>
Block deadlifts (nothing above the knee)
Stiff-legged deadlifts
Romanian deadlifts
Trap bar deadlifts
Sumo/conventional deadlifts (use the opposite to your competition-style lift)

## Muscular Movements

The second part of selecting movements is to develop the muscles primarily used in the big three. For bench pressing, that's the chest, shoulders and triceps. For squatting, it's the quads, adductors and glutes. For deadlifting, it's the entire posterior chain (let's focus on hamstrings, glutes and upper back). These movements are more focused on "making the muscles work".

Muscular Movements for the Bench Press
Pecs: Flye (flat, incline, decline)
Triceps: Pushdown, French press, Dumbbell skull crusher
Shoulders: Laterals (front, side, rear)

Muscular Movements for the Squat
Quads: Leg extension, Sissy squat
Hamstrings: Leg curl
Adductors: Adductor machine (I also call this the "good girl" machine)
Abductors: Abductor machine (I also call this the "bad girl" machine)
Glutes: Glute bridge, Split squat

Muscular Movements for the Deadlift
Erectors: Hypers, Good morning
Glutes: Glute bridge
Rhomboids and upper back: Dumbbell row, Barbell row, T-bar row

## Transition Movements

This is a list to help you decide, based on musculature, what weak area may be holding you back. This will help you make better choices about where to focus on with regards to volume and specifics in training. This also assumes that your technique is dialed in. Remember, if you miss a lift, it's either because your technique was off or because you're weak somewhere along the muscular chain. That, or you're not yet strong enough to lift that particular weight.

Transition Movements for the Bench Press
Bottom position: Pectorals
Mid-range: Shoulders and triceps
Lockout: Triceps

Transition Movements for the Squat
Bottom: Quads
Mid-range: Adductors, abductors and glutes
Finish: No one normally misses a squat at "lockout". If you get through the transition point, you generally finish.

Transition Movements for the Deadlift
Off the floor: Quads and hamstrings
Mid-range: Erectors
Lockout: Rhomboids and glutes

**Note:** This is not an all-inclusive list of everything that can be done. This is only a general recommendation of movements to improve musculature or areas of the lift that may be weak.

One way you can test to see if you are weak in an area is to perform a movement that places more emphasis on it. If that movement feels difficult, it is very likely that you need to do that movement.

An example of this is when I was focused on improving my squat. My thoughts told me that my quads were lagging, and my testing of both the front squat and hack squat—which are far more quad-dominant— cemented that idea. I sucked terribly at both fronts and hacks. So, I made it a big priority to improve them over that off-season. My quads grew, and my squat improved.

Of course, all of this depends on your technique being dialed in. For example, if your deadlift lockout sucks, getting your glutes superhumanly strong won't do a damn thing for you if you don't pronate your toes (point them slightly outwards) during your set-up. This is because you need some external hip rotation in order to get full gluteal contraction.

You need to make sure that you have perfected your technique to take advantage of your stronger and more massive musculature—or all the work will be worth very little.

## Building the Stabilizers: Secondary Support Movements

As you looked through the list, you probably felt like there were a lot of areas left off. That's because we dealt with the muscles involved as primary and secondary movers. Now we can deal with the stabilizers for those movements.

Despite what you've read on the internet, or from supposed "experts", you cannot bench press with your lats. Their primary function is internal rotation of the humerus; that is, to adduct the arm. They pull the arm towards and behind the trunk, like a lat pulldown or row.

Since this is also the same motion in the eccentric portion of the bench press, they still perform as stabilizers for the shoulders throughout the entire range of motion.

The lats and upper back play a significant role in the execution of the bench press; however, their role is as a major support/stabilizer. If your lats or upper back are weak, you will not be able to provide the support the shoulders need to be able to press powerfully and with stability. Therefore, they cannot be ignored.

The best part about the big three with regards to support and stabilizer work is that there is great overlap, as hitting all of the support muscle groups "fills in the gaps". The transverse abdominus and erectors also perform support work in the squat, but more significantly in the deadlift. The lats and upper back perform as stabilizers in the squat and bench press. They are also major performers in the deadlift. The biceps help to stabilize the elbow joint in bench pressing. The calves help to support the knee.

As you can see, you don't need to pick support work for each movement independently of each other since there will be overlap in many cases.

What we want to do is cover as many support groups in as few movements as possible in order to achieve good training economy. We also want to use the "make the muscle work" idea as well, since we're not trying to make these movements transfer directly into the big lifts. We want to use them to build the muscles involved so that, when the competitive lifts are performed, the support musculature is bigger and stronger; this will give you a much larger base to support the lifts with.

Secondary Support Musculature for the Bench Press
Upper back: Bent lateral, Face pull, Row
Lats: Lat pulldown, Chins
Biceps: Curls of various types

Secondary Support Musculature for the Squat
Calf work: Seated and standing, Donkey calf raise
Upper back and lats: Same as bench press
Abdominals: Ab wheel rollout, Plank

Secondary Support Musculature for the Deadlift
Abdominals: Same as squat

**Note:** Because the deadlift starts from the floor and is mostly a concentric movement, everything working to move the weight off the floor generally works in a "support" or isometric role. This lack of eccentric before the concentric portion of the movement is what separates the deadlift from the squat and bench press.

Also of note is that any of the movements described in the Primary Support Movements section can and often are listed as "support" work. For this outline, however, we aren't concentrating on really building the lifts—just the muscles involved in them.

## Injury Prevention and Balance

It's hard to train when you feel beat up, or are beat up. The single most important factor in avoiding injury is proper technique. After that, a very close second is maintaining balance throughout the body.

By balance, I mean that you don't want one leg to be significantly stronger than the other, one glute firing more than the other, etc. You may feel this if you can feel the load in a squat dramatically shift from one leg to the other. That means your body is moving the load to your stronger and more dominant side, and not dispersing it evenly across the musculature. This is also an issue when you see someone with uneven lockout on the bench press. This is a telltale sign that something bad is forthcoming, especially if it happens often or when loads approach the 90 percent range. It should not be ignored, and should be remedied right away.

That is why it is important to do enough unilateral work to keep your body in balance, and not overly favor one side over the other. If your technique is dialed in and you have great muscular balance, you will significantly reduce your chance of injury.

For lower body, this generally means one-legged work such as split squats, one-legged dumbbell deadlifts, one-legged leg presses and walking lunges. You can still build plenty of muscle with these movements by either loading them progressively (with one-legged deadlifts or holding dumbbells for split squats) or simply by voluming them with bodyweight (walking lunges or split for tons of reps).

This is also why you need to include plenty of dumbbell work and do variations such as one arm dumbbell extensions for triceps, one arm dumbbell bench presses, dumbbell rows, or basically one arm anything in movements for the upper body. That's if you know you have imbalance issues.

Even if you feel you do not, it doesn't hurt to keep some unilateral work in your program. Most people have one leg and arm stronger than the other, and this is the same for pecs, lats, deltoids, etc. I don't know that you can ever be perfectly balanced but, if you're completely out of whack, getting that in order is highly imperative.

Lastly, don't leave out rotator cuff work. This can simply be a part of your warm-up on upper body days. Let me also add that you probably don't need anything heavier than 5 pounds to actually strengthen the rotator cuff. I cringe when I see people doing cuff movements using even 10 pounds. The rotator cuff is comprised of four very small muscles and, to target them effectively, you need to be very strict and deliberate in your movements—not "overload" them with progressive resistance.

To keep things simple, my recommendation is to do an external and internal rotation movement as part of your warm-up. It's beyond the scope of this book to cover everything rotator cuff-related (again, it's a mass-building book!) but in regards to injury prevention for the powerlifter, who bench presses a lot, take care of your rotators by doing some prevention work. I recommend three to four sets of 15 to 20 reps using a *very light* weight.

## Maxing Out in the Off-Season

Because of YouTube and social media, many people have developed a very bad habit of "maxing out for the camera".

Ego-driven training has no place in an intelligent strength or mass program.

Maxing out is nothing more than strength demonstration. You should be saving those attempts for competition. I'm not sure what else there is to say about that.

If you enjoy maxing, there is a more intelligent way to go about it. You can set single PRs based on the RPE scale referenced above. For example, hitting a single at a RPE of 9 is not a terrible option. That usually means it should have been somewhat fast, and it looked like a double was possible.

But you need to be honest with yourself about this and not believe that, when your whole body was shaking and it took 13 seconds from the time you started the concentric portion of the lift, another rep could have been done.

Even with all of that said, I just don't see much of a point in maxing out at any point in training. Yes, I've done it before, and sometimes it is just for the sake of testing yourself. However, as I have gotten older and wiser, I've learned to save my big lifts for competition or to rely on setting new rep PRs as a more intelligent and efficient way of gauging progress.

## Movement Rotation

Because I have thrown so much at you, you're probably wondering how in the hell you're going to put all of this together into a program to cover each area.

This isn't really an issue if you understand that you don't have to hit the same movements at every session each week. That would make your workouts very long and cumbersome.

Movement rotation is a perfectly viable option and, actually, it is more ideal because you can avoid overtraining certain movement patterns and allow yourself to cover more bases over time.

I recommend making a list of all the movements you need to hit to cover everything thoroughly, and then limit the number of movements you will perform in each training session. I usually try to limit the number of movements per training session to four. However, five is also an option, depending on what movements were performed.

Your frequency will also decide your split.

If you are training three times a week, you won't be able to cover as much ground as you would if you trained four or five times per week—meaning that you'd have to train longer per session than if you split movements out over more days.

This doesn't mean that training three times per week is always inferior. The law of individuality means that recovery rates will play a part in deciding training frequency.

I have found that older and more experienced lifters can get by on training three times a week and, in some cases, as little as twice a week, whereas younger guys with less experience can often train more. This is generally because you can apply a greater amount of stress in training as you become more advanced. What a dirty little trick our own physiological system plays on us. As we get stronger and more efficient at applying training stress, the bigger the hole we can dig with regards to fatigue—especially if the body isn't trying to adapt to a new training stimulus.

We covered this, remember? But let's do a refresher.

1. A new movement is added, or a movement is changed in execution.
2. This creates a new stimulus.
3. Over the next few weeks, you gain strength and neural efficiency in that movement.
4. As you adapt, efficiency becomes maximized and strength gains slow down.
5. Once efficiency is maximized and the stimulus decreases, fatigue increases in relation to those factors.

This is why movement rotation is important for advanced lifters trying to pack on new mass. There is a longer period of time where the body is trying to adapt, and fatigue is delayed. Applying some common sense here, this is also why focusing on the competition lifts going into a meet are so important as well: you want to be as efficient as possible with them for said competition.

But, when training for mass, we want to stave off fatigue and increase stimulus adaption time for as long as possible.

There are obviously outliers to these rules, but we need to look at rules and not exceptions. So, how does that apply to frequency with movement rotation?

Most people can train four days a week and recover, if they don't overdo the volume or intensity (both in terms of one rep max and degree of energy applied to the working sets) at each session. When you add in movement rotation, you extend adaptation time; thus, recovery isn't tapped out as quickly as when you perform the same movements day in and day out.

## Putting This Together

Now that your head is spinning with what to select and how to approach this, I will make this quite easy for you to set up your own off-season mass-building template designed to help you improve in the powerlifts.

We're going to lay this template out as four days a week.

Day 1: Lower Body A
Day 2: Upper Body A
Day 3: Off
Day 4: Lower Body B
Day 5: Upper Body B
Day 6 and 7: Off

Lower Body A
Movement 1 - Squats: Warm-ups, then 2 sets of 5 @ RPE 7
Movement 2 - Deadlifts: Warm-ups, then 3 sets of 3 @ RPE 7
Movement 3 - Muscular Movement for Squat: 5 sets of 10 reps @ RPE 10 on last set
Movement 4 - Muscular Movement for Deadlift: 5 sets of 10 reps @ RPE 10 on last set
Movement 5 - Secondary Support Movement for Squat *or* Deadlift: 3 sets of 15 @ RPE 8 on last set

Upper Body A
Movement 1 - Bench Press: Warm-ups, then 2 sets of 8 @ RPE 7
Movement 2 - Primary Support Movement for Bench Press: 4 sets of 8 @ RPE 8 on all sets
Movement 3 - Muscular Movement for Bench Press (pecs/triceps/delts): 4 sets of 12 @ RPE 10 on last set
Movement 4 - Secondary Support Movement for the Bench Press (lats/upper back): 5 sets of 12 @ RPE 10 on last set

Lower Body B
Movement 1 - Primary Support Movement for Squats: Warm-ups, then 4 sets of 8 @ RPE 9 on last set
Movement 2 - Primary Support Movement for Deadlift: Warm-ups, then 3 sets of 6 @ RPE 8 on last set
Movement 3 - Muscular Movement for Squat or Deadlift: 5 sets of 12 @ RPE 10 on last set
Movement 4 - Secondary Support Movement for the Squat *or* Deadlift: 3 sets of 12 @ RPE 8 on last set
Movement 5 - Injury Prevention Movement (Unilateral Leg Work): 2 sets of 20 @ RPE 8 on last set

Upper Body B
Movement 1 - Primary Support Movement for Bench Press: 5 sets of 12 @ RPE 10 on last set
Movement 2 - Muscular Movement for the Bench Press: 5 sets of 15 @ RPE 10 on last set
Movement 3 - Secondary Support Movement for the Bench Press: 4 sets of 12 @ RPE 10 on last set
Movement 4 - Secondary Support Movement for the Bench Press: 3 sets of 20 @ RPE 8 on last set

## Example Week

Before you skip ahead to the example week, let me add that it is up to you, the lifter, to be introspective enough to decide what you need to focus on. This is not a cookie cutter program and you need to make intelligent decisions as to what you will focus on.

This is one of the most important aspects regarding improvement: to diagnose your lifts and your weaknesses, and then attack them with a plan.

Remember, this is a template designed to help you do that, but you should be the one to fill it in with the right choices. If you never develop the ability to be honest with yourself about what you need the most, you will struggle to get better.

With that said, here is an example week.

Lower Body A
Movement 1 - Squat: Warm-ups, then 2 sets of 5 @ RPE 7
Movement 2 - Deadlift: Warm-ups, then 3 sets of 3 @ RPE 7
Movement 3 - Leg extension: 5 sets of 10 reps @ RPE 10 on last set
Movement 4 - Good mornings: 5 sets of 10 reps @ RPE 10 on last set
Movement 5 - Ab wheel roll out: 3 sets of 15 @ RPE 8 on last set

Upper Body A
Movement 1 - Bench press: Warm-ups, then 2 sets of 8 @ RPE 7
Movement 2 - Dumbbell incline press: 4 sets of 8 @ RPE 8 on all sets
Movement 3 - French press: 4 sets of 12 @ RPE 10 on last set
Movement 4 - Bent lateral: 5 sets of 12 @ RPE 10 on last set

Lower Body B
Movement 1 - Hack squat: Warm-ups, then 4 sets of 8 @ RPE 9 on last set
Movement 2 - Stiff-legged deadlift: Warm-ups, then 3 sets of 6 @ RPE 8 on last set
Movement 3 - Glute bridge: 5 sets of 12 @ RPE 10 on last set
Movement 4 - Seated calf raise: 3 sets of 12 @ RPE 8 on last set
Movement 5 - Split squat: 2 sets of 20 @ RPE 8 on last set

Upper Body B
Movement 1 - Incline press: 5 sets of 12 @ RPE 10 on last set
Movement 2 - Flat flye: 5 sets of 15 @ RPE 10 on last set
Movement 3 - Lat pulldown: 4 sets of 12 @ RPE 10 on last set
Movement 4 - Cable row: 3 sets of 20 @ RPE 8 on last set

Remember that you can't possibly cover every single thing in each workout, and that's not the idea. Movement rotation allows you to cycle through movements as often as you feel you need to. My own suggestion is to focus on improving just a few aspects at a time for six weeks, and then focus on improving something else.

For example, if you are weak off the chest in the bench press and weak off the floor in the squat, focus on more chest and quad movements in your exercise selection for six weeks. After the cycle is over, assess where you are. If you still feel as though you need more improvement in those muscle groups, run another six weeks to focus on those areas but with different movements.

This template is sound and concrete in terms of usefulness and improvement with regards to mass for powerlifting, but you must massage it to fit your specific needs.

For example, you may have giant biceps and triceps but small shoulders. So, there may not be a need for direct biceps and triceps work, and you can ignore those support movements while you focus on muscular movements for your shoulders.

Virtually everyone will have weak areas and strong areas. Keep your strong areas strong, and focus on what is holding you back. Plug in the movements that will help you do that into the template, and focus on growing those areas as much as possible for several cycles.

## Conclusion:

Pure powerlifting training is not optimal for muscle growth, especially the minimalist approach of focusing almost exclusively on the competitive lifts and their variations. Unless you are perfectly balanced to start with and have perfect leverages for all three lifts, you will always emphasize the development of certain muscle groups with heavy, basic training. As a result, other important muscles will be left lagging behind.

Specific hypertrophy training is the way a powerlifter can target those weaker areas that are likely holding him back. As such a powerlifter should not shy away from "bodybuilding" work but rather embrace it. People forget that despite being known for the max effort and dynamic effort method, the popular Westside Barbell training systems has around 80% of its volume in the form of targeted hypertrophy work!

Use isolation work to develop a weak link without overstressing the nervous system and your big lifts ***will*** go up!

# Chapter Eight: Hypertrophy for the CrossFit Athlete

~ Christian Thibaudeau

There is this idea that CrossFit guys are small. That may be true when you look at those who only do group classes (which is often more of a cardio session with weights than heavy work), but if you look at the elite-level Regional and Games competitors you will find plenty of very solid physiques.

Of course, you won't find any IFBB pro physiques among them. But guys like Nick Urankar, Jason Khalipa, Neil Maddox and Dan Bailey, to name a few, look very muscular and lean with full muscle bellies.

The competitive guys need to be strong. Unless you have some crazy bodyweight skills and an unstoppable engine to compensate if you can't clean and jerk at least 325 pounds, snatch at least 265 pounds, deadlift more than 500 pounds and squat in the high 400s, you can forget about being competitive. These aren't even high numbers; there are several competitors who can snatch in the 300s and clean and jerk above 385 pounds.

### More Muscle to get Stronger

Neural efficiency, technique and leverage are all nice and well, but they have their limitations. And, ultimately, *muscle moves weight.* Neural efficiency, technique and leverages will only allow you to make the most of the strength that your muscles have.

At an equal level of neural efficiency and technical mastery, if you have more muscle you will lift more weight; just look at elite Olympic lifters who add 20 to 30kg to their total (or even more) when they go up a weight class.

If you want to be strong overall, adding muscle mass to your frame is a surefire way to get there.

## Muscle as Your Armor

Another aspect of adding muscle is that it can help prevent injuries. For example, more muscle mass in the muscles of the shoulder girdle will greatly increase your body's capacity to handle physical stress at the shoulder joint. In that regard, see muscle mass like your armor. It will help protect you by increasing joint integrity and stability.

In addition, athletes invariably suffer muscle imbalances (some muscles being proportionally too weak for the others) which can cause injuries or at least chronic aches and pains, and can also decrease performance. Hypertrophy work for these lagging muscle groups is a great way to solve the issue; when you have a lagging muscle group, big compound lifts with heavy weights aren't the solution because the body will always prefer to use its strongest muscles to do the job, which will only accentuate the imbalance.

## Hypertrophy to Fix Leakage Points

I like to explain strength in the big lifts (and bodyweight work) as a pipeline, through which water runs down towards the endpoint. If the pipeline has some leakage points, the force of the water at the end of the pipeline will be decreased. It is the same thing with lifting strength. Each muscle involved directly (prime mover or synergist/agonist) or indirectly (stabilizer or fixator) can be a potential force leak if it's too weak. The more leakage points you have, or the larger the leaks are, the less capable will you be of demonstrating your strength potential. I was reminded of this recently when I was doing isolation work for the lower body with my friend, Nick. He used more weight than I did on leg extensions, leg curls and leg press, yet I can squat 100 pounds more than he can as I have less strength leaks in the glutes, lower back, mid-section and upper back.

Hypertrophy work is a good way to fix leakage points once you have diagnosed the problematic muscle group. A weak muscle is normally smaller in proportion to the stronger ones; it is underdeveloped relative to what it should be. The activation of that muscle will also likely be deficient, meaning that you will not be good at contracting it properly. Both elements can be better developed with isolation work (where it's hard to compensate with another muscle), using lighter weights and more focus on the quality of the contraction. Once the weak muscle has gained some size and activation is improved, it will more easily be "included in" when doing bigger, heavier lifts.

## Hypertrophy as a Confidence Booster

Charlie Francis (Ben Johnson's former coach) was once asked why Ben put so much emphasis on the bench press and upper body development. Charlie mentioned that the shoulders and arms can contribute to up to 10 percent of running speed. However, the biggest benefit was that the athlete liked the way he looked, which increased both his confidence and his performance.

I can confirm that. When I coached at the CrossFit Games this year, I saw a lot of posturing, competitors discretely comparing their physiques, and so on. It can help with intimidating your opponents, which can hurt their confidence.

We've all had days where we looked and felt small (even though, to the external eye, we didn't look any different). On these days, you can't perform well because your confidence and drive just isn't there.

This might not be the best reason to do hypertrophy work, but it is a real phenomenon nonetheless and it should not be dismissed.

## Hypertrophy Work to Improve Specific Elements of a Competitive WOD

One of my favorite ways to use hypertrophy work with CrossFit athletes is to combine it with a technical skill (as a superset, if you like).

The purpose is to use the hypertrophy work to pre-fatigue a key muscle involved in the skill, thereby making the skill more difficult to complete. At first, your performance will decrease but you will then adapt. Keep in mind that you might very well have to do a rope climb or hang power clean with your hands and forearms gorged of blood and lactic acid in competition. Doing a combination of bodybuilding work with skill work can therefore prepare you for that. There is more on this specific strategy later in this chapter.

## Isolation Work is Not the Devil

**Important:** When I mention "hypertrophy" in this chapter, I am mostly referring to using isolation work and special techniques that are normally in the realm of bodybuilding. Technically, sets of 6 to 12 reps on big compound lifts are also "hypertrophy work" and these should definitely be part of the training of a CrossFit athlete, but this chapter, and especially this section, will discuss how to integrate isolation work which is designed to increase the size of a specific muscle in the training of the CrossFit athlete.

If there is one thing I love about CrossFit it is that it did more to popularize the big lifts (deadlift, squat, front squat, overhead press, snatch and clean and jerk) than any other lifting sport has ever done. People are now comparing their squat instead of their bench press, and talking about how they must make their legs bigger instead of how their biceps are too small. CrossFit made the big lifts mainstream and it rewards those who focus on them.

Sadly, while powerlifters, Olympic lifters, strongmen and gymnasts are all well-perceived by CrossFit athletes since they learn a lot from them, there is still a schism between CrossFitters and bodybuilders. For that reason, CrossFitters tend to disregard everything that bodybuilders do. Isolation work is often seen as a worthless waste of time and seeking muscular development is seen as an unworthy practice. Hopefully, after the introduction to this chapter, you are beginning to see otherwise.

Isolation work to build a specific muscle is not an inferior form of training. True, it isn't as rewarding and it doesn't require the same physical and mental investment as working hard on the big lifts does.

But it serves a very real purpose. You can't build a house with only a hammer and, with training, sometimes doing more work on the big lifts isn't the best option; it may not be the "tool to do the job".

When you perform a big compound lift, your body doesn't know that you are trying to develop a specific muscle group. All it knows is that there is a big ass weight that is trying to fight you and, in the interest of survival, it will use the muscles best-suited to do the job. If you have a certain muscle dominance, your body may very well focus on shifting more of the workload to your stronger muscles rather than your weak link. It is thus these stronger muscles that will receive the most stimulation and will progress/grow the most; this simply augments their strength and accentuates their natural dominance while the weak link stays the same. For example, if you have super strong shoulders and weak pectorals and triceps, the deltoids will take on more stress when you bench press and the pectorals will be left relatively unstimulated.

Chinese and North Korean Olympic lifters do 30 to 45 minutes of isolation/bodybuilding work after their main lifting sessions several times a week. If a group of athletes who are already training 20+ hours per week see fit to add some more work on top of their grueling schedule, they must certainly see a benefit in it, don't you think?

They understand that muscles move weight; the more muscle you have, the greater your strength potential. Why are they using isolation/bodybuilding work to build their muscles at the end of the session? Because their training is already full of neurologically-demanding exercises; the last thing they want is use a high volume of more neurologically-demanding movements to work on hypertrophy too! The same is true for CrossFit athletes: most of what they do is hard on the nervous system. They should give it a break when doing a portion of training aimed only at muscular development.

Isolation/bodybuilding work allows you to further stimulate muscle growth while not imposing more stress on the nervous system, which has already been taxed from the rest of your training.

## The Four Ways to Do Hypertrophy/Bodybuilding Work if You Are a CrossFit Athlete

A CrossFit athlete who wants or needs to increase their muscle mass has four options. The best one will depend on how much mass the athlete needs, if they need to add muscle mass overall or just to fix a weak link, how much time they have before their next competition or not, and their skill level.

For example, someone who has a competition in two months or less or who doesn't have the best skill consistency will be ill-advised to devote an entire phase of training to gaining muscle mass. For that person, reducing their CrossFit training to a minimum while shifting their focus to strength and muscle mass might not be a smart option.

But a CrossFit "Ninja" (to steal the term from Ben Bergeron) who is smaller, has great bodyweight skills and conditioning but lacks strength and size, and also has a lot of time to prepare for their next competition might do well to invest in a six to eight week period where they focus solely on getting much stronger and larger, while putting their skill/metabolic conditioning at maintenance level.

Regardless of your needs, goals and time available to train, it is possible to integrate hypertrophy work into your performance training. There are four options as follows.

**Option 1: Adding 15 to 25 minutes of hypertrophy work to the end of your training day**
This option has the least impact on how you program the rest of your training. You can keep up with your regular programming and add a small amount of isolation/hypertrophy work at the end of your session. This works best when you only have one or two muscles you want to "fix". This way, you can focus on only one muscle group for 15 to 25 minutes, and you will be able to "hit" each of the two target muscles twice or even three times per week.

One of the main benefits of this approach is that your nervous system will be firing on all cylinders after your big lifts/skill/metcon and muscle recruitment will be more effective during the isolation work. The drawback is that when you get to the isolation work, you might be glycogen-depleted and tired, which will make it harder to get a good pump and apply enough effort to make it work. For that reason, it is important to consume protein and carbs intra-workout to at least keep your glycogen levels at an acceptable level.

This first option can be done with pretty much everybody, but it works best if you only have one or two weak muscles to fix. I believe that if you are trying to develop all your major muscles by training each one once a week for 15 to 25 minutes, you won't get many results compared to training them two or three times per week.

**Key Information**: Keep in mind that often a weak muscle is weak because you are simply not good at utilizing it. For that reason, during a big lift your body won't integrate that muscle as much as it should. You can view isolation work not only as a way to build muscle, but also as a way to improve your capacity to use that muscle. And, the better you become at utilizing it, the more easily you will integrate it into the performance of the big lifts. In return, those big lifts will begin to "work", and therefore develop those weak muscles.

**Option 2: Complexing isolation moves into your training**
By complexing, I mean combining isolation/hypertrophy work with your strength or skill work. In both cases, for CrossFit athletes, I like to do the isolation work prior to doing the skill or strength move.

Why? Because this can prepare you for a very real problem that might occur in competition: having to do a skill when a key muscle is fried or full of lactic acid. For example, you might be good at doing legless rope climbs but, when your arms and forearms are pumped, it's a different ball game. Doing a snatch might normally be fine but if your shoulders are toasted, it will suddenly become a circus act! By doing an isolation exercise for an important muscle involved in the skill or strength lift, you get used to doing the latter under sub-optimal conditions. At first, your performance will decrease (better to have that in training than in competition) but, over time, you will become just as efficient doing the skill/strength movement with a tired/pumped muscle; your performance drop will be very low.

Here, the goal isn't so much to fix a weaker muscle but, rather, to use the isolation work to fatigue a muscle that will then limit the performance of a skill or strength move. The result is that this muscle will become larger but also that it will become more resilient to fatigue—both will make you a better athlete.

You can even include isolation work like this for a WOD/metcon session. For example, you could do a triplet where you have one metcon exercise, one isolation/hypertrophy movement and one skill or strength exercise.

Here are some examples:

<u>Four Rounds for Time</u>
20 calories Assault bike
12 Dumbbell hammer curls with a two second hold at the top of each repetition
1 Legless rope climb (15 feet)
1 Normal rope climb (15 feet)

<u>Couplet (no rest between first and second exercise)</u>
Deltoid triple set (8 seated lateral raises + 8 seated front raises + 8 cuban presses)
3 Snatches @ 75 to 82%

<u>Triplet (no rest between exercises one and two, and two and three)</u>
Barbell curl modern 21s (7 full reps, 7 top-partials, 7 bottom-partials)
Lying dumbbell triceps extension 1 ½ reps (lower down, lift halfway up slowly, lower back down, and then lift completely up to complete *one* rep) x 10 reps
Maximum unbroken muscle-ups (or strict muscle-ups, depending on level)

This approach should be used mostly by more advanced CrossFit athletes, or at least by those who already have a solid technical mastery of the bodyweight (muscle-ups, handstand push-ups, pull-ups, rope climbs, etc.) and barbell (Olympic lift variations) skills. Fatiguing a key muscle involved in the skill makes its performance much harder. If your level of mastery isn't high enough, it will be impossible to do the skill properly and you will learn bad motor habits.

**Option 3: Having a hypertrophy day during the week**
This is a fairly non-invasive approach to hypertrophy. By non-invasive, I mean that it doesn't interfere much with your normal programming. Hypertrophy work isn't really that demanding on the nervous system, so it won't affect your capacity to perform due to neural fatigue. Muscle damage is normally overplayed; a trained muscle can be re-trained again after very little time if proper nutrition is used. Furthermore, CrossFit athletes often use the same muscles several days in a row, so that's not something new or out of the ordinary for them. The only thing I recommend is to consume enough carbs on the hypertrophy day to avoid local glycogen depletion.

You can thus devote one day a week to building muscle mass. Normally, I like to do some strength work in there, too. Firstly, because the strength movement(s) activate/potentiate the nervous system, making the recruitment and stimulation of the muscles by isolation work more effective, but also because the strength movements themselves can contribute to developing muscle mass.

There are two approaches to that training day:

A) For three to four weeks, pick one weak muscle group to be the focus point of your hypertrophy session. The template for that training day would then become:

Exercise 1: Big lift involving the target muscle (for example, close-grip bench press if you want to work on triceps development), using four to six sets of three to seven reps. I like the 1 x 7, 1 x 5, 1 x 3, 1 x 7, 1 x 5, 1 x 3 loading scheme.

Exercise 2: Assistance exercise for the big lift, focusing on the target muscle (in our example, it could be a half close-grip bench press from pins or a close-grip floor press) for three to four sets of six to eight reps.

Exercises 3 and 4: Superset of two isolation exercises; one for the target muscle group (dumbbell triceps extension, in our example) and one for its antagonist/opposing muscle group (preacher curl, for example). Use three to four sets of 10 to 12 reps for both, focusing on the quality of contraction.

Exercises 5 and 6: Superset of two isolation exercises; one for the target muscle group (cable triceps pushdown, for example) and one for its antagonist/opposing muscle group (dumbbell hammer curl, for example). Here we use a max pump technique; something like slow tempo, extended sets, 21s, or double contractions. The technique itself doesn't matter as much as creating a huge accumulation of lactic acid and fluid inside the muscle (big pump, bro). Three sets are done in this matter.

The downsides to this approach are that you will only hit the lagging muscle directly once a week and that you will not work on improving the whole body at once. In both cases, it is important to remember that you are already doing plenty of work for the whole body during your regular programming; you are likely doing squats, deadlifts, push presses/strict presses, pull-ups, dips, etc. So it's not like your body isn't receiving any stimulation. This approach is more about building up a lagging muscle group, so it will work even though the target muscle is only worked once a week for hypertrophy. Since our goal is to correct a weakness, and not win a bodybuilding contest, it's fine if you don't train the whole body for hypertrophy all at once. Especially since the whole body will already receive some stimulation from your regular programming.

B) Doing a whole-body hypertrophy session. Here, I like to use an antagonist superset approach whereby you pair two exercises targeting opposing muscle groups.

You can use basic hypertrophy loading schemes (sets of six to eight or eight to 12 reps) or use intensification methods for some of the exercises.

A good template looks like this:

Exercises 1 and 2 (antagonist superset): One movement targeting the quadriceps (could be a Bulgarian split squat, squats doing only the middle portion of the range of motion, a hack squat machine, etc.) and one targeting the hamstrings (any form of leg curl, glute-ham raise, reverse hyper, etc.). Do not rest between exercises 1 and 2.

Exercises 3 and 4 (antagonist superset): One movement targeting the pectorals (could be dumbbell or kettlebell flyes, a pec deck machine, a wide-grip bench press, a dumbbell bench press, etc.) and one for the mid-back (face pull, bent-over barbell row to chest, chest-supported dumbbell row, rear delt machine, rear delt raise, etc.). Do not rest between exercises 3 and 4.

Exercises 5 and 6 (antagonist superset): One exercise for the lateral or front deltoid (dumbbell lateral raise variations, dumbbell front raise variations) and one exercise for the lats (straight-arm pulldown, dumbbell pullover, kayak row, one-arm dumbbell row/lawnmower, etc.). Do not rest between exercises 5 and 6.

Exercises 7 and 8 (antagonist superset): One exercise for the biceps (any form of curl) and one for the triceps (lying or standing dumbbell triceps extension, lying barbell triceps extension, cable or elastic band pushdown, etc.). Do not rest between exercises 7 and 8.

The upside of this option relative to the preceding one is that you place some stimulation on all the major muscle groups in your body. The downside is that you can't place a lot of stimulus on any single muscle because you will be using a restricted volume for each muscle group. So, while you will touch everything, growth might be slower than expected. This is a decent option for a beginner who lacks overall muscle mass and will respond positively to everything; however, it's not the best option for the more advanced athlete, especially if he has some specific weak points to address.

**Option 4: Devoting a training block to maximizing hypertrophy**
This option involves putting your metcon work on maintenance. This obviously means doing less skill work, too. Basically, for four to six weeks (or even six to eight if you really lack muscle mass), you will train primarily for strength and hypertrophy. It is also important to eat a caloric surplus during that phase as we are shooting for an increase in bodyweight of about 4%. Eat a lot but don't let yourself gain too much fat.

A good template looks like this:

Day 1: Lower Body (Squat)
Exercise 1: Major squat variation (back low bar, back high bar or front) trained for strength. Ramp up to a 1, 2 or 3RM, then do three sets of three to five reps with 90% of the maximum reached for that day.

Exercise 2: Squat assistance. I like to use a compound movement (which can be another squat variation), targeting a weakness in your squat, for three to four sets of four to six reps.

Good options include:
*Zombie squat* (front squat with arms extended in front of you, so the bar is resting on the deltoids only) if keeping an upright torso is a problem in your front squat.

*Paused squat* (front or back, three to five second pause at the bottom) if your weak point is getting out of the bottom position.

*Double-contraction squat* (squatting all the way down, getting back up to parallel, going back down, and then standing up completely to complete *one* rep) is another option if you are weak at the bottom position.

*Half-squat from pins* (starting the bar on the pins, with your legs at a 100 degree angle) if your main issue is feeling intimidated by a heavy load, or if your core strength is a limiting factor.

*Super-slow squats* (going down and up in five seconds) if your problem is getting out of position during the squat. Do the movement slowly, focusing on pushing only with the legs and maintaining a static torso angle.

Exercise 3: Quadriceps movement, where the goal is to get a good quad pump. We want the muscle to be under tension for 45 to 60 seconds. You can use a leg extension machine, do leg extensions with a dumbbell between your legs, do leg extensions with a resistance band or (my favorite) dragging a sled backwards while staying in a "seated/crouched" position. Perform three to four sets using whatever rep number or intensity technique you want—as long as the time under tension is between 45 and 60 seconds.

Exercise 4: Glutes movement, following the same guidelines as for the quads: keep the muscle under tension for 45 to 60 seconds per set and perform three work sets. You can do hip thrusts, wide Bulgarian split squats or push a prowler forward focusing on long, full strides contracting the glutes hard.

Day 2: Upper Body (Horizontal)
Exercise 1: Horizontal press variation (bench press, close-grip bench press, incline bench press or decline bench press) trained for strength. Ramp up to a 1, 2 or 3RM, then do three sets of three to five reps with 90% of the maximum reached for that day.

Exercise 2: Assistance movement for the horizontal press. Like with the squat, perform a compound movement to strengthen the weak link in the horizontal press movement, for three to four sets of four to six reps.

Good options include:

*Floor press* (bench press lying on the floor, pause for one to two seconds with the elbows on the floor before pressing) if the sticking point is right around or just prior to the mid-range point.

*Partial bench press from pins or board* (elbows at 90 degrees before pressing) is another option if the sticking point is right around the mid-range point.

*Extra range press* (doing lower than if the barbell is stopped by the chest, either with dumbbells or a cambered bar) if your sticking point is from the start of the movement.

*Incline press* (dumbbell or barbell at a 15 or 30 degree angle performed with a two second pause at the bottom) is another option if your weak point is from the start of the movement.

*Spotto press* (paused bench press, completely relaxing in the bottom position) is another option to strengthen the start of the bench press.

*Close-grip incline press* if your sticking point is in the last-third of the movement.

*Partial bench press from pins or boards* (from the last-third of the range of motion, with elbows at around 110 degrees) is another option if your sticking point is near the lockout.

Exercises 3 and 4: Superset of one triceps isolation exercise and one mid-back isolation exercise, with both done for three to four sets of eight to 12 reps. Do not rest between exercises 3 and 4, but rest about 90 seconds after exercise 4.

Exercises 5 and 6: Superset of one deltoid isolation exercise and one lats exercise, with both done for three to four sets of eight to 12 reps. Do not rest between exercises 5 and 6, but rest about 90 seconds after exercise 6.

Day 3: Bodyweight Skill Maintenance and Metabolic Conditioning
On this day, you will spend about 30 minutes working on your bodyweight skills and then perform two short and intense WODs/metcon sessions, with a total of about 20 to 25 minutes.

Day 4: Lower Body (Pull)
Exercise 1: Olympic lift variation (snatch or clean variation) to stay sharp with the movement and to activate the nervous system for the deadlift work. Perform six to ten sets of two repetitions with a moderate weight (70 to 80 percent). Focus on technical perfection as well as speed and crispness of execution.

Exercise 2: Major deadlift variation (conventional powerlifting deadlift, sumo deadlift, Olympic/clean deadlift). I don't like ramping up to a max on a deadlift in training. I believe that doing plenty of work in the 80 to 90 percent range, focusing on perfect position, is much more effective in the long run. Shoot for about 15 to 20 total work reps with 80 to 90 percent in the form of five to seven sets of three reps. Every rep must start from a dead-start on the floor.

Exercise 3: Deadlift assistance exercise. Pick an exercise to focus on your weak point in the deadlift. Do three to four sets of three to five reps.

Good options include:

*Deadlift from a deficit* (deadlift, standing on a two to three inch platform, focus on leg drive off the floor) if your weakness is getting the bar moving from the floor.

*Floor-to-knees/first pull* (lift the barbell from the floor to the knees only, and pause there for two seconds per rep; can also be done on a podium) is another option if you are weak off the floor.

*Barbell back squat/behind the back deadlift* (with your heels raised on a block, hold the barbell behind you and deadlift it) is another option to strengthen the first pull but, specifically, if your quads are holding you back.

*Romanian deadlift* if your weak area is the passage from below to above the knees.

*Arched back good morning* is another option if your weak area is the passage from below to above the knees.

*Partial deadlift from pins* (from just below knees) is another option to strengthen the transition from below to above the knees.

*Barbell hip thrust* if your problem area is the lockout.

*Partial deadlift from pins* (from just above the knees) is another option to strengthen the transition from below to above the knees. Be sure to mimic your actual pull (posterior chain/lower back) and do *not* cheat by "sliding' your knees forward to leverage the bar.

Exercise 4: Posterior chain exercise involving the glutes and hamstrings (glute ham raise, reverse hyper, kettle bell Romanian deadlift or back extension) for three to four sets of eight to 12 reps.

Exercise 5: Hamstring isolation exercise (any form of leg curl) using various intensification techniques (drop set, double-contraction, slow eccentric, added partial reps at the end of the set, 21s, etc.) for three sets. Aim for maximum pump to failure.

Day 5: Upper Body (Vertical)
Exercise 1: Major overhead lift (strict press, behind-the-neck press, push press or thruster) trained for strength. Ramp up to a 1, 2 or 3RM, then do three sets of three to five reps with 90 percent of the maximum reached for that day.

Exercises 2 and 3: Superset of one exercise for the lats and one isolation move for the deltoids, with both done for either three to four sets of eight to 12 or using intensification techniques to create a maximum pump.

Exercises 4 and 5: Superset of one isolation movement for the biceps and one isolation exercises for the triceps, with both done for either three to four sets of eight to 12 or using intensification techniques to create a maximum pump.

"Exercise" 6: Short but very intense WOD involving six to eight minutes of all-out effort.

Day 6: Olympic Lifting Skills
Exercise 1: Snatch variation. Again, the focus is on technique and speed. Do six to eight sets of three reps with 75 to 80 percent.

Exercise 2: Clean variation. Same principles as for the snatch.

Exercise 3: Jerk variation. Same principles as for the previous two exercises.

Day 7: Rest Day

This fourth option is better left to what Ben Bergeron (coach of the 2015 female Games winner and male runner-up) calls "Ninjas": the smaller athletes (170 pounds or less) with great bodyweight skills and conditioning (who can therefore afford to reduce their amount of both for six to eight weeks) but lack size and strength.

Those who are stronger than they are skilled and conditioned would be better off selecting another option— the exception being team athletes who have a specific role on their team (to be a strength beast).

Regardless of the strategy you decide to use, as a CrossFit athlete you should not neglect the importance of increasing your muscle mass. It will help you become stronger on both your lifts and advanced bodyweight skills.

# Chapter Nine: Mobility for Health and Mass

~ Paul Carter

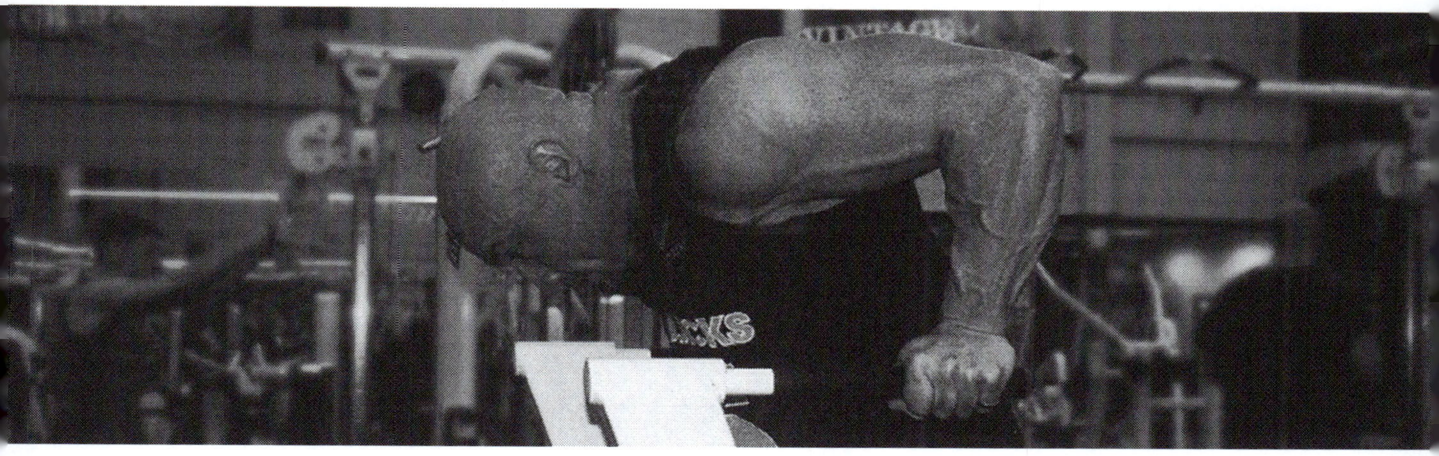

I am not a huge fan of mobility training. I am not saying it is not needed, but I think it's become a very overrated and overstated part of getting better in the gym.

One principle I discuss with lifters regarding mobility work is: "Are you immobile, or are you too weak to hold a certain position?"

The second one is: "You only need to be mobile enough to perform the movement with proper execution through a full range of motion without pain."

These are the two principles I look at, and you need to look at, to decide if you actually need mobility work as a part of your training paradigm, or if you're just not strong enough to hold position in a movement.

One of the things I like to do, rather than spend time doing "mobility drills", is incorporate movements into training that fit into the training economy plan. That is, pick movements that develop the musculature, but also have many other benefits with regards to becoming mobile and staying mobile.

I'm not going to blow your mind with my suggestions here. I've read almost every conceivable article you can imagine on mobility and, to be honest, I often end up rolling my eyes. I don't mean to sound like a sarcastic asshole, but I just don't think that needing to put yourself into some contorted position with your ankle behind your head while you extend your thoracic spine to stretch your psoas is really the reason you can't squat to depth. Every single morning you get up and you squat to depth after your first couple of cups of morning coffee. So why can't you do that with a barbell on your back?

Generally, it is just a matter of movement execution—or lack of—holding you back.

Nevertheless, staying flexible enough to perform the movements and keep your joints healthy *is* a huge part of training success. Let's venture into my suggestions for doing that to keep training productive and consistent.

## Ankle/Knee/Hip Mobility

One of the first things I look at when diagnosing how well someone's hips move when they squat is their ankles. Most people look at adduction or abduction of the knees and, if someone has valgus (knee cave) when they squat, they automatically assume that said lifter's glute medius is just not strong enough to hold that position.

This may be true, but it also may not be—which is why I look at what the ankles do.

In order to properly engage the hip extensors during squats, there needs to be enough external rotation of the hips to allow that to happen. In layman's terms, this means that the knees should travel outwards, slightly outside the feet, in order to bring the glutes into play in the squat.

While it's true that maximum gluteal contraction cannot happen without some external hip rotation, and you need to pronate your feet slightly for external rotation to occur (meaning to point the toes slightly outwards), if the ankles have internal rotation during the concentric portion of the squat the adductors will take over, and steal tension from the glutes to complete the movement.

This is not ideal as we want to load and bring the glutes into play in the squat—unless we are using the squat as a primary knee extensor movement—in which case we want more knee flexion and extension.

If all of that confuses you, I will make it simple. If you want to shift the load in the squat to be more hip-dominant, break harder at the hips (meaning sit back more). If you want the squat to be more quadricep-dominant, break more at the knees.

In both cases, however, we want the ankles to have enough flexibility to do two things:

1. Have external rotation so that the knees can travel in a path that loads the primary mover.
2. Be flexible enough to keep the load over the mid-point of the foot.

If ankle flexibility is poor, what often happens is that the lifter shifts the load more onto the balls of the feet and proper leverage over the bar is lost. It doesn't matter if someone is trying to be more hip- or quad-dominant; the weight of the bar still needs to be directly over the mid-foot position the entire time. Without proper ankle mobility, the knees and hips cannot move in an ideal manner to create and hold this position.

So, in this case, it's a mobility issue. Rather than lay out 14 different calf mobility movements, I am going to give you a very simple cure here.

Start all of your leg sessions with calf work, standing and seated. Hold the stretch portion of the reps for five seconds. At the bottom of the movement, roll on to the outside of the feet, then rotate on to the big toe as you perform the concentric portion of the rep.

This is not the time to try and become calfzilla by piling on 1000 pounds of weight. In fact, if you're holding that stretch for five seconds, it will eliminate that altogether. Perform four to five sets of each movement for 10 to 15 reps. Not only will this give you some new-found calf mass, but it will also help with ankle mobility during your squats. This is smart training economy.

After you do these two movements, do four sets of 12 to 15 reps for your anterior tibialis. You don't need added weight. Find something to stand on with your heels planted firmly and your toes hanging off, and then simply raise your toes towards your knees and hold for three seconds.

Regarding knee stability, most people have one of two issues: either their vastus medialis (VMO) isn't strong enough to create proper knee-tracking, or their hamstrings are too weak to stabilize the knee.

The VMO is the only knee flexor with a medial pull to it. Once it gets weak, the knee tends to track outward, and this often results in patella pain (below the knee cap). As noted in earlier chapters, exercise selection won't do a lot to improve this issue if you cannot get the VMO to start firing in the first place.

Despite the fact that exercise "scientists" often argue over the effectiveness of the leg extension machine, I have found it to be the best option to get someone's VMO recruitment back on track. I know many prefer exercises like step-ups and split squats; once the lifter can get the VMO involved in a movement, those are indeed great options to help further development. However, if the lifter cannot get the VMO to fire and become involved, they will keep resorting to using the other knee and hip extensors to execute the movement.

My recommendation is to use the top 1 quarter of the leg extension in a slow and deliberate manner with a five second hold at the top, for 5 sets of 15 to 20 reps. Again, adding weight is not the goal here—it is the recruitment of the VMO. Once the trainee can consistently feel the VMO working very hard, they can graduate on to using other movements to introduce progressive overload and further strengthen and develop that area.

Why not full range leg extensions? Because the bottom quarter of the movement tends to recruit the rectus femoris to perform the movement, and the tension isn't shifted to the VMO until about halfway up in execution. What a lot of people do is perform the bottom part very explosively to get the weight moving, and then use that momentum to finish the rep. We aren't after that. We want total recruitment of the VMO at the exclusion of the other knee extensors.

When a lack of hamstring strength or mobility is an issue, the pain is often felt on the outside or back of the knee. A lack of hamstring strength is closely related to ACL injuries, this is because when the hamstrings are too weak to provide stability in the knee the ACL takes the brunt of the load. When the ankles, knees and hips have a lack of flexion, the soft tissue/tendons will be the areas that receive the greatest amount of torque. Obviously, this is bad.

That is why it is vitally important, for proper knee health, that the VMO and hamstrings are very strong to provide adequate knee tracking and support.

The good ol' leg curl is great for curing this issue, and it will help to create a strong and stable environment for the knee. How you execute the leg curl matters. You need to press your hips into the leg curl pad and not allow them to rise off of it for the entire set—like most people do. This creates separation between the hips and the pad, and decreases how short the hamstrings can become in the contracted position and how long they can get in the bottom of the eccentric position. This therefore lessens the effectiveness of the movement. Remember, we want the contraction to be as strong as possible by creating a position where the muscle shortens as much as possible and lengthens as much as possible during the range of motion. Forget the weight and instead focus on pushing your hips hard into the pad, contracting the hamstrings as much as possible, and then lowering under control all the way down. Do four sets of eight to twelve reps in this manner before your leg work.

The final movement is nothing more than walking lunges. The best thing about the lunge is that it brings all of the knee extensors into play, while also stretching the usually tight hip flexors at the same time. This can also be done with split squats, where your leg is on a bench behind you. Either of these are great choices and can be done at the beginning or end of the training session. But make sure to include them in every workout. These are often what I call my "finisher" for most workouts. I set either a total number of reps I want to do, or simply set a timer for how long I want to do them and try to beat the number of reps I do in that time each week.

## Shoulder Mobility

Due to the fact that the bench press is probably the most popular exercise in America, and maybe even all over the world, the majority of lifters are heavily internally rotated in their shoulders. That is, their shoulders are slightly rolled forward, and some guys even end up with imaginary lat syndrome from it.

Stand upright and look down at your hands. If your palms are basically facing your front pockets, you have some serious internal rotation going on and this is a great sign that shoulder problems are probably forthcoming.

The obvious solution is to do external rotator work, such as L-flyes. However, in my own personal experience, this has a somewhat limited fix capability.

The first step to solving this is to prioritize rear delt, mid-trap and rhomboid development. Most guys spend a lot of time pressing shit, and far less time pulling shit, and this is how the imbalance gets set in place.

The other movement I've found that constantly ensures that shoulder mobility is on point is the behind-the-neck press.

I've heard all the groaning about this movement, and I groan back about it. Olympic lifters do behind-the-neck movements on a consistent basis and never have the same kind of shoulder issues that non-Olympic lifters do; this is because they don't tend to be as internally rotated in their shoulders.

Why? Because they do a great deal of work that involves the posterior chain and back. Thus, there is no issue with front to back balance.

It's the guys who spend too much time bench pressing that often say they can't do this movement due to shoulder pain. Then, they blame the movement as being "bad" when in actual fact their training habits are the culprit.

Charles Poliquin once told me that he used the behind-the-neck press as the barometer to see if someone did in fact have good shoulder mobility. I have done behind-the-neck presses consistently for more than 20 years, and have never had a single shoulder problem from them. Dmitry Klokov does snatch grip behind-the-neck presses with 300 pounds each week and, as far as I know, doesn't have shoulder issues.

If you cannot do them, I suggest developing the shoulder flexibility/mobility to be able to. You can start working on this by doing shoulder dislocates with a band. This is where you hold a flexible band in front of you, bring it over your head and then down behind you, allowing your hands to travel as far apart as they need to in order to do this without pain.

At first, you will likely have your hands very, very wide in order to do this. But, over time, the space you need between your hands to complete this movement will decrease. When you can do this with comfort, make behind-the-neck pressing a part of your shoulder work and keep it in there from then on out. You don't have to go super heavy for them to be effective (although I have many times in the past, and with no issues). In addition, they are a supreme delt developer—far superior to any other overhead pressing movement, in my opinion.

## Elbow Pain

I can't tell you how many guys I've talked to over the years whose training takes a massive hit due to elbow pain. I've had it so bad that picking up a gallon of milk sent shockwaves up my arm.

One of the issues with self-diagnosing elbow pain is that most guys think it's attributed to a triceps problem when, in fact, it's most often due to the muscles in the forearm—especially the pronator teres.

Try this: do a dumbbell curl where you supinate the dumbbell, supinating very hard at the top and trying to turn the pinkie over as much as possible. Do you feel some relief in the area where you generally have pain? More times than not, you will.

This is common because of too much over-pronation by the wrist and hard flexion in the hand and fingers. What is one of the things you are constantly told to do during an exercise like say, the bench press? Squeeze the bar as hard as possible. Of course, you do this in virtually every upper body movement, and more movements cause the hands to be in either a pronated or semi-pronated position.

Powerlifters generally suffer from this more than bodybuilders because they do so much bench pressing and deadlifting, and tons of triceps work. They often do very little biceps work to correct this imbalance, and then end up with significant elbow problems due to overworked/tight pronators.

The solution here is simple: lots of curls. Empty barbell curls tend to remedy this very quickly. Do 100 reps non-stop with no weight on the bar. This will do a few things: it forces a tremendous amount of blood into the area, decreases inflammation, and offers a ton of repetition to correct the imbalance in the supination/pronation problem.

If someone is in really bad shape, start with hammer curls for four sets of 25 reps, and then graduate on to the barbell curls. At that point, pain should be minimal and doing supinated dumbbell curls should then become a mainstay in arm/support training.

## Lower Back Pain

I cannot tell you how many guys I've talked to at seminars or online who told me that they had to quit deadlifting or squatting for a while because "man, I blew my back out."

What the fuck does that even mean? You blew your back out? How are you not in a wheelchair? How are you even standing right now?

I am not talking about guys with disk issues. I cannot address that here. And, to be honest, few things irritate me as much as someone asking me online how in the hell to fix their blown-out disks. Go to a doctor! They will help you.

What I *can* help you with, if you've "blown out your back" from deadlifting, is to offer up this simple piece of advice: More times than not, when someone does some deadlifts or squats and then thinks they have "blown out their back" it's nothing more than a piriformis strain.

Can't bend over? Pain radiating up your lower back? Feels better to sit down and elevate your feet? Yeah. It's the piriformis.

This is a simple and easy fix, and you'll be back to lifting in no time. Sit in a chair and put one foot on your knee. Sit upright with tall posture and then push forwards at the chest, until you feel a nice stretch down in that glute/lower back area where the pain is. If you're doing it correctly, you should feel a bit of relief right away just from the stretch. Hold that stretch for 10 to 12 seconds, relax, and repeat four to five more times. Do this four to five times throughout the day, and within a few days you should be good to go.

If that's not it, you blew out your back. Seek medical attention.

## Conclusion

This chapter is short. I could make it super long, however, I am not a doctor, and I didn't even stay at a Holiday Inn Express last night (older people will get that joke). I also don't want to present myself as an expert on rehabilitation as there are professionals that do that for a living.

What I am giving you is the things I have dealt with and solutions I have used for myself and my clients to help keep me and them on track for productive training.

If you have issues falling outside of the scope of this very simple chapter, seek professional help. I cannot emphasize that enough. The internet is not a place to go to when you're dealing with serious health issues. Go to WebMD and enter the symptoms for a cold and you'll find out that you're dying from lung disease.

Be smart. This chapter was about minor aches and pains and some mobility, not fixing your torn ACL.

# Chapter Ten: Body Part Specialization

~ Paul Carter

I have to preface this entire chapter with a very important piece of information about specializing in body part selection: if you can't get a muscle to fire very hard during the execution of a movement, then movement selection becomes completely irrelevant.

Let me draw up an anecdote to show you why that is. Think about your most developed body part. Now, think about how quickly it gets a pump and how much of a connection you have with that body part when training it. You can get it to contract very hard, and feel it working through the entire range of motion in a movement.

Now, think about a body part that is lagging, and think about how hard it is to get a pump in that area, and how much trouble you have "feeling it" when performing movements for it.

It is of paramount importance that you perform each movement for your weak body part by concentrating on starting the movement with that body part. Furthermore, if the movement offers resistance at the top or finishing portion, you need to hold that contraction for a few seconds before performing the eccentric/negative portion of the movement.

In order to bring a body part up as quickly as possible, you need to actually get it to fire as intensely as possible during training. Without this, all the specialization in the world will mean very little.

A very good idea to help increase this ability is to simply flex that body part as often as possible throughout the day. If you want more pecs, simply contract them, hold the contraction for 5 to 10 seconds, and repeat 10 to 12 times. Do that 10 to 20 times throughout the day, and apply that to your time in the gym as well.

The more time you spend asking a muscle to contract, the faster you will develop a great connection to make that muscle do so. This cannot be emphasized enough; you will never bring a body part up to speed without learning how to get it to fire as hard as possible against the resistance you provide. Keep this in mind throughout your training and you will improve very rapidly.

Now we can begin.

After you have built a solid base level of mass, it's going to become very apparent to you what areas in your musculature are lagging. This will vary greatly from person to person and each of you will need to be body aware enough to identify what those areas are.

Let me emphasize that this is *after* a large base level of muscle mass has been built. There is nothing quite as annoying as some dude that is 155 pounds who has been training for three years and thinks he needs to specialize a body part.

Before you decide to worry about specializing on bringing up a particular body part, you need to make a decision based on self-assessment and a few questions.

1. Have you been training and eating properly and consistently for at least five years?
2. Has your training over that time been thoroughly balanced?
3. Are your base levels of strength at least adequate?
4. Have you had any nagging injuries or a history of injuries that have kept you from training a particular muscular group?

In order to decide if you should venture into body part specialization, consider these answers:

1. If the answer to this is no, you need to do that first. Your base level of mass isn't high enough to decide if you actually need to specialize first.
2. If the answer to this is no, then you need to decide on a more balanced training routine for a significant span of time. For example, if you were an Olympic lifter, or have only been doing half a dozen total movements, or full body workouts only, you don't need body part specialization.
3. If you're not even in the 300/400/500 club for bench/squat/deadlift, then your base level of strength is probably not adequate to decide on specialization.
4. If you've had injuries that have kept you from training certain muscle groups hard enough, obviously you can't specialize on them when you can't train them properly.

To sum it all up, if you haven't built a very solid base level of muscle mass and strength, and you haven't put in enough time to do so, you don't need specialization. Obviously, you also need to be able to train an area pain-free before specialization can be a viable option. All of this must be considered before you can entertain the idea of specializing.

One thing that some guys don't understand either is that you often need to simply get bigger overall before you can make these kinds of assessments. If you want an inch on your arms, and you still have a long way to go in terms of overall mass, you don't need arm specialization. It's not for you. If you want an inch on your arms, plan on adding about 10 to 15 pounds of *lean* muscle mass to your whole body. You can't really just slap on five pounds of muscle to a single area—the body doesn't really work that way.

I am also talking about lean muscle mass. Bulking is still a staple for a lot of guys, and many of them don't even get their body fat taken before and after they decide to run a 64-month bulking cycle. Fatceps do not count. If you put on 20 pounds of fat mass then, yes, your arm measurement will go up. But, if it's not lean mass under there, then when the fat comes off, your arms are going to be the same size—or even smaller due to a longer dieting cycle that possibly resulted in a loss of muscle mass.

I have to write all of this because there will be guys who think they need to specialize on body parts when they can't bench 315 or squat 400, and are still lightyears away from maxing out their complete muscular development, yet, they think they need to work on a single body part. No, you need to worry about filling out a size "L" t-shirt first.

The 155 pound guy that is hammering away at concentration curls, barbell curls, preacher curls and machine curls to bring up his "small arms" is literally approaching training backwards, and putting the cart before the horse. When you're 155 pounds, *everything* will be small.

Until you have put in a significant amount of consistent work dedicated to growing your entire body, you don't need to specialize. Be honest with yourself when you make that assessment.

## Specialization Splits

There are a few options split-wise regarding specialization.

### 1. Every Workout Option

You can train that body part every training session, either at the beginning or at the end, with one movement. With this option, you work up to one all-out set to failure with possible intensity techniques thrown in. This is a high frequency, high intensity, and low volume approach.

### 2. Blast Option

You can dedicate two full training sessions a week to improving that body part while you put everything else in maintenance mode. In other words, you dial down the workload and intensity for all the body parts you are not trying to specialize on. This is a moderate frequency, high intensity, and high volume approach.

### 3. Total Workload Option

You can set a total workload as a goal to meet for the week for a certain body part, and then slowly increase the volume over the coming weeks. This is a higher frequency, periodized volume approach.

In my personal opinion option two is best; this is because you can pour a lot of volume and intensity techniques into those sessions. That is my opinion based on what I've done and seen with others, but I've seen the other two options work excellently as well. The one reason I believe that the two times a week idea is best is because you can incorporate a great many principles of hypertrophy into those sessions and really pour on the volume, whereas I feel the everyday option and total workload option are more limited in that fashion.

However, for someone who is really busy with "life", the everyday option or total workload option is very useful. One could merely pick up a few dumbbells from a sporting goods store and get that extra work in at home during their free time, rather than making trips to the gym for each session.

Someone is going to look and ask "can I combine option one and two?".

No. One is a low volume, high intensity approach, and the other is a high volume, low intensity approach. Glad we could clear that up.

Let's consider each option in more detail.

## Every Workout Option

The idea here is to pick one movement per training session, and either begin training with it or throw it in at the end. I think it's a better idea to start the training session with it, because you will have more energy to devote to that body part.

Pick one body part and go after it, and be specific about that area. In other words, "legs" are essentially comprised of quads, adductors and hamstrings. But you want to be more specific than "legs", because you're trying to bring up a weak area. That means you aren't training quads one day and hamstrings the next; you're picking one or the other.

Likewise, the "back" is comprised of lats, rhomboids, traps and erectors. You don't want to focus on all of those; instead, pick just one area. Being as specific as possible is key because you want to concentrate all of your work towards improving a single area, and not spreading the work across multiple muscle groups.

This is why, for the every workout option, it's best to choose mostly single-joint movements or movements that isolate that area well. Some multi-joint movements do that better than others. For example, front squats are a multi-joint movement but place an enormous amount of emphasis on the quads at the exclusion of everything else (better than the back squat, in my opinion).

If you need more quads, you could focus on leg extensions, sissy squats and hack squats. For biceps, focus on all variations of curls. For triceps do pushdowns, overhead extensions, French presses, and so on.

The following is a list I recommend if you want to go with this option.

Traps: Shrugs and all variations, Dumbbell lawnmower, Upright row
Medial Delts: Side lateral (one-arm, two-arm, behind-the-back cable)
Front Delts: Front raise (one-arm, two-arm, with a plate or cable)
Rear Laterals: Bent lateral (one-arm, two-arm, cable, rear delt machine)
Triceps: Pushdown, Dumbbell skull crusher, Overhead rope extension, Kickback, French press with EZ curl bar or cable
Biceps: All forms of curls (after all, curling is really all you can do for biceps)
Forearms: Behind-the-back wrist curl, Reverse curl, Hammer curl, Various wrist curls
Pecs: Flyes at all angles, Pec deck, Cable crossover
Abs: Plank, Crunch, Leg raise, Sit-up, Ab wheel roll out
Quads: Leg extension, Sissy squat, Hack squat, Sissy hack squat, Front squat

Hamstrings: Seated, lying or one-legged leg curl, Swiss ball leg curl, Stiff-legged deadlift, Glute-ham raise, Good morning
Calves: Seated or standing calf raise, Donkey calf raise, Calf press on leg press machine

Set performance goals for each movement you pick and go after them. By performance goals, I mean set some goals in terms of reps to hit with certain weights. The way I would work this is to do your warm-ups, then do one top set trying to break rep PRs in the eight to 12 rep range. Start with a weight you can get around eight to nine reps with and, once you break past 12, increase the weight the next time you perform that movement.

This is what sets the total workload option apart from the every workout option. With the total workload option, you're going to have a determined amount of volume to get in during the week, whereas with the every workout option, you should be more focused on performance goals—that is, breaking rep and weight PRs in that single set.

You should merely apply this to a normal training split where you are still working the whole body over the course of the week. This is a great option for someone who is advanced, but has not quite filled out their muscular potential and needs a little work in a specific area. Essentially, the guy with five years of very solid and consistent training who is training at least four times a week. The body part you focus on will get hit during those sessions.

You can also train every day using this option and just do the one or two movements on the days you're not doing full training sessions.

Below is an example of someone who is training four times a week, still hitting their whole body in that span, but adding in the extra work on those workouts. In this example, he or she wants to improve their quads. I will also demonstrate how to work it in as "everyday work" as an optional routine.

Day 1: Leg extension, then chest and shoulders
Day 2: Sissy squat, then back work
Day 3: Off (Optional - hack squats)
Day 4: Normal leg day
Day 5: Single-leg leg extension, then arm work
Day 6: Optional - front squat
Day 7: Optional - sissy hack squat

## Blast Training and the Resistance Curve

In my opinion, the blast training option is the best option to bring weak areas up the fastest. Rather than blather on any more about why I believe that, I'm simply going to show you how to set up two days each week to achieve that purpose.

In my opinion, the best way to make sure that you are stimulating as much muscle growth as possible, is to use the resistance curve of various movements and apply them to each body part.

*"What the hell are you talking about?"*

Each movement you do has a point of low to medium to high resistance. That means that, over the course of the range of motion, there can be little to no resistance (like in the first few inches of a barbell curl), to very high or peak resistance (like the very mid-point of a barbell curl). After the mid-point of a barbell curl to the finish, the resistance is significantly less.

But let's take an incline dumbbell curl, for example. Where is the resistance highest at in this exercise? Generally, in the first quarter of the range of motion (shortly after you begin the motion). After resistance is overcome in the first quarter of the range of motion, it reduces substantially.

Finally, let's look at a bent-over, free-hanging arm concentration curl. Where is the resistance the least and most in this movement? There is very little—if any—at the start, and maximal resistance is at the top, or completion, portion of the movement.

You should choose movements that offer resistance at each selected position:

1. Starting resistance
2. Mid-range resistance
3. Completion resistance.

To make things simple, just choose a movement that offers resistance at each point in the range of motion. There are a variety of movements to select from, of course. In my opinion, it's best to select loading and overall volume based on the movement itself. This requires some actual training knowledge, which again is why prioritizing isn't for beginners.

**Starting Resistance:**
Dumbbell flyes, for example, offer more resistance during the first quarter range of motion than at the finish, where there is virtually none. But, because it is a stretch-dominant movement, you don't want to go heavy on them, as it increases the risk of injury to the shoulder, pec and biceps. My opinion, is that these respond well to higher rep ranges like 12 to 20 reps per set.

**Mid-range Resistance:**
Most movements that offer the greatest amount of resistance in the mid-range point are the compound movements, like the bench press, squat, barbell curl and overhead press. These should be done with a greater degree of intensity—that is, weight on the bar—with lower to medium rep ranges, like five to eight reps per set.

**Completion Resistance:**
Movements that offer the greatest degree of resistance at the top, where the muscle is maximally shortened in the movement, tend to respond very well to heavy weights with high reps. In this case, as always, "heavy" is a relative term. A heavy set of five reps is obviously not going to be the same as a heavy set of 12 reps, but the set of 12 can still be "heavy" for that rep range. For these, I like sets of eight to 12 reps.

Let me also add that some machines, such as Hammer Strength machines, will have resistance curves that are maximal at two points in the range of motion like, say, the start and finish. This is fairly common with most of their pressing machines. Adding accommodating resistance to a movement, whereby you incorporate bands or chains, can also induce resistance at two points in the range of motion. Usually, this is done with compound barbell and dumbbell movements.

If bands are used, it means that resistance usually starts off low and then peaks from the mid-range position until the completion of the rep. If chains are used, it usually means that resistance is suddenly increased at the point where the majority of the chain weight has come off the floor. These are two very good tools you can use in your training to manipulate the resistance curve, and often kill two birds with one exercise.

**Finishers**
To top all this off, we want to add a "finisher": a movement to be done for a significant amount of reps that induces an incredible amount of metabolic stress/fatigue. In this option, you will do a movement for a total of three minutes, using essentially a rest/pause technique for as many reps as possible until the three minutes are up. Count the total reps done in those three minutes and continuously try to beat that number each session. As the set wears on, your time between rest/pause breaks will probably get longer but, if you are striving to beat the previous workout's total number of reps for that movement, you will be forced to push hard on each round.

Let's take push-ups as an example of a finisher.
First set: 55 reps, rest 30 seconds
Second set: 30 reps, rest 30 seconds
Third set: 22 reps, rest 10 seconds, do three more reps, time runs out.

This is, of course, hypothetical. You may only rest 20 seconds between the first round of rest/pause and the second. Again, you want to get as many reps in as possible in those three minutes, and try to break those total reps in that time.

Unlike the every workout option, with the blast option we will attack more of a "whole" area than be quite as specific. So, if someone needs more quads, legs will be worked as a "whole"; however, if their hamstrings were a strong point, less effort could be devoted to improving that area. This all comes back to the lifter being body aware enough to adjust the training accordingly.

Below is a template to help you create a plan that incorporates all of these ideas.

Chest
Mid-range: Flat/incline/decline barbell or Dumbbell bench press. All exercises with mid-range resistance should be performed for 3 sets of 5 to 8 reps, heavy.
Starting: Flat/incline/decline dumbbell flye. All exercises with starting resistance should be performed for 5 sets of 12 to 20 reps.
Completion: Cable crossover, Pec deck, Hammer Strength machines with peak resistance, Accommodating resistance using bands. All exercises with completion resistance should be performed for 3 sets of 8 to 12 reps.
Finisher: Push-ups, Dips. All finishers should be performed for as many total reps as possible in a 3 minute time frame.

Legs - Quad-dominant
Mid-range: Squat, Leg press, Front squat, Safety bar squat.
Starting: Sissy squat, Various machine squat (if the resistance curve for the machine is highest at the bottom).
Completion: Leg extension, one- or two-legged.
Finisher: Walking lunges, Split squat, Bodyweight squat.

Legs - Hamstring-dominant
Mid-range: Good morning, Stiff-legged deadlift, Leg curl.
Starting: Glute-ham raise, High deficit stiff-legged deadlift, Leg curl.
Completion: Hyperextension with bands, Leg curl with bands added.
Finisher: Swiss ball lying leg curl (I'm being serious—these are hard as hell).

Shoulders
Mid-range: Any form of barbell or dumbbell overhead pressing.
Starting: Cable side lateral.
Completion: Dumbbell side, front and bent-over laterals.
Finisher: 10 or 25 pound front plate raise.

Biceps
Mid-range: Barbell or dumbbell curl.
Starting: Incline dumbbell curl, Preacher curl.
Completion: Bent-over barbell or Dumbbell concentration curl.
Finisher: Empty bar barbell curl.

Triceps
Mid-range: Close-grip bench press, Dips.
Starting: Seated French press, One-arm triceps extension (overhead), overhead rope extension.
Completion: Pushdowns (one-arm, rope, v-handle, etc.).
Finisher: Bench dips, Diamond push-ups.

Lats/Lat Width
Mid-range: Chin-up variations of all kinds (wide, curl-grip, parallel, etc.).
Starting: Straight-arm lat pulldown, Pullover (dumbbell, barbell, machine).
Completion: Lat pulldown of any kind (v-bar, wide, behind-the-neck, curl-grip, etc.).
Finisher: Ab wheel roll out (yes, the ab wheel will hit the abs *and* lats hard if you get a full extension).

Mid-back/Back Thickness
Mid-range: Deadlift off blocks, Rack pull.
Starting: Various machine rows (I often find that most row machines put the greatest amount of resistance at the beginning, but you will have to experiment).
Completion: Bent-over barbell row, Cable row, Pendlay row.
Finisher: Bodyweight row (hanging with your body parallel to the floor).

*Again, an important notation that different machines will offer different levels of resistance throughout the range of motion. Experiment to find out where you feel the greatest amount of resistance and then apply it appropriately to the template.

## Setting Up the Two Days

There are about a zillion ways you can spread all of these movements across two days. Here are a few things I believe are optimal for doing so.

1. Always train biceps and triceps together. I have found that the synergistic approach to doing this caused more overall arm growth than splitting them up.

2. Do the same thing for legs. Address legs in this particular scenario as a whole; that is, quads and hamstrings.
3. My own personal opinion is to use the big compound movements with a lower degree of volume, but a higher degree of intensity (weight on the bar). My reason for this is that you should consider the overall volume of the workout. For the five to eight rep sets, go heavier but limit it to one to two "top" sets (that is, one to two hard working sets). The big movements tend to have a more significant degree of impact on the recovery curve. While they do offer the best bang for buck in regards to growth in terms of movement selection, it's better to temper the volume on them a bit while specializing.

One to two really hard, ball-busting sets of squats, while trying to keep an eye on adding weight to the bar each week, can become brutally demanding. Five to six brutally hard sets of squats while adding in 15 to 20 sets of other types of movements can sometimes be too much. Remember, more is not always better. Optimal is what is best. Some people may need to adjust the volume up on some movements, and some people may need to adjust it down slightly. However, I think it's a good idea to start by using a lower degree of volume on the big lifts, with more weight.

You can do a tremendous amount of volume with single-joint movements, without blunting the recovery curve. The systemic recovery factor with these kinds of movements tends to be less.

From an anecdotal standpoint, you can probably walk into the gym every day and go all-out on leg extensions without overtraining or getting burned out. However, if you walk into the gym every day and do ball-busting set after set of squats, the likelihood of injury or burnout becomes substantially higher.

A great way to incorporate this into the split is to move the big movements to the third spot in terms of movements. Start with a movement that offers resistance in the finish position—something with a hard contraction—and then move on to a movement that offers resistance or a stretch in the start position, and then finish with a heavy mid-range movement. This pre-fatigues the muscle group, so it doesn't require as much weight on the bar during the big movement to stimulate muscle growth while also keeping recovery in check.

Again, this is my own experience in this matter so, if you're looking for scientific text, you're not going to find it. But I truly believe that more weight on the bar takes a significantly higher toll on the overall recovery system. In a fatigued state, you can still stimulate lots of muscle growth while using less weight on the bar with a big compound movement.

For example, on leg day you might move squats to the third position after leg extensions and sissy squats.

<u>Leg day - Quad-dominant</u>
Leg extension: 5 sets of 8 to 12 reps, with intensity techniques
Sissy squat: 5 sets of 12 to 20 reps, bodyweight-only
High bar squat: 1 to 2 top heavy sets of 5 to 8 reps

By the time you get to high bar squats in this scenario, you will be using far less weight for those one or two top sets than if you had started the training session with them.

Some people will equate more weight on the bar to the only factor in stimulating muscle growth, but your body doesn't know how much weight is on the bar; it only knows how hard it must work to overcome the resistance.

The following is how I recommend you should set the two days up.

Completion Resistance Movement: 5 sets of 8 to 12 reps, with the same weight on all five sets after warm-ups. 90 seconds between sets. 5 second eccentrics.
Starting Resistance Movement: 3 sets of 12 to 20 reps, with the same weight on all three sets after warm-ups. 90 seconds rest between sets. 3 second eccentrics.
Mid-range Resistance Movement: 2 "top" working sets of 5 to 8 reps. 3 minutes between sets. 3 second eccentrics.
Finisher: As many reps as possible in a 3 minute window.

## Total Workload Training

With total workload training, it's all about getting the work in over a week. This one is pretty simple—you're going to increase the volume dedicated to one movement over the course of four weeks, shooting for a total number of reps achieved each and every week.

My suggestion here is to pick a movement that can be done without going to the gym. If you need to run to the store and pick up a light set of dumbbells, this is an option. But, most likely, you will also need to do part of the training in the gym (either at the beginning or end of the workout).

This volume can be spread out over the course of the day. In fact, that will eventually have to happen as the volume reaches epic proportions.

Here are some movements I suggest to use during this time.

Chest: Push-ups, Dumbbell flye
Yoke: Pull-aparts, Face pull
Anterior/Medial/Posterior Deltoids: Front/side/bent laterals
Triceps: Dumbbell skull crusher, French press
Biceps: Dumbbell or barbell curl
Legs: Lunges, Bodyweight or "light" squats (135 is sufficient for even a heavy squatter)
Hamstrings: Band leg curls or even ankle weights
Glutes: Bodyweight glute thrust, Split squat
Back: Chins (if you are strong enough; if not, two-arm dumbbell rows)

There are reasons I suggest these movements:
1. All of these can be done at home with minimal equipment. You only need a barbell or set of light dumbbells.
2. They are mostly joint friendly. You may have to be careful on the dumbbell skulls but, other than that, these are easy on the joints.
3. These aren't going to be heavily-loaded movements. The key with this program is that there is daily stimulation to the area. Oftentimes, if someone has a lagging body part it's because they simply don't

have great blood flow to that area or because they don't have a great mind-muscle connection to it. This training develops both of those factors.

Below is how the four weeks of this program are laid out.

Week 1: 500 total reps for the week.
Week 2: 700 total reps for the week.
Week 3: 900 total reps for the week.
Week 4: 1,100 total reps for the week.

Below is the daily average needed to hit all the reps in a week.

Week 1: 71 reps per day.
Week 2: 100 reps per day.
Week 3: 128 reps per day.
Week 4: 157 reps per day.

At first, this may look daunting. But remember that this workout is supposed to be spread out over the course of the day. So, even for the last week, when it will be difficult, I suggest figuring out a set/rep scheme for various times of the day to get this work in.

For example, (during the last week):
Upon waking (after coffee, so relax!): Get in 40 reps
After lunch: Get in 40 reps
During workout: Get in 40 reps
After dinner: Get in remaining reps (37)

If you miss a day, you can either make it up the next day or just up the reps for the remaining days of the week. Remember, it's about getting in the total reps each week. But I do suggest getting in an average rep count each day. This isn't just about getting the reps in, but about constantly asking that body part to fire. Oftentimes, as mentioned, the reason a body part is behind is not only because it's lacking in strength, but because the lifter doesn't have a great connection with it mentally.

If you find that is the case with a certain area, this would be the most ideal solution to remedy that problem.

## Set-Extending Techniques

There are a multitude of ways to increase the duration of a set, thus increasing the perceived intensity of it. I write perceived intensity because that's a basic way of saying how difficult it was, outside of weight on the bar or RPE. Basically, "doing that was fucking brutal to get through".

Any of these techniques can be applied to your sets, but some apply better to certain movements than others. For example, I don't really recommend applying a set-extending technique to anything where the lower back takes a great beating in the movement, like bent-over barbell rows or deadlifts. Outside of that, I don't have an issue with applying these to any exercise.

So as not to overload you with too many variables, I'm going to stick to three that can be applied and work exceptionally well, and show you how I would implement these.

**Rest/Pause Sets**
This is where you take a set to failure, or close to it, and rest for a short period of time before resuming the set. Generally speaking, what I do is take 30 deep breaths, and go again. This was the staple set-extending technique in DC training and it works very, very well.

I do two rest/pause sets, which extend the initial set. It looks like this:
Leg curls: 150 x 12, 30 deep breaths, 150 x 9, 30 deep breaths, 150 x 6.

The weight stays the same on rest/pause sets. The benefit of this is that you aren't lightening the load but simply extending the amount of time under tension with it. You should tally up the total number of reps you do with these, and try to beat that number each week until you feel the need to add weight.

What total number is that? Arbitrarily, I would say 30 total reps, but there is no hard and fast rule here. In the example above, I tallied 28 total reps. I would stay there until I beat a 30 rep total, and then add weight.

You also want to pick a weight that is light enough so that after the first set a moderate amount of reps can still be achieved. A weight that only allows six reps on the first set will limit you to possibly three reps on the second rest/pause set, and maybe only one or two on the second. In my opinion, this is not as conducive to growth as sets with moderate or higher rep ranges to start with.

I would implement rest/pause sets with movements that have resistance in the completion portion of the movement.

**Strip Sets**
These can also be called drop sets. The idea is to take a weight to failure then immediately, with no rest, grab a lighter weight and continue doing reps. You can continue this protocol for as few as one drop set, or as many as 50. It all depends on how much of a masochist you are. The reps and load can obviously be varied to a high degree.

What I prefer to do here is to pick a rep range for the initial set, and each drop set, and then find a weight that allows me to hit that rep range or something pretty close to it.

For example:
Bench Press: 365 x 8, drop to 295 x 8, drop to 245 x 8.

In this example, we are obviously using 8s as the drop set "base". You can use 5s, 8s or 10s here. I don't think your drop set base should be below five reps, however, if you are trying to stay uniform in reps across the board.

With that said, you can still vary the reps in each drop as well. Something like six reps on the first set, followed by a drop where you achieve 12 reps, and then another drop with 20 reps is very productive and a style I often use.

The reason I prefer the uniform version of drop sets is because, when my initial set increases, the drops after that tend to be all over the place when my reps vary significantly. Conversely, with a uniform rep standard, I can concentrate on increasing the load across the board a bit more evenly, and can apply simple progression to this intensity technique. Try both, and see which one you like better.

I would use strip/drop sets with movements that have resistance in the starting portion of the exercise.

**50% Sets**

This is a technique where you take the first set to failure, and then rest 60 seconds and do another set, trying to achieve at least half the number of reps you attained on the first set.

For example:
Incline Press: 315 x 10, rest 60 seconds, 315 x 5.

In this example, the goal was achieved: I got at least half the number of reps on the second set as I did on the first set.

I love this technique for a few reasons. For one, it allows you to still train fairly heavy, and keep the intensity somewhat high. Secondly, it gives you a goal to beat not only on a week-to-week basis, but on a daily basis based on how you feel. Whereas with other progression methods, people can get discouraged by a bad day because they didn't beat last week's PR, this method allows you to still shoot for goals, even on shitty days.

This method can also incorporate the RPE system very well for both the initial set, and the 50 percent set.

I also like this method because it can be used for movements that put the low back into a static position; this is because you're simply just reducing the rest time between two sets in order to sort of extend the set. In a way, it's really two sets; however, it's also like a longer version of rest/pause training but with an immediate goal built into it.

I would use 50 percent sets with mid-range resistance movements.

## Length of Time to Specialize

You already know the total workload option is four weeks. What about the length of time for the blast and every workout option?

For the every workout option, I recommend six weeks.

For the blast option, it's also six weeks; however, with this option you can extend it out even longer—though, I do suggest changing movements at the six-week mark if you aren't satisfied with your improvements.

## Conclusion

Remember that specialization is mainly for advanced lifters. If you have small arms, you need to gain more total body mass. This doesn't mean you do zero arm work; it just means you don't need two arm workouts a week dedicated to that. Focus on progressive resistance and building a larger strength and mass base first.

I cannot possibly cover everything about specialization in one chapter. I could write a Bible-length book on how to specialize. However, the principles described here and the template laid out is a great place to start. Put it to work, and bring those lagging body parts up to speed.

# Chapter Eleven: Maximum Muscle Bible Program

~ Paul Carter

As my training has progressed over the years, I've learned that frequency plays a huge part in hypertrophy development. The more often you can stimulate growth and recover from it, the faster you will grow. The key is being able to recover from training more often.

As I've touched on before, the three main variables for meeting the recovery equation are frequency, volume and intensity. If you are going to train often, and with a lot of volume, the intensity should be dialed down slightly.

However, when I speak of intensity in this regard I am talking about percentage of one rep max. I don't mean you should train like that guy texting while he's doing a "brutal set" of leg presses. What it means is that you need to dial down the weights on the bar, but still train very hard.

My reasoning here is that close to maximal poundages used in training take a much larger systemic toll on recovery than hard training done with submaximal loads. When submaximal loading is done, most of the tension is applied directly to the musculature structure. When the poundages start creeping up into the 90 percent range and above, there is a strong degree of neural taxation that requires more recovery time.

When we talk in terms of recovery, there's muscular recovery, which actually happens fairly quickly if rest and nutrition are dialed in, and nervous system or neural recovery, which takes far longer to recover from.

In my opinion, anyone can train three days a week. However, I believe that only training three times a week presents a myriad of problems in regards to maximizing hypertrophy.

Three workouts a week generally means cramming a lot of movements into each session, making them last longer than what is ideal for recovery. It also means less variation in training, unless you are using the principle of rotating movements to keep stimulus adaptation high. Finally, it reduces your ability to bring up lagging areas in musculature.

Anecdotally, I don't know many people with ultra-developed physiques who only train three days a week. I do know a few, but I consider them to be exceptions rather than rules. I mean, can you imagine a guy trying to get better at tennis or basketball telling you he's trying to get his game to the highest level by only practicing three times a week?

This doesn't mean training three times a week is not a viable option. It can—and does— work for some. I just find it to be a less desirable option if one *can* train four to six times a week.

Falling right in the middle of all of that is training five days a week, which is the template we are going to use.

Day 1: Legs - heavy
Day 2: Arms
Day 3: Off
Day 4: Chest and Back
Day 5: Legs - light/unilateral work
Day 6: Shoulders
Day 7: Off

This routine is not laid out haphazardly. There is a reason for the entire layout.

Day one is a heavy leg day, which will be the most taxing day of the week. Rather than follow it up with another taxing day, we will do an arm day that is focused on metabolic stress and reps, rather than break-neck poundages (which you shouldn't be using for arm work, anyway). The arm work will have very little in the way of system taxation, and a full rest day follows to offer recovery from the two days of training. Also, as mentioned before, I believe there is a synergistic growth effect that comes from training agonist and antagonist muscles groups together. Anyway, doing biceps and triceps together for a massive and swole up arm pump is fun and enjoyable.

After the rest day, we're back to a heavy and hard chest and back session. I like to throw in chest and back together in alternating set fashion for the same reason I like biceps and triceps together: to work the agonist and antagonist together. I feel this is a good recipe for success and growth.

After chest and back day, we're on to the second leg day of the week. This time, however, we won't be piling weights on the bar. We will use this session to push as much blood through the muscles as possible, and once again pursue metabolic stress. This will mean focusing more on isolation movements as the mainstay, decreasing rest time between sets, and getting in a lot of reps.

After this day, we move on to shoulders. Because shoulders play a huge role in chest and back movements, we don't need to overdo the overhead pressing, and rather focus on "filling in" the gaps like the medial and rear delts. This doesn't mean no overhead pressing is done; it's just that it doesn't need to be the focal point of shoulder development.

After shoulders, we take the next day off to eat, recover and revamp for the next week of growth-producing training.

Use the following template for this split.

## Day 1: Calves, Hamstrings, Quads and Glutes

**A.** Standing/seated/donkey calf raise: 4 to 5 warm-up sets.

Here we will do one set of 12 to 15 reps, holding the stretch position of each rep for five seconds before coming to a full contraction that is held for three seconds. After reaching failure, rest for 30 seconds and repeat. After reaching failure again, rest for another 30 seconds and repeat for one last awful set. If you haven't been working calves recently, expect extreme soreness for the next few days. Rotate between the three movements listed each week.

**B.** Lying leg curl: 3 to 4 warm-up sets, then 4 sets of 8 to 10 reps to failure, with partial reps to finish.

Make sure you press your hips into the pad as hard as possible during each set. Do not let them rise off the pad. Hold the contraction at the top, squeezing the hamstrings as hard as possible, then lower each rep in five seconds. Once you hit failure, do 5 to 8 partial reps from the bottom.

**C.** Paused hack squat*/Smith machine squat/Front squat/Barbell squat: Rotate between each movement each week. 3 to 4 warm-up sets, adding weight each set, then 1 set all-out of 12 to 15 reps.

*Paused hack squat description: After 3 to 4 warm-up sets, work up to an all-out set of 12 to 15 reps. Use a slow and controlled three second negative, pause at the bottom for two seconds, and then explode upwards.

**D.** Sissy squat: Bodyweight only.

This is the final movement and one you should really punish yourself with. 5 sets of as many reps as possible for each set. Don't skimp on the range of motion; really push those knees forward and stretch those quads really well. Reverse the motion by pushing through the toes, through to the floor.

## Day 2: Arms

Now that you can't walk properly, it's a fun day to get in the gym, get your pump on, and then head to the club after. I'm just joking. Although lots of guys do go to the gym before the club for that "club pump".

Arms will be done in alternating set fashion, so you will do one set for biceps, then one set for triceps. You can also choose to superset if you're short on time; however, I prefer resting between sets for each movement.

**A1.** Barbell curl: Elbows in, wrists wide. 4 sets of 6 to 8 reps + cheat reps.

Almost everyone does barbell curls. And almost everyone grabs the bar at about shoulder-width and curls away. However, you must remember that the biceps are made up of two heads: the long and short head. You can direct more tension on one or the other, depending on the angle of your wrist and elbow during the execution of a curl.

With the elbows in and the wrists wide, this tends to bring the short head of the biceps more into play. If you're one of those guys who has great looking biceps from the side, but they look thin from the front, this is your movement. This is the starting movement, regardless. Remember to get long in the arms so that the movement is initiated by the biceps, and not the shoulders or traps. Watch a lot of guys curl, and you will see that they often bend slightly at the elbows as the starting position before they begin the curl. This takes tension off the biceps to start the curl, and displaces it elsewhere. We want to start the movement by engaging the biceps.

Do 3 to 4 warm-up sets, then 4 sets of 6 to 8 reps using a three to five second negative. After failure is hit in that 6 to 8 rep range, you can loosen up just a bit to eek out another 4 to 5 reps—but only after failure is hit while being strict.

**A2.** Alternate with: Rope pushdown with pronation and then a neutral hand position: 4 sets of 30 to 40 reps.

This movement seems simple enough. However, most people do not lock their elbows into place, and turn it into a sort of back, rear delt and lat-style movement where the tension isn't on the triceps as much as possible. Think about turning the index fingers downwards as hard as possible and holding it for a peak contraction for two seconds before performing the eccentric.

Shoot for 20 reps with a hard degree of pronation. Once you get to 20 reps, do 10 to 20 more reps with a forward lean, without pronation. Keep the hands in a neutral position (meaning straight up and down like in a hammer curl) and use some cheating to eek out the next 10 to 20 reps.

Alternate between these two movements for 4 sets each.

**B1.** Incline dumbbell hammer curl/Standing supinating curl: 3 sets of 10 to 12 reps + alternating curls for AMAP.

This is actually two movements done together. The first one is the incline hammer curl. Use a low incline with a neutral hand position and perform 10 to 12 very strict reps with 3 to 5 second negatives. Once you hit failure, stand up and do alternating dumbbell curls with a focus on supinating very hard. You want to think about turning the pinkie over as much as possible. Once again, you can cheat slightly, but don't turn it into something akin to dumbbell dancing. Do as many reps as possible on the standing dumbbell curls with a slight bit of cheating.

**B2.** Seated EZ curl French press: 3 sets of 15 to 20 reps.

After a short rest from your dancing dumbbell curls, do the seated French press using the EZ bar. Do not let the elbows get wide on you; keep them facing as forward as possible to get maximal tension on the long head of the triceps. You do not need to use break-neck poundage here. Do 3 sets of 15 to 20 reps using the same weight or adding a little bit of weight to each set.

**C1.** Incline bang curl: 3 sets of 12 reps, with a 3 second hold at the top.

I learned these from John Meadows and I have yet to find another movement that causes as severe of a contraction in the biceps as these.

Lie chest-down on an incline bench with your arms hanging down. Press the insides of the dumbbells together and do not let them separate. Squeeze them together hard throughout the entire movement. Curl up and hold the contraction for three seconds, then lower under control. Do 3 sets of 12 reps this way and your biceps will be absolutely done.

**C2.** Triceps bench dips with pause: 3 sets of AMAP, shooting for 20+.

At this point, your triceps should be warm and fairly fatigued. We will finish with a somewhat joint-friendly movement: the bench triceps dip. The caveat here is that we are going to hold the bottom position for three seconds before performing the concentric. The other caveat is to perform the concentric in a controlled fashion, not explosively. Once again, we're trying to create as much tension and push as much blood into the muscle as possible. Between your sets of bang curls, do these for as many reps as possible. I also recommend elevating your feet to make these more difficult. If you're really a strong son of a bitch, have someone place a couple of 45 pound plates on your lap and go to town like that. However, bodyweight-only will probably be enough here.

## Day 3: Off

## Day 4: Chest and Back Day

We're going to employ the same agonist/antagonist strategy here that we did with the arm day: going back and forth between a press and a pull.

One reason I like doing this is because it keeps the lifter in check in regards to keeping balance between pressing and pulling and, as I said before, I believe there is a synergistic growth that happens when using opposing muscle groups together.

**A1.** Incline/decline/flat bench press (rotate each week): 1 over warm-up, 1 50% set.

For the main pressing movement, we will employ a neural technique that I have used for a long time. This is to allow the lifter to use more weight for his rep sets, and also adds on an intensity technique that I am fond of.

For the first press, you will work up to a nice crisp single—something that is maybe 20 percent or so above the weight you plan on doing the main working set with. For example, if you plan on doing 315 for 10 reps on the bench press, you'd work up to a single at around 375 pounds, then drop back to 315 for your rep-out set.

My strategy to properly warm up for this method is as follows.

Bar x 40, 20
135 x 15
185 x 5
225 x 4
275 x 3
315 x 2
375 x 1

315 x AMAP, shooting for 10 to 12 reps, + 50% set.

The 50 percent set was covered in chapter 10. But in case you skimmed it, this is what you do: perform as many reps as possible with the working weight, then rest 60 seconds. At that point, do another set, trying to get at least half as many reps as you did in the first set.

So, if you hit 10 reps on the first set with 315, you'd rest for 60 seconds, then try to hit at least five reps for the 50 percent set. Despite the fact that this is simple, every time I tell people to use it they get very confused about it. If you don't understand it simply reread that part again until it sinks in. This is a very simple method.

Between your warm-up sets for the first pressing movement, do a set of chin-ups or lat pulldowns. I recommend cycling through the following three exercises each week.

**A2.** Parallel-grip chin-ups: A set of five, bodyweight-only, with a 2 second hold at the top. On the final set, do as many reps as possible. Try to beat this number each time chins are brought back into the rotation.
**A2.** Parallel-grip pulldown with curve bar: Work up to a top set of 10 to 12 with a 3 second hold at the contraction point, with a 50% set.
**A2.** Curl-grip pulldown: Work up to a top set of 10 to 12 with a 3 second hold at the contraction point, with a 50% set.

My favorite lat pulldown handle is the parallel-grip bar that is about shoulder-width in length, and has a slight curve to it. I feel like this bar offers the greatest stretch/contraction combination for the lats in relation to other bars.

**B1.** Low incline dumbbell press/Flat dumbbell bench press.

Here, you will do 2 to 3 acclimation sets to get in groove with the movement. Then, do 1 heavy set of 6, pausing the reps at the bottom and concentrating on squeezing the pecs together to perform the concentric. After you perform your back movement (described below), you will come back and choose a weight that is a bit lighter—something that allows you to perform about 12 to 14 reps before you hit failure. Then, do another set for back/lats. For the final set, you will pick an even lighter weight—something that allows you to hit about 20 to 25 reps before reaching failure. Again, all reps should be paused for one to two seconds at the bottom while concentrating on squeezing the pecs to perform the concentric.

**B2.** Curl-grip barbell row.

You will perform these in between sets of the chosen dumbbell bench presses. The format for these will be the same: 1 set of 6, 1 set of 12 to 14, and then a final set of 20 to 25 reps.

These are *not* sloppy. I've read every excuse in the book as to why sloppy rows are okay, and none of them make sense to me. You're trying to contract your rhomboids, traps, lats and lower lats. If you're doing rows like a monkey mid-seizure, I'm not sure what it is exactly you are working, and neither are you.

Stop making excuses to sling around weight you cannot control with shit form, and learn how to stretch and contract the targeted muscles against proper resistance. Pull the bar into your lower abdominals, squeeze, and lower. *Make the muscles work.*

Another great reason not to go heavy on these is because they can put you in a position to tear a bicep. So, why choose them? Because they hit the back and lats so efficiently compared to most other types of rows. But use them properly; not as a "power" movement.

**C1.** Incline flye: 2 rounds of triple drops at 15/15/15.

Once again, set the incline at a slight angle. You want to keep tension throughout the pecs, which means you're not going to bring the dumbbells all the way together. How close should you bring them? From the bottom, squeeze and contract your pecs as hard as possible against the resistance, and see how far the dumbbells move; that will be about the range of motion you need to keep constant tension on the pecs.

The other key here is to have the palms facing forwards, and not facing each other. This offers up a greater stretch to the pecs and should keep you from turning it into a half flye/half press bullshit movement.

These should not be heavy. They should be heavy enough to allow you to hit failure at around rep 15, then grab a lighter pair of dumbbells and continue doing another set of 15. Grab one more pair that are lighter again and do a final 15.

**C2.** Dumbbell shrug.

After the first drop set, rest a few minutes and do a set of dumbbell shrugs, holding the dumbbells at the top for a count of five, trying to squeeze your traps so hard you feel as though your head might explode like that scene in Scanners. You can alternate between dumbbells and a barbell here, or even the Hammer Strength shrug if your gym has one. Do a set of 20, focusing on making the contraction as hard as possible.

Rest a few minutes, and then repeat another triple drop set of flyes, and then another set of 20 shrugs.

## Day 5: Legs - Light/Unilateral work

The "big" leg workout was earlier in the week. While this won't be a big session, it will still be hard—just in a different way. The aim of this session is to put things into place to simultaneously keep the lower body healthy, happy and growing.

**A.** One-legged calf raise.

Follow the same protocol as before: five second hold on the stretch, then a three second hold on the contraction. No weight is really needed. Do 5 sets per leg for maximum reps that your pain tolerance will allow. Just don't be a bitch about it; do all the reps you can.

**B.** Walking lunges: 200 per leg.

Find a place to do walking lunges. Do 200. Yes, that's 200 *per leg*. I can't believe people ask this question: "Is that 200 total or 200 per leg?" TWO HUNDRED FOR EACH LEG!!!!

Take big steps and really stretch those adductors out, get a good stretch in the hip flexor of the rear leg, and keep the torso upright. Don't turn this into zombie lunges where you sort of hunch over with your upper body because you're tired or lazy. Maintain good core stability and posture. Also, make sure you that you don't turn your toes in when you step forward; try to get either a neutral foot position or possibly some pronation on the stepping leg.

**C.** One-legged leg curl: 3 sets of 8 rep triple drops.

Once again, press your hips hard into the pad, and contract the hamstring as hard as possible. Do a set of 8 with a five-second negative to failure, then drop the weight and repeat. Do one more drop like this, and then do the other leg. Repeat this whole nightmare twice more after this (yes, rest in between all three triple drops).

**D.** One-legged leg press (feet high on platform): 4 sets of 20 reps.

This is a great ham and glute movement. Since we're doing one leg at a time, it will help to correct any strength imbalances between the hips, hams and glutes. There is a kicker here: there's no rest between all 4 sets. Do a set of 20 with your right leg, then a set of 20 with your left leg, and then straight back to the right leg with no rest. Repeat this until all 4 sets are done. You need to be cognizant of the weight you use in order to get all the reps in.

Do *not* let your hips or lower back come off the pad. Lower to the point where you feel your butt trying to come off the pad, and cut the range of motion about an inch shorter than that. On the concentric, do not lock out the weight; keep all of the tension on the glutes and hams.

**E.** Good morning: 4 sets of 15, using the same weight all 4 sets.

This is the only bilateral movement in this session. Stay light here and focus on pushing the glutes back and the chest into the wall in front of you as you bend over. When I was deadlifting over 700 pounds, I never used more than 185 pounds on these. That should give you an idea of how light you should be going. Think about having strong hip extension on the concentric portion of the movement; that is, pushing the glutes through to finish.

## Day 6: Shoulders

**A.** Seated side laterals: Giant set of 25/15/10, then 10/15/25.

This is one of my favorite delt combinations. Start with a few light sets to get warm, and then pick a light pair of dumbbells and do 25 perfect reps. Immediately, grab a heavier pair and do 15 perfect reps. Then, grab an even heavier pair and do 10 reps. On this last set of 10, you can get a little more loose with your form. Rest for three minutes, and then repeat the process in reverse: do 10 reps, grab a lighter pair and do 15 reps, and then grab a lighter pair and do 25 reps. Keep the sets of 15 and 25 very strict, using only the medial delts to do the work.

**B.** Rear delt machine or Bent laterals: 4 sets of 20 reps.

The key to making sure that you do not turn this into a trap/rhomboid movement is to make sure you have scapular protraction when performing this exercise. What the means is let your shoulders relax and hang forward. Hold this position and, with straight arms (not bent), squeeze the rear delts together against the resistance. Hold at the top for three seconds, and then reverse the motion. 4 sets of 20 of these will have your rear delts screaming.

**C.** Overhead press (machine/behind-the-neck/Smith/standing barbell): Work up to two top heavy sets of 8.

Choose an overhead press variation and perform 3 to 4 acclimation sets to get into the groove with the movement, adding weight each set. Then, find a weight that lets you hit 8 reps before you are at failure. Rest for a few minutes, reduce the weight a little bit (10 percent should suffice), and then repeat.

**D.** Plate front raise: 100 reps non-stop, with a 25 pound plate.

I love this finisher. It's simple, and it tests you. Grab a 25 pound plate and do 100 reps, bringing the weight *all the way* over your head. Don't stop in front of your face. Yes, doing it this way will shift the last portion of the range of motion to the traps, but who cares? No one in this life has ever been told their traps were too big. And, if they were, their reply should have been "thank you for noticing."

## Day 7: Off

## Intentional Overlap

Some people will look at this layout and think that, outside of legs, body parts are only hit once a week. But, upon inspection, that is just not true. The fact is there's no such thing as truly isolating a muscle group. We do want to isolate off a muscle group as much as possible in order to drive the greatest amount of tension to that area, however, it's virtually impossible to do that. So, we do not mind *some* overlap and actually look for it in some of the movement selection here.

You cannot train chest and back without the shoulders being involved. And you cannot train shoulders without the rhomboids and traps coming into play. You can't train chest and back without arm work coming into play as well. So, each muscle group is not *really* getting hit only once a week, outside of legs.

This is fine. This is why we have legs set up for two direct workouts per week, while dedicating one day to chest, shoulders, back and arms. All of those get hit either directly or indirectly during each session, so there's plenty of opportunities for growth.

## Conclusion

This routine is designed to take advantage of many of the factors that have been discussed in this book including progressive overload, metabolic stress, prehabilitation, mobility, intensity, frequency and volume.

No routine is perfect for everyone. The most important part of any program is *your* buy-in to how successful it can be for you.

Apply it, work your ass off, benefit and grow. It's that simple.

# Chapter Twelve: Thib's Mass Training Program

~ Christian Thibaudeau

This program is designed to maximize muscle growth while adding a significant amount of strength all around. It thus relies on more big lifts as well as training methods that involve lifting heavier weights. The bulk of the muscle growth will be stimulated via mechanical loading and muscle damage, but we will conclude every session with pump work to encourage the release of growth factor, too. I find that pumping/constant tension techniques work best after having done heavy work: it seems like, since the nervous system is already firing, muscle recruitment and the quality of the muscle contraction are better when you perform the constant tension work.

The template is as follows.
Day 1: Upper body (horizontal pressing)
Day 2: Lower body (quad-dominant)
Day 3: Upper body (pulling)
Day 4: Off
Day 5: Upper body (vertical pressing)
Day 6: Lower body (posterior chain)
Day 7: Off

### Day 1: Upper body (horizontal pressing)

**A.** Bench press (barbell)
**Sets**: 6
**Reps**: 3 sets of 3 reps, then 3 cluster sets of 4 to 6 reps with the same weight
**Rest**: Long enough to be able to maintain performance level.

Gradually warm up until you find a weight that is challenging for 3 repetitions, but that leaves a little bit in the tank—this should fall between 85 and 90 percent of your maximum. You will perform 3 sets of 3 repetitions with that weight. When you have done those three sets, move on to cluster sets, keeping the same weight. The goal is to perform between 4 and 6 repetitions, taking 10 seconds of rest (re-rack the bar) between reps. If you reach 6 reps with good form, you can add weight. If you can't reach 4 reps, lower it slightly. Perform 3 of those cluster sets.

**B.** Flat dumbbell press
**Sets**: 4
**Reps**: 3 sets of 6 to 8 reps, then 1 rest/pause set at the same weight
**Rest**: Go fast but don't let performance drop too much (max 2 minutes).

Use a weight that you can lift 8 times with good form. I give a rep range of 6 to 8 reps because I want you to not rest completely between sets; therefore I will allow a 2 rep decrement in performance but no more. Lower the weight under control, pause for one second at the bottom, and lift smoothly. Do 3 regular sets and the fourth one is a rest/pause set. After you have completed your 6 to 8 reps, rest for 15 to 20 seconds and then try to get as many additional reps as possible. For the extended portion of the set, tempo can go out the window but keep form strict.

**C.** Isometric dip or push-up*
**Sets**: 5
**Reps**: 60 seconds
**Rest**: 60 seconds.

Here I give you the choice between a dip and a push-up because not everybody can do dips, especially not after 10 sets of pressing work. The exercise consists of lowering your torso to the low position of the exercise, contracting the chest and holding that position for 60 seconds. If you do push-ups, elevate both your hands and feet on blocks or plates so that you can reach the low position without your chest touching the floor. If you can't reach 60 seconds in one shot, you can rest for a few seconds before resuming the set, but you must do 60 seconds of work (meaning that you only count the time you spend in the low position). If you can handle 60 seconds for 5 sets, you can move up to 75 seconds per set, and then eventually 90 seconds.

**D.** Rope triceps pushdown
**Sets**: 4
**Reps**: 3 sets of 6 to 8 reps, then 1 rest/pause set at the same weight
**Rest**: Go fast but don't let performance drop too much (max 90 seconds).

Use a weight that you can lift 8 times with good form. I give a rep range of 6 to 8 reps because I want you to not rest completely between sets, so I will allow a 2 rep decrement in performance but no more. Use a peak contraction style: split the rope up as you extend your arms and squeeze for two seconds per rep in the peak contraction (when you hold the peak contraction try to split even wider). However, if you are splitting the rope, avoid moving your elbows away from your body at any point in the set. You do three sets like that then on the fourth you complete your 6 to 8 reps, then rest 15 seconds before resuming the set trying to get as many additional reps as possible. On the rest/pause reps you don't have to hold the peak contraction or split the rope.

**E.** Pec deck flye
**Sets**: 4
**Reps**: 3 sets of 6 to 8 reps, then 1 rest/pause set at the same weight
**Rest**: Go fast but don't let performance drop too much (max 90 seconds).

Use a weight that you can lift 8 times with good form. I give a rep range of 6 to 8 reps because I want you to not rest completely between sets, so I will allow a 2 rep decrement in performance but no more. Use a peak contraction style: squeeze the pecs hard at the peak contraction position for two seconds then lower back down slowly. Do 3 sets like that and the fourth set is a rest/pause set: once you have done your 6 to 8 reps, rest for 15 seconds then get as many additional reps as possible. The reps after the pause do not need to be squeezed, but don't cheat either.

## Day 2: Lower body (quad-dominant)

**A.** Front squat
**Sets**: 6
**Reps**: 3 sets of 3 reps, then 3 cluster sets of 4 to 6 reps with the same weight
**Rest**: Long enough to be able to maintain performance level.

As a quad-builder, I prefer the front squat over the back squat, especially if you have longer limbs (in that case, the back squat pretty much becomes a posterior chain movement). I do not like the use of a crossed-arms grip; either use an Olympic clean front rack or straps to hold on to the bar. The crossed-arms grip tends to round the upper back more than the two other grips. Gradually warm-up until you find a weight that is challenging for 3 repetitions, but that leaves a little bit in the tank—this should fall between 85 and 90 percent of your maximum. You will perform 3 sets of 3 repetitions with that weight. When you have done those three sets, move on to cluster sets, keeping the same weight. The goal is to perform between 4 and 6 repetitions, taking 10 seconds of rest (re-rack the bar) between reps. If you reach 6 reps with good form, you can add weight. If you can't reach 4 reps, lower it slightly. Perform 3 of those cluster sets.

**B.** Bulgarian split squat
**Sets**: 3
**Reps**: 3 sets of 6 to 8 reps per leg, with a low double contraction
**Rest**: A short period (20 to 30 seconds) between legs and a moderate period (60 to 75 seconds) between sets.

A low double contraction is also called 1 ½ reps. Go down completely, stand halfway up, go back down and then stand up completely—this is *one* repetition. The Bulgarian split squat is a split squat with the back foot elevated. Do not use a lifting bench to elevate your leg, as that's too high. Use a block, a bar set in the power rack, or something that is about 12 inches from the floor. The key thing is to go down fairly slowly and, most of all, do the "half-rep" slowly. The half-rep should take the same time as a full rep, which means that you need to move twice as slowly as you would during your normal rep.

**C.** Leg extension
**Sets**: 4
**Reps**: 3 sets of 8 to 10 reps, then 1 rest/pause set at the same weight
**Rest**: Go fast but don't let performance drop too much (max 2 minutes).

Use a weight that you can lift 10 times with good form. I give a rep range of 8 to 10 reps because I want you to not rest completely between sets, so I will allow a 2 rep decrement in performance but no more. Lower the weight under control, and initiate the upward lift very slowly, you don't want to jerk/accelerate from the bottom in the leg extension, as it both makes the movement ineffective and potentially dangerous. At the top, hold/squeeze the peak contraction as hard as you can for two seconds. Do 3 regular sets and the fourth one is a rest/pause set: after you have completed your 8 to 10 reps, rest for 15 to 20 seconds and then try to get as many additional reps as possible. For the extended portion of the set, tempo can go out the window but keep form strict.

**D1 and D2 (superset).** Sprint on stationary bike with lots of resistance and body weight squats
**Sets**: 3
**Reps**: 45 seconds on the bike and max reps in 60 seconds on squats
**Rest**: Go fast but don't let being out of breath affect your performance.

Use a stationary bike and add a lot of resistance. You want to not be able to spin rapidly, but you shouldn't have choppy spinning either. Basically, use as much resistance as possible without the movement becoming choppy. Try to go as fast as possible for 45 seconds. Stay seated on the bench (so that you don't use your bodyweight to your advantage instead of having the muscles do the work). Do this for 45 seconds, then rest for 15 to 20 seconds and do as many bodyweight squats as possible in 60 seconds. I prefer slower squats with better form: maintain an upright torso, and do not completely lock out the knees.

## Day 3: Upper body (pulling)

**A.** Deadstart barbell row
**Sets**: 6
**Reps**: 3 sets of 3 reps, then 3 cluster sets of 4 to 6 reps with the same weight
**Rest**: Long enough to be able to maintain performance level.

Start each repetition with the barbell on the floor. Your torso should be as close to parallel to the ground as possible and stay in that position when you pull. Gradually warm up until you find a weight that is challenging for 3 repetitions, but that leaves a little bit in the tank; this should fall between 85 and 90 percent of your maximum. You will perform 3 sets of 3 repetitions with that weight. When you have done those three sets move on to cluster sets, keeping the same weight. The goal is to perform between 4 and 6 repetitions, taking 10 seconds of rest (rest the bar on the floor) between reps. If you reach 6 reps in good form, you can add weight. If you can't reach 4 reps, lower it slightly. Perform 3 of those cluster sets.

**B.** Chin-ups (supinated) or lat pulldown (supinated)
**Sets**: 4
**Reps**: 3 sets of 6 to 8 reps, then 1 rest/pause set at the same weight
**Rest**: Go fast but don't let performance drop too much (max 2 minutes).

If you do chin-ups, make sure that you are able to do at least 8 technically solid and strict repetitions. If not, use the lat pulldown machine. Use a weight that you can lift 8 times with good form. I give a rep range of 6 to 8 reps because I want you to not rest completely between sets, so I will allow a 2 rep decrement in performance but no more. Hold the peak contraction for one to two seconds per rep. Do 3 regular sets and the fourth one is a rest/pause set: after you have completed your 6 to 8 reps, rest for 15 to 20 seconds and then try to get as many additional reps as possible. For the extended portion of the set you don't need to hold the peak contraction, but keep form strict.

**C.** Extreme barbell shrug
**Sets**: 5
**Reps**: 50/40/30/20/10
**Rest**: Go fast but don't let performance drop too much (max 2 minutes).

You will use the same weight for all your sets, even though the reps decrease significantly from set to set. However, you will change the way the reps are performed from set to set.

**Set 1:** normal, relatively rapid reps, with a slight cheat of the lower back and legs allowed
**Set 2**: strict but normal reps
**Set 3**: strict reps holding the peak contraction for one full second per rep
**Set 4**: strict reps holding the peak contraction for three seconds per rep
**Set 5**: strict reps holding the peak contraction for five seconds and the stretched position for two seconds per rep.

*At the end of every set, hold the stretch/low position for 30 seconds.

**D.** Standing barbell curl
**Sets**: 6
**Reps**: 3 sets of 3 reps, then 3 cluster sets of 4 to 6 reps with the same weight
**Rest**: Long enough to be able to maintain performance level.

Gradually warm up until you find a weight that is challenging for 3 repetitions, but that leaves a little bit in the tank—this should fall between 85 and 90 percent of your maximum. You will perform 3 sets of 3 repetitions with that weight. When you have done those three sets, move on to cluster sets, keeping the same weight. The goal is to perform between 4 and 6 repetitions, taking 10 seconds of rest (re-rack the bar) between reps. If you reach 6 reps in good form, you can add weight. If you can't reach 4 reps, lower it slightly. Perform 3 of those cluster sets.

**E.** Multi-technique machine curl
**Sets**: 3
**Reps**: 5 one-arm negatives + maximum two-arm pump reps + maximum iso hold
**Rest**: 90 to 120 seconds.

Start each set with the 2/1 technique on the curl machine. Lift rapidly with two arms and lower in five seconds with one arm. Alternate arms and do 5 reps (use a weight so that the fifth rep is hard). Continue your set by doing pump reps with both arms (pump reps mean not going all the way down or all the way up) until you can't tolerate the pain anymore. Finish the set by holding the mid-range point for as long as you can.

## Day 4: Off

## Day 5: Upper body (vertical pressing)

**A.** Standing shoulder press (barbell)
**Sets**: 6
**Reps**: 3 sets of 3 reps, then 3 cluster sets of 4 to 6 reps with the same weight
**Rest**: Long enough to be able to maintain performance level.

Gradually warm up until you find a weight that is challenging for 3 repetitions, but that leaves a little bit in the tank—this should fall between 85 and 90 percent of your maximum. You will perform 3 sets of 3 repetitions with that weight. When you have done those three sets move on to cluster sets, keeping the same weight. The goal is to perform between 4 and 6 repetitions, taking 10 seconds of rest (re-rack the bar) between reps. If you reach 6 reps in good form, you can add weight. If you can't reach 4 reps, lower it slightly. Perform 3 of those cluster sets.

**B.** High incline (60 to 75 degrees) dumbbell press
**Sets**: 4
**Reps**: 3 sets of 6 to 8 reps, then 1 rest/pause set at the same weight
**Rest**: Go fast but don't let performance drop too much (max 2 minutes).

I like the high incline for dumbbell shoulder presses as it allows you to use a bit more weight and will hit the muscles from a slightly different angle compared to the standing press. Use 60 or 75 degrees—whatever feels best for you. Use a weight that you can do 8 reps with, and perform 3 sets of 6 to 8 reps (going to failure) with fairly short rest intervals. The last set is a rest/pause set: after hitting failure, rest for 15 seconds and try to get as many additional reps as possible with the same weight.

**C1, C2 and C3 (mechanical drop set).** Dumbbell seated lateral raise, Dumbbell seated front raise, Dumbbell seated clean and press
**Sets**: 3
**Reps**: 8 to 10 of the first exercise (lateral raise), max reps on the other two using the same weight
**Rest**: 75 to 90 seconds.

Start with seated dumbbell lateral raises: keep the form strict and the movement smooth. When you hit a point close to failure (after 8 to 10 reps), switch to seated front raises using the same weight without taking any rest. Do as many quality repetitions as possible on the front raises and, when you reach failure, switch to a seated dumbbell clean and press: lift the dumbbell from the hanging position to your shoulders, then press them all the way up. Use the same weight and do as many quality reps as possible.

**D.** Behind-the-neck shoulder press with constant tension
**Sets**: 3
**Reps**: 12 to 15
**Rest**: Short rest periods, incomplete rest.

Use a constant tension style of repetition: lift the barbell up in about two to three seconds and lower it down in about three to four seconds. At the top, try to touch the ceiling by bringing your delts to your ears (shoulder shrug). Don't focus on the weight; focus on the quality of the muscle contraction and range of motion.

## Day 6: Lower body (posterior chain)

**A.** Sumo deadlift
**Sets**: 6
**Reps**: 3 sets of 3 reps, then 3 cluster sets of 4 to 6 reps with the same weight
**Rest**: Long enough to be able to maintain performance level.

For all your sets, utilize a deadstart approach. Reset on every rep, even the non-cluster sets. Gradually warm up until you find a weight that is challenging for 3 repetitions, but that leaves a little bit in the tank—this should fall between 85 and 90 percent of your maximum. You will perform 3 sets of 3 repetitions with that weight. When you have done those three sets, move on to cluster sets, keeping the same weight. The goal is to perform between 4 and 6 repetitions, taking 10 seconds of rest (re-rack the bar) between reps. If you reach 6 reps in good form, you can add weight. If you can't reach 4 reps, lower it slightly. Perform 3 of those cluster sets.

**B.** Romanian deadlift
**Sets**: 3
**Reps**: 3 sets of 6 to 8 reps, with a low double contraction
**Rest**: Moderate. You do not want full recovery but no more than a 2 rep drop-off between the first set and the others.

A low double contraction is also called 1 ½ reps. Go down completely, bring the barbell halfway up, go back down and then stand up completely—this is *one* repetition. The key thing is to go down fairly slowly and most of all do the "half-rep" slowly. The half-rep should take the same time as a full rep, which means that you need to move twice as slowly as during your normal rep.

**C.** Seated leg curl
**Sets**: 4
**Reps**: 3 sets of 8 to 10 reps, then 1 rest/pause set at the same weight
**Rest**: Go fast but don't let performance drop too much (max 2 minutes).

Use a weight that you can lift 10 times with good form. I give a rep range of 8 to 10 reps because I want you to not rest completely between sets, so I will allow a 2 rep decrement in performance but no more. Release the weight under control and initiate the contraction very slowly. At the bottom, hold/squeeze the peak contraction as hard as you can for two seconds. Do three regular sets and the fourth one is a rest/pause set: after you have completed 8 to 10 reps, rest for 15 to 20 seconds and then try to get as many additional reps as possible. For the extended portion of the set, tempo can go out the window but keep form strict.

**D.** Multi-technique machine lying leg curl
**Sets**: 3
**Reps**: 5 one-leg negatives + maximum two-leg pump reps + maximum iso hold
**Rest**: 90 to 120 seconds.

Start each set with the 2/1 technique on the lying leg curl machine. Lift rapidly with two legs and lower in five seconds with one leg. Alternate legs on each rep and do 5 reps for each side (use a weight so that the fifth rep is hard). Continue your set by doing pump reps with both legs (pump reps mean not going all the way down or all the way up) until you can't tolerate the pain anymore. Finish the set by holding the mid-range point for as long as you can.

**Day 7: Off**

# Chapter Thirteen: HIT Routine 1

~ Paul Carter

Despite all the studies that exist that might tell you that high intensity training (HIT) is somehow inferior to other methods of training, or that it doesn't work, I am here to tell you that it is indeed a very valid and productive training methodology.

Back in the early '90s when Dorian Yates rose to bodybuilding popularity using a HIT style of training, it gained a resurgence from the '70s when Mike Mentzer and Arthur Jones first put it on the map.

Dorian used it very effectively to win six Mr. Olympia's and to build a level of muscle mass that had not previously been witnessed.

Of course, this caused a lot of people to adopt his training methods without fully understanding how Dorian applied them. There were camps of HIT disciples who took the "it's too hard to recover from training too often" to extreme levels, and things got weird from there—like guys training once every 10 days, using two movements for one set each.

This caused people to abandon HIT-style training because they lost focus on the style that Dorian used, and instead focused on fringe movement. They decided it was for idiots or "hardgainers" who saw overtraining as the boogeyman.

As both Christian and I have covered in this book, no single type of stimulus will carry you forever. It's vitally important that you are open-minded enough to change training stimulus from time to time in order to move past plateaus and keep improving.

I successfully used the Dorian-style HIT methodology for years and years with great success. However, Dorian never completely married himself to someone else's ideas because he was a great thinker, and often manipulated his training to fit what he felt worked best for him. For example, Dorian believed that if one set was hard and focused enough, a second set probably wasn't needed. But, he also knew that training days didn't always work that way, and sometimes a second set might be needed in order to elicit growth.

The other part that gets lost on people is while Dorian wasn't a huge believer in counting the speed of the eccentric, he did use very controlled negatives and explosive concentric movements. However, he also believed that the concentric portion had to create an incredibly strong contraction at the finishing portion of the rep, where the muscle is in its most-shortened position. In other words, when you do a lat pulldown, you don't just release slowly then yank the weight back down. You release under control then pull with explosiveness, but in a manner where you can contract the lats as hard as possible.

I cannot emphasize this last part enough. I see so many people train using movements where the concentric is so explosive that there is almost no way that the muscles involved can keep the greatest amount of tension throughout the movement.

If you are going to train in this manner, you need to be cognizant of these principles:

1. Controlled negatives
2. Strongly initiated positives, where the contraction is powerful and strong at the finished position of the rep.

If you cannot accomplish this, or don't have a great mind-muscle connection, this style of training may not work for you as well as you would hope. I'm not trying to dissuade you from using it; I'm saying that in order to make it as efficient as possible, these are two important requirements.

Dorian was also big on progressive overload, but *not* at the expense of losing tension on the muscle. He wanted to move greater and greater amounts of weight while still applying the two principles above: controlled negatives, then initiating the movement with the muscle he was trying to work, then achieving a contraction as strong as possible to stimulate growth.

The fact is that these principles should be being applied to your training regardless of whether or not you use a low or high volume approach. This is because they are vitally important to encouraging those muscle groups to grow.

Dorian also liked extended set techniques, but didn't often overdo it either: some strip sets here, some rest/pause sets there, and some forced reps here and there. You don't have to throw the kitchen sink at every working set you do to make up for lower volume. Just make sure the above principles are intact, and make this work for you.

Let me close by emphasizing that this is not a routine for beginners or intermediates. They absolutely do not have the ability to generate the mind-muscle connection needed for this to work as effectively as possible. It requires a great deal of muscle control and "feeling" to isolate an area as much as possible to make it do the majority of the work.

The four day routine is as follows.
Day 1: Legs (Quads, Hamstrings and Calves)
Day 2: Shoulders and Arms
Day 3: Off
Day 4: Back
Day 5: Off
Day 6: Chest
Day 7: Off

## Day 1: Legs (Quads, Hamstrings and Calves)

**A.** Standing/seated/leg press calf raise (rotate through each week): After warm-ups, do 2 sets of 12 reps holding the stretch position for five seconds.
**B.** Lying/seated leg curl (rotate each week): After warm-ups, do 2 sets of 12 reps, plus 2 rounds of rest/pause with 30 seconds between each one.
**C.** Leg extension: After warm-ups, do 1 set of 12 to 15 plus 2 to 3 forced reps.
**D.** Leg press/Hack squat/Barbell squat (rotate each week): After warm-ups, do 1 set of 12 to 15 reps.

## Day 2: Shoulders and Arms

**A.** Seated behind-the-neck/Military press (rotate each week): After warm-ups, do 2 sets of 6 to 8 reps.
**B.** Side laterals: Drop set of 15/15/15 reps.
**C.** One-arm dumbbell/cable side laterals (rotate each week): 2 sets of 12 to 15 reps.
**D.** Concentration curl/Incline dumbbell curl (rotate each week): After warm-ups, do 1 set of 8 to 12 reps.
**E.** EZ bar/barbell curl (rotate each week): 1 set of 8 to 12, with 2 rounds of rest/pause with 30 seconds between each one.
**F.** Pushdown with rope/straight bar (rotate each week): After warm-ups, 2 sets of 12 to 15 reps plus 2 to 3 forced reps.
**G.** Seated French press/Skull crusher: After warm-ups, do 2 sets of 8 to 12 reps.

## Day 3: Off

## Day 4: Back

A. Dumbbell pullover/Pullover machine (rotate each week): After warm-ups, do 1 set of 12 to 15 reps.
**B.** Curl-grip chin-ups/V-bar pulldown (rotate each week): After warm-ups, do 2 sets of 8 to 12 reps plus 2 to 3 forced reps.
**C.** Barbell/Dumbbell row (rotate each week): After warm-ups, do 1 set of 6 to 8 reps.
**D.** Cable/Hammer Strength row: After warm-ups, do 2 sets of 10 to 12 reps.
**E.** Hyperextension: 1 set of 12 to 15 reps.

## Day 5: Off

## Day 6: Chest

**A.** Incline/decline barbell bench press: After warm-ups, do 2 sets of 6 to 8 reps plus 2 forced reps.
**B.** Incline/flat dumbbell bench press: After warm-ups, do 1 triple drop set of 8/8/8 reps.
**C.** Incline/flat flye: After warm-ups, do 2 sets of 12 to 15 reps.
**D.** Dips: 2 sets of as many reps as possible, bodyweight only.

## Day 7: Off

# Chapter Fourteen: The Hybrid Mass Program

~ Paul Carter

program is what I believe encompasses ally every facet of not only the scientific data e seen about hypertrophy, but also the dotal evidence we've seen in regards to it as

ther words, the decades of n=1 results people found through experimentation that led to rch showing the most optimal ways to grow, und within this routine.

own experimentation with it, and my results clients have cemented this belief in regards to program I dub "The Hybrid."

n a high-level overview, I will go over the s involved in it, why the program is designed the way it is, and what purpose each function serves.

## Frequency

There's no doubt that traditional splits where muscle groups getting trained in a direct fashion one time a week produce results. There's been countless numbers of bodybuilding champions that have trained this way, and research has shown that such a split offers enough stimulus to induce growth.

However, training a muscle group directly twice a week has been shown to be more optimal in regards to hypertrophy potential, than training it directly once a week.

One of the common problems many face with trying to train a muscle group twice a week is that meeting the demands for recovery become more difficult because they don't cycle their intensity and volume appropriately to do so.

In other words, the program from top to bottom tends to follow the same protocol for each workout.

Every leg day is a balls-out leg day. Every back day is high volume. Whatever ideology gets implemented into the program, tends to get spread across every workout in that same fashion. Therefore, if someone has a chest day, and its high volume, then every other muscle group gets lots of volume as well.

I'm not sure why people ended up designing routines where each session is basically a carbon copy of the other in regards to intensity and volume, but that most often is the case.
20 sets for biceps also means 20 sets for triceps. Then 20 sets for legs, chest, back, etc.
Or the other side of the coin is they do less volume, but do lots of forced reps, drop sets, etc. If they are doing high reps, then everything gets high reps. The same "theme" gets painted across each and every workout.

With The Hybrid, it takes into account that frequency is one of the greatest facets of inducing growth, but implements that frequency in a way that is manageable by cycling the frequency, intensity, and volume throughout the cycle.

With The Hybrid, a muscle group gets trained directly twice one week, and one time the next week. Not only that, each session offers two very different types of stimulus, and manages volume and intensity differently.

## Performance workouts and Pump Workouts

Most often, lifters fall within a couple of camps. The one camp that is constantly chasing more weight on the bar through progressive overload, and the camp that goes in and does a ton of volume but lots of pumping style sets and reps. Neither is wrong in their approach, and decades have shown that both types of styles can and will induce growth. Some people do incorporate a bit of both types of training into one ideology but more or less end up doing so within single sessions. They do some heavy squats, then some pumping high rep leg curls and leg extensions, etc.

Once again, there's no "wrong" here. But I do believe it can be made more efficient by focusing on one or the other in opposing training sessions.

My reasoning for this is because the systemic recovery curve is influenced by the sympathetic nervous system and parasympathetic nervous system.

The sympathetic nervous system is your "flight or fight" nervous system. The one that gets turned on when you're psyching up for that heavy balls to the ball set of a big movement like deadlifts, squats, or any other big compound movement. This is something Thibs and I call "training on the nerve". Meaning you have to turn on the sympathetic nervous system each time you have sets you have to approach in this manner.

The problem with this is that in order for systemic recovery to take place (that is, your nervous system is allowed to calm down, reduce cortisol, and find balance again) the parasympathetic nervous system has to be allowed to come back into the picture while you turn the "animal in the cage" mode off.

When too many flight-or-fight training sessions follow one another, something I dub "workout hangover" will generally follow. This is where you are fatigued, the weights feel ultra heavy, and your mind isn't really into the training session. This is where recovery takes a hit from a systemic standpoint, and can create a gap in the recovery process. During the time when your sympathetic nervous system is depressed, your ability to generate power and explosiveness will be diminished. It's not until the upwards curve in recovery for the parasympathetic nervous system happens that training can be "turned up" again.

I do believe that setting performance goals is not only a great way to spur on growth, but also a great way to keep one focused and goal oriented in their training. But it shouldn't be something that is done on an every workout basis due to the above factors. If you are chasing rep PRs on every set of every workout, and those sessions are comprised of mostly big lifts, you will hit the wall after a few weeks and often see progress decline.

This is where "pump workouts" come into play.

With "pump workouts" there's no mental pressure to hit rep PRs, and each session tends to leave one feeling better after they walk out of the gym than when they arrived. During these, the sympathetic nervous system gets turned off for the workout, allowing room for the parasympathetic nervous system to allow for systemic recovery.

Performance workouts are low volume in regards to "work sets". A work set being defined as a set where you will be going all out to failure, trying to break the number of reps you hit previously in that kind of session, and often has set extending techniques implemented.
A pump workout consists of straight sets, where no sets are taken to failure, but rest times between sets are short, and you "chase the pump" by pushing blood through the muscle to facilitate localized recovery, but also allow for systemic recovery.

In essence, each session builds on the other for growth by complimenting the other. One day of that week for chest you might go all out on incline press with forced reps and strip sets, exerting maximal effort to break rep PRs. The next time you walk into the gym to do chest work, you will do far more sets, but well short of failure, get a pump and leave feeling good.

## Rotational movements

Another facet of this program is the flexibility in which it can be implemented to keep adaptation at bay. The body does a very good job at adapting to the stimulus that you throw at it. This is why most programs see the trainee tend to peak at a specific number of weeks into the program, and then hit a wall due to detraining. Detraining defined as, the body has made all the requirements needed to adapt to the program, and is no longer progressing forwards to meet demands imposed on it.

Therefore, there will be two types of performance days, and two types of pump days that get rotated in over the course of "one cycle" of the routine.

One need not worry about losing strength due to not squatting weekly because the movements will be similar in nature that are implemented. And while front squatting is not the same as back squatting, at the end of the day, you're still performing knee and hip flexion and extension under a loaded barbell. So, there is enough similarity to keep you dialed in for both in regards to performance.

The split is broken up like this, body part wise –
Chest/Shoulders/Triceps
Back/Biceps
Legs – Quads, hamstrings, calves

To eyeball all of this, here is how the routine will be laid out.
Workout 1 – Chest/Shoulders/Triceps – performance day #1
Workout 2 – Back/Biceps – pump day #1
Workout 3 – Legs – performance day #1
Workout 4 – Chest/Shoulders/Triceps – pump day #1
Workout 5 – Back/Biceps – performance day #1
Workout 6 – Legs – pump day #1
Workout 7 – Chest/Shoulders/Triceps – performance day #2
Workout 8 – Back/Biceps – pump day #2
Workout 9 – Legs – performance day #2
Workout 10 – Chest/Shoulders/Triceps – pump day #2
Workout 11 – Back/Biceps – performance day #2
Workout 12 – Legs – pump day #2
Workout 13 – repeat starting from Workout 1

## Performance Days

On the performance training days, this is where you will be shooting for setting new PR goals in regards to reps and weight on the bar. You will also be using various set extending techniques that increase intensity within those sets.

Some various types of set extending techniques are the followingÈ
Rest/Pause sets – This is where you take a set to failure, then rest for a brief period – around 20-30 seconds – then do another set. This can be repeated several times but generally I don't advise doing more than 3 total "sets" in this manner. You would do the initial set to failure. Rest 20-30 seconds, repeat to failure, rest 20-30 seconds, and do the last set to failure.

**Drop/Strip sets**
This method is where you would take a set to muscular failure, then immediately take weight off the bar, or move the pin in the stack to less weight, and continue doing the set. Again, this can be done many times, but again I advise only around 3 drop sets when using this technique.

**Micro-drop sets**
Similar to normal strip sets, but in this case, then reduction in weight is very minor. Once you hit failure, the drop in weight is very small, only allowing you to achieve a maximum of around 3 reps on the drop set. So, if you did a set of barbell curls with 100 pounds, and hit failure at 10 reps, you would drop to around 90 pounds and continue. If you find yourself getting more than 3 reps on the micro-drop, then your reduction in weight was probably too great.

**Forced reps**
This is where a partner assists you in doing more reps after you've hit failure in a movement. One mistake I see in how partners assist in helping with forced reps is that they only offer enough help so that the lifter is having to grind and struggle very hard to complete the reps. In a proper

forced rep, the speed of the rep should be about the same as it was during the last few reps achieved before the partner started assisting. This means you need a good spotter who you help to understand how much assistance to apply during those reps post-failure.

## Pump days

On the "pump day" workouts, there will be more volume done, with shorter rest period, and no intensity techniques will be done. It will be all straight sets, with none of them taken to muscular failure. There should never be "psyching" up for any sets, yet this workout should have you pouring buckets and breathing pretty hard. Almost akin to a bit of metabolic conditioning type work.

The other factor here is movement selection. Pump workout days should be centered around lots of dumbbell, machine, and cable work.

The reason for this are a few.

Dumbbells and cables especially, allow for a more natural path for the joints to travel in during the execution of the movement. This means less stress on the connective tissue during training. A lot of lifters end up with aching joints and pains because they select so many "fixed" barbell movements that also are performed without good technique; this then leads to a lot of unwanted torque on the joints and soft tissue.

Therefore, pump days make sure to take the joints through ranges of motion that tend to be more natural, and pain free. Furthermore, because the load selection is lighter, there's less stress on the soft tissue and joints.

It offers up recovery at both the kinetic chain level, soft tissue level, and systemic level. And these things are needed in order to be at your best during the days when you're going to go in and press the accelerator hard during the performance training days.

## Layout of the "hybrid"

The one thing about the hybrid that makes it ideal for the advanced lifter who knows his or her body is that it allows flexibility within the routine for them to choose the movements they want to base their training around, and to choose whatever intensity methods they want to apply.

I highly advise being smart about this and picking movements that focus on bringing up weak areas, and not just designing the program around doing your favorite movements. I also advise using intensity methods you actually DESIRE to do because we tend to work the hardest when we choose training methods we actually enjoy.

The other flexible part of it is that if you're having a "down day" where energy is low, and you know you're not really "up" for one of the performance days, it's perfectly acceptable to substitute in a pump day instead. There should never be a fear of "losing your gains" based on doing so. Fluctuations in drive and motivation are actually tied into components of nutrition, sleep, and nervous system recovery. A day of feeling run down or having "workout hangover" is simply a sign that the body is lacking in a component required for recovery. Remember that training is the tearing down of the body, and without recovery, no progress will be made. Pushing the envelope while the body is working to get back to a state of recovery only means you dig an even deeper hole into recovery debt.

## Performance Days

<u>Chest/Shoulders/Triceps</u>
Chest Press Movement – 2 working sets of 8-12 reps to failure, plus an intensity technique.
Flye Movement – 2 workout sets of 8-12 reps to failure, plus an intensity technique.
Shoulder Pressing Movement – 1 working set of 8-12 reps to failure.
Lateral variation – side, front, rear – 2 working sets of 12-15 reps, plus an intensity technique.
Triceps Movement – 3 working sets of 10-12 reps to failure, plus an intensity technique on each set.

Back/Biceps
Vertical Pull – Chin up – Lat Pulldowns using various handles or grips – 2 working sets of 8-12 reps to failure, plus an intensity technique.
Row or Deadlift Variation – 2 working sets of 8-10 for rows, and 1 working sets of 5-8 for the deadlift variation. No intensity techniques unless the rowing variation offers low back support such as a t-bar row with chest support. Deadlifts should never be taken to failure. Leave 1-2 reps left in the set.
Shrug Variation – 2 working sets of 10-12 reps to failure. No intensity techniques.
Biceps movement 1 – 2 working sets of 12-15 reps, plus an intensity technique.
Biceps movement 2 – 1 working set of 8-10 reps plus an intensity technique.

<u>Legs – Quads/Hamstrings/Calves</u>
Leg Curl Variation – 3 working sets of 6-8 reps, plus intensity technique.
Quad machine based movement – 2 working sets of 12 reps to failure. No intensity technique. This would be a leg press variation in most cases.
Squat Variation – 1 working set of 15-20 reps. 1-2 reps shy of failure.
Calf Movement – seated, standing, calf press – 2 sets of 15-20 reps taken to failure, holding the stretch portion for 5 seconds on each rep.

## Pump Days

<u>Chest/Shoulders/Triceps</u>
Dumbbell Chest Press Variation – 5 sets of 12-15 reps, 60 seconds between sets. Same weight each set, last set only moderately difficult.
Chest Press Machine Variation or Flye/Pec Deck Variation – 5 sets of 12-15 reps, 60 seconds between sets. Same weight each set, last set only moderately difficult.
Side Lateral Variation – 4 sets of 12 reps, 60 seconds between sets. Same weight each set. Intensity low on all sets.
Rear Lateral Variation – 4 sets of 12 reps, 60 seconds between sets. Same weight each set. Intensity low on all sets.
Triceps Movement – 5 sets of 20 reps. 60 seconds between sets. Same weight each set. Last set only moderately difficult.

Back/Biceps
Lat Pulldown or Straight Arm Pulldown – 5 sets of 12 reps, 60 seconds between sets. Same weight each set. Last set only moderately difficult.
Row Variation - 5 sets of 12 reps, 60 seconds between sets. Same weight each set. Last set only moderately difficult.
Row Variation #2 - 5 sets of 12 reps, 60 seconds between sets. Same weight each set. Last set only moderately difficult.
Biceps Movement #1 - 5 sets of 20 reps. 60 seconds between sets. Same weight each set. Last set only moderately difficult.
Biceps Movement #2 – 3 sets of 12 reps. 60 seconds between sets. Same weight each set. Last set only moderately difficult.

Legs – Quads/Hamstrings/Calves
Walking Lunges or Split Squats – 100 reps per leg. As many sets as it takes to get the 100 reps in.
Leg Curl Variation – 8 sets of 8 reps. 60 seconds between sets. Same weight each set. Last set only moderately difficult.
Leg Extensions – 1 legged or two legged – 4 sets of 15 reps. 60 seconds between sets. Same weight each set. Last set only moderately difficult.
Calf Movement – seated, standing, calf press – 5 sets of 10. 5 second hold on the stretch position. 60 seconds rest between sets. All sets moderate intensity.

## Conclusion

The hybrid is not a program for novice lifters who have not spent enough years under the bar to have an understanding about the natural recovery patterns of their body in regards to training stress. It is a flexible program based on both anecdotal evidence and scientific data; it sets up a very optimal method of training for advanced lifters to massage the template in a way that best suits their needs, ability to recover, and ability to implement intensity techniques into their training.

I can say with certainty that it is without a doubt the most effective training protocol I've used in my training life; this is because of its flexibility and pliability when it comes to manipulating training at both the daily, weekly, and monthly basis. But the lifter must have had enough years under the bar to understand how to apply all the principals involved in it to make it work maximally for them.

# Chapter Fifteen: Thib's Strength/Pump Program

~ Christian Thibaudeau

This program is based on the training method of the former great bodybuilder and strength athlete Chuck Sipes. It will look very unconventional to those used to the more traditional ways of training but it will bring amazing results in terms of strength, size and hardness. The principals involved are:

Repeating the same strength movement over and over again, doing a very high amount of heavy lifting to develop neural efficiency and fatigue as many fast-twitch fibers as possible.
Adding episodes of pump work in the middle of the heavy work to take advantage of the high neural activation of the muscles involved in the big lift. It represents a lot of work and will seem counterintuitive to many because of the high frequency but, if you stick with it, it will build muscle and strength at a very fast rate.

The template is as follows.

Day 1: Upper body (pressing)/Quads
Day 2: Upper body (pulling)/Posterior chain
Day 3: Arms

Day 4: Off
Day 5: Upper body (pressing)/Quads
Day 6: Upper body (pulling)/Posterior chain
Day 7: Off

## Day 1: Upper body (pressing)/Quads

**A.** Incline bench press/Pec deck machine
**Sets**: 16/4
**Reps**: 3 to 5 reps for the press, 8 to 10 double contraction reps for the pec deck
**Rest**: Long enough to be able to maintain performance level.

Here, we will use the "series" loading pattern. One series is 4 sets of the main lift (incline bench press). You do these as sets of 3 to 5 repetitions, taking about two minutes between sets. When the fourth set is completed, quickly go to the pec deck machine and perform one set of 8 to 10 double contraction reps. During each double contraction rep, do a full rep followed by a half-rep in the last portion of the range of motion. For the incline press, lower the bar under control and push as forcefully as possible. For the peck deck, go with a slower tempo and aim for maximum contraction. You perform 4 such "series" which will total 16 (yes, that's right) sets of incline press and 4 sets of pec deck. For the incline press, a load of about 80 to 85 percent is optimal; you can adjust the weight if fatigue is hurting your performance, but I prefer that you lower the reps to 3 per set than lower the weight.

**B.** Front squat/Leg extension
**Sets**: 16/4
**Reps**: 3 to 5 reps for the squat, 8 to 10 double contraction reps for the extension
**Rest**: Long enough to be able to maintain performance level.

I will not repeat the information about series loading, since it will be used for every single workout, and even though Paul is obsessed with having the highest word count possible, I prefer to save trees by not writing unnecessary stuff. For the front squat, ideally use a clean front rack position (like an Olympic lifter catching a clean). If you lack the mobility or your arms are too big, I'd prefer you to use straps attached to the bar than to use the bodybuilding crossed-arms position. The latter gives you much less control over the bar and increases the tendency to round the upper back when front squatting. For the leg extension, the double contraction is at the top. Make sure to squeeze the peak contraction for a good second or two on each rep.

## Day 2: Upper body (pulling)/Posterior chain

**A.** Chest-supported barbell row/Rear delt machine
**Sets**: 16/4
**Reps**: 3 to 5 reps for the row, 8 to 10 double contraction reps for the rear delt machine
**Rest**: Long enough to be able to maintain performance level.

The chest-supported barbell row is my favorite exercise for the upper back. The bent-over row allows for too much cheating and also fatigues the lower back, which will be a big no-no since we have to deadlift later in the session. Elevate a weight bench on some blocks or plates, and put the loaded barbell on the floor, underneath the bench. Lie chest-down on the bench and row. You don't have to pull the barbell all the way to the bench (you can, but some bigger guys won't be able to); the important thing is to get a maximum squeeze in the upper back. For the rear delt machine, do the double contraction at the peak contraction position and focus on squeezing both shoulder blades together (we are using it to build the mid-back and not the rear delts).

**B.** Romanian deadlift with shrug at the top/Leg curl
**Sets**: 16/4
**Reps**: 3 to 5 reps for the RDL, 8 to 10 double contraction reps for the leg curl
**Rest**: Long enough to be able to maintain performance level.

The goal of the Romanian deadlift is to load the hamstrings, so don't focus on bending forward or lowering the bar down; focus on pushing the hips back to feel a stretch in the hamstrings. If you feel your lower back lose its arch, that's the lowest you should go. Most people will lower the barbell slightly below the knees. At the top of each rep, shrug the barbell up. Since you will likely use less weight on the RDL than you can shrug, hold the shrug peak contraction for two to three seconds per rep. For the leg curl, the double contraction will be at the bottom of the rep. To make the leg curl effective, that first half of the repetition has to be done *slowly;* do not build any momentum at all during the first half of the repetition.

## Day 3: Arms

**A.** Standing barbell curl/Preacher curl
**Sets**: 16/4
**Reps**: 3 to 5 reps for the barbell curl, 8 to 10 double contraction reps for the preacher curl
**Rest**: Long enough to be able to maintain performance level.

Even though we are shooting for heavy weights and low reps on the curl, it doesn't mean that you can use bad technique whereby you use the lower back to create momentum; do not extend your arms fully and use the traps and front delts as prime movers. You should still use picture perfect form, keeping your chest up, shoulders back and down and arms fully extended, and do not use momentum. For the preacher curl, the double contraction is at the peak contraction point. Do that half-rep very slowly and squeeze extra hard when you reach the peak contraction.

**B.** Lying EZ bar triceps extension/Rope triceps pushdown
**Sets**: 16/4
**Reps**: 3 to 5 reps for the extension, 8 to 10 double contraction reps for the pushdown
**Rest**: Long enough to be able to maintain performance level.

In the triceps extension, lower the bar to your forehead slowly (take a good three seconds) and, even though the goal is to go heavy, still use perfect form. Most importantly, keep your upper arms tucked close to your body. Most people let the elbows flare out when they go heavy and this shifts the tension on to the deltoids, which we want to avoid. For the rope triceps pushdown, the double contraction is at the peak. Use zero momentum for the pushdown. You can produce a lot of momentum by exploding at the top and that really takes all the stress off the triceps for most of the movement. Try to use a constant, slow speed of movement so that your muscles must fire during every single inch of every single repetition.

## Day 4: Off

## Day 5: Upper body (pressing)/Quads

**A.** Dumbbell shoulder press/Lateral raise combo
**Sets**: 16/4
**Reps**: 3 to 5 reps for the press, 8 to 10 reps per exercise in the combo
**Rest**: Long enough to be able to maintain performance level.

For the dumbbell shoulder press, even though we are lifting for strength, stop about one inch before lockout to keep constant tension on the deltoids. I recommend using a very steep incline instead of a 90 degree bench (just one pin setting lower than 90 degrees); it will allow you to use a bit more weight without reducing involvement of the deltoids. For the lateral raise combo, we will do 8 to 10 reps of three different variations of the lateral raise done as a triset, using the same weight: 1) lateral raise, seated on a 30 degrees bench 2) lateral raise, standing 3) front raise, standing.

**B.** Back squat/Leg extension
**Sets**: 16/4
**Reps**: 3 to 5 reps for the squat, "improved 21" for the leg extension
**Rest**: Long enough to be able to maintain performance level.

The only thing I want to say about the squat is: *don't use a low bar squat.* Our goal is to build the quadriceps, not lift like a powerlifter. Use a shoulder-width stance, high bar placement and upright torso for your squat. For the leg extensions, we will use a variation of the good old 21s: you will start with 7 full reps, squeezing one to two seconds at the top, then you will do 7 half-reps at the top of the movement, again squeezing at the peak contraction, and then you will finish with 7 slow, momentum-less half-reps in the bottom half.

## Day 6: Upper body (pulling)/Traps

**A.** Lat pulldown with a supinated grip or chin-ups/Cable straight-arm pulldown with 3 positions
**Sets**: 16/4
**Reps**: 3 to 5 reps for the pulldown/chins, 8 to 10 reps for the straight-arm pulldown per position
**Rest**: Long enough to be able to maintain performance level.

Only pick the chin-up if you can do 10 solid, not cheated, full range of motion reps. If not, go with the lat pulldown using a supinated grip. If you pick the latter, do not use momentum by swinging your body; keep your lower back arched, chest pointing towards the ceiling and pull to your mid-chest. Those with bigger arms or who lack mobility can use either an EZ or neutral-grip bar but, ideally, use a straight bar. For the straight-arm pulldown, use a full-length bar. Perform 8 to 10 reps per position, taking about five seconds of rest between positions. The positions are: 1) very wide-grip 2) shoulder-width grip 3) narrow-grip. You might not get up to 8 reps in the last position. Do not sacrifice form and the quality of contraction just to reach a number; stay strict and focus on the muscle contraction.

**B.** Kaworksi shrug/Dumbbell shrug with 3 positions
**Sets**: 16/4
**Reps**: 3 to 5 reps for the Kaworski shrugs, 8 to 10 reps per position for the dumbbell shrugs
**Rest**: Long enough to be able to maintain performance level.

A Kaworski shrug is a mix between a barbell shrug and an upright row. Basically, shoot to pull the barbell above your navel using the traps and arms. When you reach the top position the traps should be fully contracted, with the bar about one to two inches above your navel (depending on your body type) and arms bent at about 30 degrees. Hold the peak contraction position for one to two seconds on each rep. For the dumbbell shrugs, do 8 to 10 repetitions of 3 different positions as a triset (no rest) using the same weight. The positions are: 1) pronated grip, with the dumbbells in front and torso leaning forward 15 to 20 degrees 2) pronated grip, with the dumbbells in front and torso straight 3) neutral grip, with the dumbbells to your side and torso straight.

## Day 7: Off

# Chapter Sixteen: HIT Routine 2: High Frequency HIT

~ Christian Thibaudeau

Not many people know this but for the first few years that I trained for muscle mass I was an avid HIT advocate. Arthur Jones' Nautilus Bulletin no.1 was my Bible, Dorian Yates, Casey Viator and Mike Mentzer were my models (to this day they are still my favorite physiques).

Now HIT doesn't seem to be discussed as much as it was in the earlier days of the internet; back when the HIT vs. high volume (or periodization) argument was the hottest debate on training forums. Yet HIT style training is still popular but people simply don't refer to it as "HIT" anymore.

As a reminder, HIT is a training philosophy based on:

- Low volume (1-2 work sets per exercise)
- Maximum intensity (going to failure on every work set)
- Infrequent (normally around 3 training days per week)
- Done without using acceleration/explosion and emphasizing the eccentric (focusing on more controlled reps)

The main tenet is that ***you can either train hard or train long but you can't do both***. And it is a training style that is regaining a lot of popularity in the world of body building through the philosophies of Dante Trudel (DC training) and Dr. Scott Stevenson (Fortitude Training). They don't call it "HIT" but it does respect the principles of traditional HIT.

And I admit to coming full circle with this myself. I did lots of volume for a while, burned out and I'm now back to this style of training, for the most part.

I agree with the basic tenet of HIT which is "***you can either train hard or train long, but not both. And intensity beats volume every time***". And it is especially true for the natural, non-genetically gifted or older trainee.

The one thing I disagree on with traditional HIT philosophy is the frequency of training. I believe that training more often will lead to better results, especially in natural trainees (yes it might sound counterintuitive) since they need the actual training session to trigger protein synthesis whereas enhanced lifters have an elevated rate of protein synthesis 24/7.

## The number one mistake made by natural trainees

I believe that the work mistake someone training without the help of performance enhancing drugs can make is to do too much volume.

The whole purpose of training to build muscle is to trigger protein synthesis. Once it's been triggered there is no added benefit to continuing punishing a muscle, it will not grow more. In fact, it will grow less and might even lose size!

The key to growth is having the biggest difference between protein synthesis (building muscle) and protein breakdown (mobilizing amino acids from muscles for energy). The more volume you do, the more protein breakdown you get. Why? Because the more volume you do the more glycogen you need to burn for fuel.

What does this have to do with protein breakdown? Plenty!

When you try to mobilize stored glycogen, you need to increase the release of cortisol. Basically, during training cortisol's role is to mobilize energy to be used for fuel.

The more fuel you need, the greater the cortisol release.

So, the more volume you do, the more glycogen you need to burn and the greater the cortisol release.

However, cortisol also comes with a drawback: it can hurt muscle growth. It does so 3 ways:

1. By increasing the breakdown of amino acids from muscles; basically cortisol breaks down muscle tissue to turn it into fuel. This is why we say that cortisol is a catabolic hormone.

2. By inhibiting mTor. MTor is the light switch that turns on protein synthesis (muscle building). Cortisol can inhibit mTor directly and by increasing the level of AMPK. The more cortisol you produce, the more likely you are to negate the effect of training on protein synthesis. Essentially, mTor will turn on muscle-building, and cortisol can turn it off.

3. Cortisol and other glucocorticoids increase the expression of the myostatin gene. Myostatin expression limits the amount of muscle you build. The more myostatin expression you have, the less muscle you build. High cortisol levels, and thus a high volume of work, lead to a greater myostatin expression during the recovery period after a workout.

What we want is to trigger mTor/protein synthesis but also to keep cortisol release as low as possible to maximize the growth stimulus. This means that volume must be kept low.

It also means that since you can't afford to do a lot of volume you must make sure that the volume you do is done at an intensity level that will trigger mTor activation.

Note that enhanced (drug-using) bodybuilders do not have that same problem.

Enhanced bodybuilder do not need to stimulate protein synthesis with the session: the anabolic hormones they are taking artificially increase protein synthesis 24/7. As such doing too much volume will not have the same negative impact as for a natural trainee.

## The problem with the original HIT

Because of this physiological fact it would seem that HIT/low volume training is the right approach; do a very low volume of work to failure to make sure to trigger protein synthesis and minimize protein breakdown.

However, it doesn't always work that well in real life, and when it does work it often doesn't work well for long.

In my opinion the main problem with HIT was the low frequency. I believe that to maximize growth, frequency is king. Both frequency of training a muscle per week and in the number of training sessions per week.

Why is frequency the king? Because for a natural trainee the actual training session represents the stimulus to trigger protein synthesis. In other words, the training session itself is what puts you in an anabolic mode; whereas the enhanced athlete doesn't need to use the session as a trigger.

So, the more often you train, the more your body stays in an anabolic state and the more muscle you will build.

But do not forget that frequency and volume are inversely related. You cannot do a high volume of work if you have a high frequency of training when you are natural.

And frequency works better than volume.

Dr.Brad Shoenfeld did a meta-analysis of the optimal frequency of training and he concluded that training a muscle twice a week is more effective than training it only once and that training it three times per week is likely superior. This is a something that Dr. Stuart Philips agreed with when he told me that three stimulations per week is better than two which is better than one. He even mentioned that for advanced individuals a higher frequency might even be more effective!

So, hitting a muscle three times per week is the optimal frequency for a natural trainee (with a low volume to compensate for the increase in frequency).

The original HIT by Arthur Jones (Jones' earlier work) relied on three weekly sessions, hitting the whole body at every session. And that was arguably the most effective HIT variation. It is when HIT proponents started to recommend an even lower frequency for each muscle that results started to decrease.

The only problem with three whole body workouts, especially if you go to complete failure on each work set, is that you will be burned out before you finish your session and the quality of work at the end of your workout will suffer.

Furthermore, a whole body workout burns more glycogen than training half or part of the body. This leads to a greater cortisol release during the session which makes that session less "anabolic" (less likely to lead to maximum growth).

Therefore, to optimize the protein synthesis/cortisol increase balance, it is best to divide the body in two or three. Train six days a week, doing short, low volume workouts hitting half or one third of the body each time. That's the only way to get the optimal frequency without the excessive cortisol release.

## The training split

In this program we will use a 3-ways split, with each group being trained twice a week.

GROUP A – PULLING MUSCLES
Back
Biceps
Traps

GROUP B – PUSHING MUSCLES
Pectorals
Deltoids
Triceps

GROUP C – LOWER BODY
Quadriceps
Hamstrings
Glutes
Calves (if you want to do direct work for them)

Each workout will have 5-7 exercises.

For each exercise you will perform 2 preparation sets and ONE ***all-out*** work set.

**First set** (preparation set): 10-12 reps with a level of effort that is about 5-6 on a scale of 10. This is just to get some blood flowing to the target muscle, practice contracting the main muscle and feeling it do the work and get in the groove for the exercise.

**Second set** (preparation set): 8-10 reps with a level of effort that is about 8 on a scale of 10. This means that you use a fairly heavy weight and you go hard, but you don't reach failure. This set will contribute to growth but more importantly it helps you select the weight for your work set and get you ready to handle bigger weights and produce a maximal level of effort.

**Third set** (work set): here you shoot for a weight you can get 6-8 reps with. In reality, you might get less or more because your goal is to go to true muscle failure (go until you cannot move the weight one more inch. Don't stop when you "think" you will not get the next rep). We will also use post-failure methods like rest/pause, assisted reps and drop sets to go past the point of failure. See it this way: you have ONE set to trigger maximum growth, make it count.

## Program structure

The program can be as long as you want but it works in 3 week cycles. Each cycle using a different training method. A "full program" is 4 phases long (so 12 weeks) after which you would normally take 1-2 weeks off from muscle-building training, focusing on something different like conditioning work or explosive exercises. But you can do shorter cycles of 6 or 9 weeks if you prefer. But respect the order of the phases since intensity is built up from phase to phase.

## Exercise selection

Excessive exercise variation is the enemy of muscle growth. Look at all the top bodybuilders and most elite strength athletes: they stick to a small number of exercises. They will use some variation from time to time (or when they are in a different gym) but for the most part they stick to the same movements. Dorian stayed with the same set of exercises for pretty much all of his pro career!

If you change your exercises too often you never become efficient at them. And if you are not efficient you get sub-optimal muscle fiber recruitment and stimulation. Furthermore, when you are neutrally inefficient in an exercise, the body can adapt to the stress without having to add muscle (it really doesn't want to add muscle) simply by becoming more efficient, making the muscle gains much slower. You need to stick to the same exercises and become really good and efficient at them before being able to stimulate muscle growth at the fastest possible rate.

So, for the duration of the 12 week program you will use the same exercises and your focus should be to get gradually stronger at them over time; always try to add a bit more weight, even if it is just a few pounds.

**IMPORTANT**: Only change exercises if you get stalled on one movement for 3 weeks; if you can't add weight or reps on a movement for 3 weeks (6 workouts for that lift) then switch to a different movement ***for a few workouts*** then get back to the original movement.

The exercises I recommend are:

GROUP A
Straight-arm pulldown (machine pullover are even better if you have that machine)
Supinated lat pulldown (the hammer strength high row machine is even better if you have it)
Single arm seated row machine
Deadlift
Low pulley rope upright row with thumb pointing up
DB shrugs
Preacher curl

GROUP B

Incline bench press in Smith machine
Pec deck machine
Seated shoulder press in Smith machine
DB lateral raise
Barbell front raise
Lying EZ bar triceps extension
Rope triceps extension

GROUP C
Leg extension
Leg press
Hack squat
Lying leg curl

DB Romanian deadlift with the front of the feet elevated

## Training schedule

You use a 3 on/1 off schedule. So basically: pulling muscles/pushing muscles/lower body/off / pulling muscles/pushing muscles/lower body/off / etc. Therefore, everything is trained twice every 8 days.

## Training phases

As I mentioned you have four phases lasting 3 weeks each. Each phase is more demanding than the preceding one. You must do them in order! And if you decide to start a second cycle after your 12 weeks, and your 1-2 weeks of deload/different training you still start with the first phase. A huge part of the system is progression. Progression from week to week in weights but also progression in the difficulty of the phases.

PHASE 1 – INTRODUCTION (3 weeks): After your two preparation sets you do one work set of 6-8 reps to complete muscle failure. Perform reps until you cannot move the weight one more inch. The exception is the deadlift and DB Romanian deadlift where you stop when you feel that form will breakdown.

PHASE 2 – BASE (3 weeks): You once again do your 2 preparation sets and then your work set with 6-8 reps to failure. After you hit failure your training partner will help you get an additional 2-3 reps. He should help you just enough to keep the weight moving up and stop helping during the eccentric. The eccentric should be done fairly slowly, 3-4 seconds down.

PHASE 3 – ACCUMULATION (3 weeks): After your 2 preparation sets you do your all-out work set by going to failure. Then you decrease the weight by about 25% and you once again go to failure with that new weight.

PHASE 4 – INTENSIFICATION (3 weeks): You do your 2 preparation sets then proceed to your one maximum intensity set which will be a double rest/pause set: you perform 6-8 reps to failure, rest for 10-15 seconds and go to failure again with the same weight, rest for another 10-15 seconds and go to failure a third time with the same weight.

PHASE 5 – DELOAD (1-2 weeks): Do something completely different. No intense lifting. It could be playing sport, doing more conditioning work like sprints, prowler pushing, sled pulling, sledgehammer striking, tire flipping or explosive work like jumps and throws.

**IMPORTANT**: I mentioned it previously but it is important enough to repeat it. When I talk about the work set, I give an ideal range (6-8 reps) and most of the time you should be able to pick an adequate weight to reach failure somewhere in that range, especially if you are using the second preparation set properly and also based on your previous weeks of training. But, if you misjudge how much weight to use on that set, your first priority is to hit failure, not to get the recommended number of reps. For example, if you picked a weight that is a bit too light and after you complete 8 reps you know you have more left in you, then continue on with the set until you hit failure. And if you only reach 4-5 reps it might not be ideal but if you reached failure you will be fine, just remember to make a better weight selection next week.

## Progression

Every week you should strive to increase the amount of weight you are using on you work set. It doesn't have to be a huge increase; in fact, it is likely better to stick to smaller increments to ensure a more constant progression. Heck, simply getting 5lbs more per week on each exercise would represent a 60lbs increase over the whole program! Now, chances are that you wont be able to add weight every week, but you should strive to. Even if that means getting less than the recommended 6-8 reps *once in a while*. You are training every exercise twice per 8 days period. So if you only hit 5 reps wait until you are getting 8 to add weight. You are likely to be able to add weight at least once every third workout (of a same time) which would lead to a gain of about 40lbs over 12 weeks. If you don't think that you will be able to get 6 reps if you add weight you can keep the same weight, even if that means going above 8 reps. But if you go above 8 reps make sure to add more weight next time around. Basically, always try to do either more reps or lift more weight at every workout.

**IMPORTANT**: keep pretty much the same weight for the preparation set; these are only to prepare you for your work set and you don't want to create too much fatigue by pushing them too hard.

## Workout pace

I find that a fast pace is best to keep you focused during a session. And since you only have one hard set per exercise there is really no benefit in extending the rest intervals, because you don't have to repeat the performance on a lift and the first two sets of the new exercise are fairly easy.

I find that the optimal work to rest ratio is about 1:2. For example if you train with two partners you would rotate one after the other with no additional rest. If you are training with one partner you should each go, then rest an additional 30 seconds or so. If you are training by yourself (which I don't recommend for this training style) you would rest twice the amount of time it took you to complete your set.

To give you an idea I train with two partners and our workouts last around 75 minutes so that is a good target.

## Conclusion

In my opinion this is the best approach to build muscle mass, especially if you are a natural trainee without any genetic predisposition for building tons of muscle. Older folks will respond especially well since their body doesn't recover as well as when they were younger. But really, anybody will greatly benefit from this style of training provided that they are capable of pushing themselves hard enough.

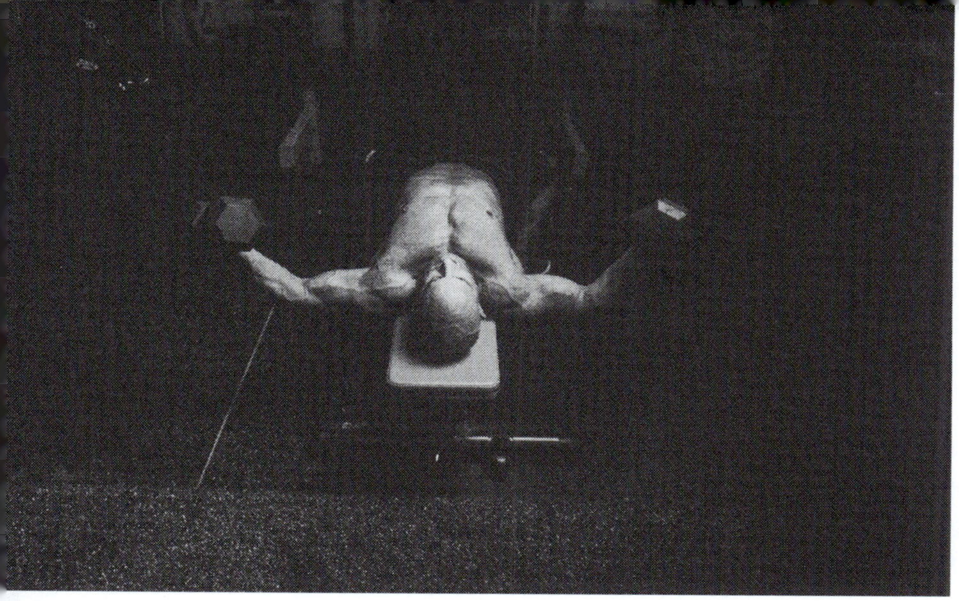

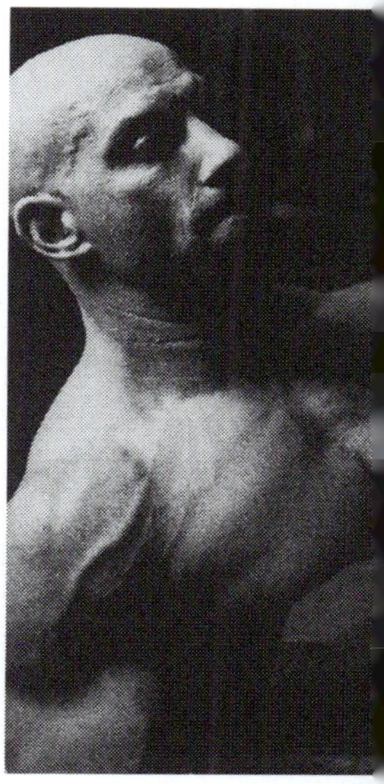

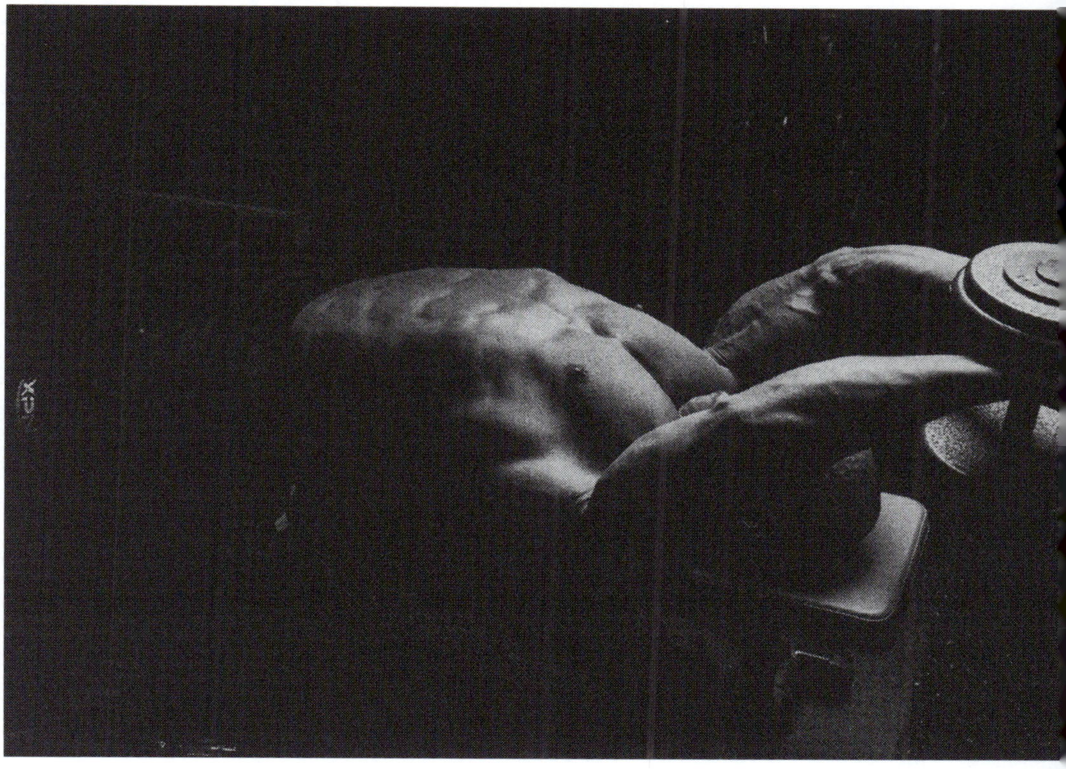

Christian Thibaudeau

www.ThibArmy.com

Paul Carter
www.lift-run-bang.com

# MAXIMUM MUSCLE BIBLE

F.Lepine Publishing


ISBN: 978-1-926659-32-9

www.MaximumMuscleBible.com

37843268R00105

Printed in Great Britain
by Amazon